The Savvy Woman's
Guide to Financial Freedom

The Savvy Woman's Guide to Financial Freedom

SUSAN HAYES

PENGUIN
IRELAND

PENGUIN IRELAND

Published by the Penguin Group
Penguin Ireland, 25 St Stephen's Green, Dublin 2, Ireland
(a division of Penguin Books Ltd)
Penguin Books Ltd, 80 Strand, London WC2R ORL, England
Penguin Group (USA) Inc., 375 Hudson Street, New York, New York 10014, USA
Penguin Group (Australia), 707 Collins Street, Melbourne, Victoria 3008, Australia
(a division of Pearson Australia Group Pty Ltd)
Penguin Group (Canada), 90 Eglinton Avenue East, Suite 700, Toronto, Ontario, Canada M4P 2Y3
(a division of Pearson Penguin Canada Inc.)
Penguin Books India Pvt Ltd, 11 Community Centre, Panchsheel Park, New Delhi – 110 017, India
Penguin Group (NZ), 67 Apollo Drive, Rosedale, Auckland 0632, New Zealand
(a division of Pearson New Zealand Ltd)
Penguin Books (South Africa) (Pty) Ltd, Block D, Rosebank Office Park,
181 Jan Smuts Avenue, Parktown North, Gauteng 2193, South Africa

Penguin Books Ltd, Registered Offices: 80 Strand, London WC2R ORL, England

www.penguin.com

First published 2013
002

Copyright © Susan Hayes, 2013

The moral right of the author has been asserted

Set in 12/14.75pt Dante MT Std
Typeset by Jouve (UK), Milton Keynes
Printed in Great Britain by Clays Ltd, St Ives plc

A CIP catalogue record for this book is available from the British Library

ISBN: 978–1–844–88290–8

www.greenpenguin.co.uk

MIX
Paper from
responsible sources
FSC
www.fsc.org   FSC™ C018179

Penguin Books is committed to a sustainable
future for our business, our readers and our planet.
This book is made from Forest Stewardship
Council™ certified paper.

To Ardle

Contents

Foreword   ix

STEP ONE: WORK OUT YOUR ATTITUDE TO MONEY

1. What is your financial temperature?   3
2. Turning up the heat   13

STEP TWO: DECIDE YOUR FINANCIAL DESTINATION

3. If I was going there, I wouldn't start from here   23
4. Getting past the First of January Syndrome   35

STEP THREE: LEARN TO LOVE BUDGETING

5. Putting the boring stuff on automatic so you can
   get to stuff that really makes a difference   55
6. Knowledge is power . . .   72

STEP FOUR: CURB YOUR SPENDING

7. If you think cost-cutting takes the fun out of
   spending . . . think again!   93
8. Savvier women think smarter . . .   106

STEP FIVE: TALK TO THE EXPERTS

9. Let others help you on the way towards
   financial freedom   125
10. Getting along with the bank manager (and everyone
    else in your financial world)   144

STEP SIX: SHARE YOUR FINANCIAL JOURNEY

11. *'I will, if you will!'* Having someone to talk to about
    your financial goals   165

12. Why having to account for your actions
    (and inactions) is good for you   185

STEP SEVEN: IDENTIFY THE COSTS AND BENEFITS
OF YOUR CHOICES

13. Revenue is vanity, profit is sanity   201

14. Profit – it's not just about the money . . .   222

STEP EIGHT: CHALLENGE YOUR BELIEFS ABOUT
MAKING MONEY

15. Can you handle more money?   251

16. Are you afraid of change?   267

17. The secret about making money . . . is that there is
    no secret   277

STEP NINE: MAKE MORE MONEY

18. The four principles of revenue generation   291

19. Grabbing the low-hanging fruit and working towards
    your own money tree   304

20. Nine steps to your first €100 of extra income   317

Conclusion   331

Acknowledgements   339

Foreword

I'm not writing this book because I know it all, but because I've learned the hard way . . . the way most of us do. I've just gone out and spent money without budgeting. I've written budgets and then forgotten all about them. I've blown money simply because it burned a hole in my pocket. I've set up a filing system to help me keep track of my finances and then let it fall into disarray. I've planned to spend €100, spent three times that sum 'just because' and then berated myself for it. I've felt under pressure when out at a nice restaurant and inwardly groaned at the prices because I couldn't afford it   nor could I afford, I thought, the 'shame' of admitting it. I've lived off my credit card. I've earned less than people I went to college with and felt less successful than them because of it. I've genuinely believed: 'This is the way it is, trying to change my life for the better will be futile.' I've been too proud to ask for help. I've pushed away thoughts of saving for a rainy day by saying, 'I will deal with it if it comes.' For a long time, I yearned to set up a business but was too afraid. You name it – I've done it. It was very easy to come up with the specific situations in this book, because I've been through many of them myself.

Of all the strategies and tips in this book, there isn't one that I haven't tried and there isn't one that hasn't helped me when it came to solving the problems mentioned above. This book is dedicated to showing you all the things that I learned to do right. I've written it with two things in mind: first, practicality; and second – the element that will make a real difference – helping you to discover and under-stand your true motivations when it comes to money.

I grew up as the elder of two, but was among the youngest of a very large, close group of cousins, so I've had the best of both worlds. I've watched all of them grow up, get married, secure mortgages and have kids. I've been privy to their many conversations about how hard it is to juggle commitments, financial and otherwise. I've watched them figure their way out of pickles. All of this meshed with my unusual interest in business from very early on: as a little girl I would hold board meetings with my teddy bears! Naturally, when the time came, I studied financial maths and economics at college and then I went on to study for the CFA (Chartered Financial Analyst) exams.

Through the years my goal was always to become a success in business. I started my first business, mentoring people in the stock market, when I was still a student. Unsurprisingly, I had gravitated towards something I love – financial training – and eventually, through my academic studies, training courses and the practical experience of dealing with people figuring out how to make real-life financial decisions, I found that I had amassed, quite early in my adult life, a lot of knowledge not only about finance, economics and the stock market but about how to manage all of these.

Mentoring people gave me an education that money couldn't buy. I would meet them in their homes, and they gave me a unique insight into their myriad of financial opinions, problems and solutions. Since then I have spoken at numerous events on topics ranging from banking to behavioural finance, equities to bonds, economics to entrepreneurship. During the course of question-and-answer sessions, or privately over coffee, participants have told me what they think, how they see things, how I was right, how I was wrong, or asked my advice on a problem. The point is that over the last decade I have talked to thousands of people from a complete cross-section of society – in terms of age (my youngest stock-market mentee was seven!), net worth (or the lack of it) and role – so I don't just bring my experiences to this book; I bring many of theirs too. I bring to it the lessons of our collective financial experiences.

I know what money means to people. It's not paper and coins or the number that appears on your bank-account statement. Money means sending your kids to college, enjoying a carefree retirement, nice restaurants, nice clothes, the ability to look after the ones you love, the freedom to take time off work, to travel the world, to extend the house, to impress those for whom outward impressions are important.

At its most basic level, not having to worry about money is probably an aspiration for most people and an everyday definition of financial success. However, I know that for many – and particularly during an economically difficult time in their lives – money is a source of perennial anxiety, a slippery commodity that never seems to stick in their wallet. It is the wedding they will never have, the opportunities their children will be deprived of, the cramped house that they cannot move out of, the relaxed lifestyle they will never enjoy. It is something they will always chase but find difficult to grasp. At a deep level, money can be inextricably linked to people's dignity and social standing, and in some cases, sadly, it is all that they live for. So some of our attitudes to money are healthy and some are not. Here, I want to show you how to take control of them and to prevent their taking control of you.

What I have learned along the way is that you define success in your own terms. I like to dream big. I've achieved some of the goals I set for myself: be a regular guest on radio and on TV; be a public speaker; have my own business; have an international company with an exports-led turnover. I'm not a millionaire yet, but I'm not quite thirty and I'm on my way.

I dream of power suits and international expansion, but your dream might be very different. I had my hair done the other day. The hairdresser and I got talking about my work. She said, 'I have no ambition to be like you. I want to have the same four walls in twenty years. I want to open on a Wednesday, I want to walk away on a Saturday, and I want to be able to take Mondays and Tuesdays off to be with the kids.' And that's perfectly fine. This book is not about replicating anyone else's success; it's about ensuring your own. If that hairdresser reads this book, in it she will find ways to make sure she achieves her goals. I'm ambitious by some people's standards, and not ambitious enough according to others. It doesn't matter what anybody else's ambitions are – your own are all that count. They are what you have the most control over.

In the chapters that follow, I'm going to simplify the jargon and cut through the bull. I'll arm you with the language you need to deal with anybody who might try to pull the wool over your eyes. I'll show you the tricks of the trade and empower you so that you can do things yourself. I've seen all the reasons why you might fail and learned all the ways you might succeed. Whatever your definition of success, this book will help you on your path towards it.

STEP ONE

Work out your attitude to money

What is your financial temperature?

Are you always spending? Or always saving? Do you have friends whose behaviour with money is the same as yours, or the complete opposite? Maybe you've heard of those lottery winners who file for bankruptcy a few years after making it big and wondered how that could possibly happen. If any of these questions has ever crossed your mind, and you've noticed that many people have a default position when it comes to money, you're well on your way towards a crucial understanding: we have an inner monitor, a sort of thermostat, that responds whenever our financial temperature falls above or below a certain set-point. So, before you embark on your financial transformation, you'll need to know where you're starting from – you need to take your financial temperature.

I'm going to ask you a series of questions about your relationship with money. Please be brutally honest – no sugar-coating or hiding anything. Nobody else needs to know, and there is a real nugget of learning contained here.

But, before we start, do you notice yourself getting tense as you prepare to look your finances in the eye? Or do you feel elated, raring to go? Afraid? Perhaps already discouraged, even?

This is perfectly normal. Money is a difficult topic and there are a lot of fears and preconceptions around it. This book will make you more aware of your money fears and help you to overcome them.

So, take this short test. Below are three hypothetical situations. Imagine what you would do in each case.

1. Stop right this second. You check your account and you have €50,000 extra in the bank. How do you feel? What are you going to

do? I would be interested to hear what you automatically say to yourself . . .

    a. Delighted! I would take €20,000 off the mortgage, book a holiday for €5,000 for the family, go on a spending spree in Brown Thomas . . .

    b. That's about a year and a half's wages. Wouldn't it be lovely to take a year off and travel or spend it at home? Although what if I didn't get my job back?

    c. That would be nice! It would be great to have such a cushion built up.

    d. It's a start, anyway . . .

    e. That equates to €1,500 interest, assuming a 3% interest rate.

2. Stop right this second. You check your bank account and see that you have to repay a €50,000 loan. How do you feel? What are you going to do? I would be interested to hear what you automatically say to yourself . . .

    a. Panic! I need to budget to find every cent available to pay that down.

    b. If anything happened to me, at least my family could benefit from the write-off of the loan.

    c. That's not bad! I might borrow more, so that I can put it to good use. After all, I can make more of a return on it than the interest the bank is charging me.

    d. So what? The repayment is about €400 a month. It's just like the electricity bill or the groceries. It's just another payment.

    e. At least when I get that reduced, I can go back to the bank and get another loan to get the conservatory I've been dreaming about.

3. Stop right this second. You check your bank account and you have zero 'net wealth' (i.e., the amount you have in the bank cancels out the amount you owe exactly). How do you feel? What are you going

to do? I would be interested to hear what you automatically say to yourself . . .

a. Relief! That's great now, I can pay it all off in the morning.
b. Why would I not just pay it off, then?
c. I wonder what I could borrow and buy?
d. OMG! I'm a pay cheque away from being destitute!
e. I need to make a lean budget and save, save, save!

In the first scenario – where you discover you have €50,000 extra in the bank – I'm testing your financial thermostat i.e., the amount of money you would feel comfortable with in your life. Here is my take on your answers:

(a) Delighted! I would take €20,000 off the mortgage, book a holiday for €5,000 for the family, go on a spending spree in Brown Thomas . . .

You are very uncomfortable with more money in your life. You no sooner have the extra money in your account than you automatically set about finding ways to spend it. Money burns a hole in your pocket. Your 'number' is well below €50,000: should you get as high as €50,000, you would find ways to get back down to your lower set-point.

(b) That's about a year and a half's wages. Wouldn't it be lovely to take a year off and travel or spend it at home? Although what if I didn't get my job back?

You feel financially insecure and dependent on your job. You don't have, or at least you don't think you have, any other way to make money and you live with the fear that the 'money will run out'.

(c) That would be nice! It would be great to have such a cushion built up.

You have probably hit on your number. If you don't particularly want to change your situation, you are comfortable with that amount of money. You don't necessarily want to spend or save at this stage. It's a nice situation to be in.

(d) It's a start, anyway . . .

We haven't hit your number yet. You may even be nervous at this stage because you don't feel 'financially safe'. You would be a lot happier if there was an extra zero on that bank balance.

(e) That equates to €1,500 interest, assuming a 3% interest rate.

You're savvy, but I would be slightly concerned about you. If you have already 'made' the interest in your head, you may not have any plans about how to spend this money. That's fine, as long as there aren't any emergencies along the way. Would you have locked away all that money in a savings account to get a higher interest rate? If so, how much liquid (immediately accessible) money could you access right now? Liquid money is your actual 'rainy day fund' – is it enough? You might end up in a tight spot just when you were thinking you had made it. Do you apply enough practicality to the theory of improving your finances? It's not all about putting it under lock and key!

With the second scenario – where you discover you are €50,000 in debt – I'm checking out your attitude to debt.

(a) Panic! I need to budget to find every cent available to pay that down.

You're allergic to owing anything. You are probably well able to save so that you can pay debt down. A feeling of overwhelming relief comes over you when you get something paid off. Conversely, you have this sense of discomfort when you know there are bills (short or long term) that are outstanding.

(b) If anything happened to me, at least my family could benefit from the write-off of the loan.

That's a thought that many people have towards debt. While that's correct, is this the only reason that you would get into debt? If it's not the only reason, it's just an added benefit, so what other answer applies to you? If it is, is this really enough of a reason to pay interest for as long as you live? Here is a quick formula used by finance people that might make you think again about the wisdom of this approach. The 'Rule of 72' is a way of calculating the length of time it takes to double your money. Conversely – and more relevant to this example – it also tells you how long it takes the bank to get back twice what it lent you. The formula is to divide 72 by the interest rate you're paying on your loan, to arrive at the number of years. So, say if you have a loan with an interest rate of 4%, then

72 divided by 4 is 18, which means that at this interest rate it will take the bank 18 years to get back twice what it lent you. To look at it from another angle, if you take out a loan and repay it back over 18 years with a 4% interest rate, the bank will have doubled its money on you.

Although it's a morbid thought, compare this to when you might die. Let's say you borrow €100,000 with the idea in the back of your mind that if anything happens your family would have the loan written off. You die halfway through the repayment period and your family gets to keep €50,000. However, let's look at how much interest you will have paid by that point. With a simple-interest loan at 4%, €100,000 at 4% over 12.5 years = €50,000. But, based on simple interest, if you died after 12.5 years, your family would make a net loss, as you will have already laid out at least this amount in interest repayments. I accept that lending does not operate on this basis, and that as you pay down the loan, the interest due every month falls along with it. Without getting into complex maths here, the point stands that this attitude to money doesn't make a whole lot of sense (or cents . . .). What happens if you don't die? Is it worthwhile paying interest for the foreseeable future, just so others can make money out of your death? I don't think so.

(c) That's not bad! I might borrow more, so that I can put it to good use. After all, I can make more of a return on it than the interest the bank is charging me.

That's some smart thinking and maybe you're someone who already has a certain amount of confidence about money, and you're reading this book just to pick up a few extra tips. I have a feeling that you selected (e) in the first situation and I would raise the same point: are you sure everything is going to go according to plan and that nothing will happen which might require money in the future, emergency or otherwise? I'm not a fan of pie-in-the-sky theories but for the sake of argument, let's look at an example here. If you have a way of making a 5% return and you can get money at 3% (this is called arbitrage), you could borrow unlimited funds and make unlimited profits. That's great, but what happens if anything ever threatened that 5% return?

Dividends on shares might provide that sort of yield, but what if they were cut? Maybe you could make 5% on a loan to someone (we call this a bond), but what happens if they ever default? They won't, you say? Think about the Bank of Ireland dividend that was rock solid all the way back to time immemorial. Or what about those who held Russian and Argentinian bonds? Russia and Argentina did default, the former in 1998, and the latter in 2002.

The other thing I would say is: what if interest rates go up? If it's a variable loan, it could happen at any stage. If it's fixed, you should be safe enough. In either case, if you're borrowing today to pay off yesterday, at any stage the tap could switch off. Run some 'scenario analysis' on yourself and see what's the worst that could happen to you. What if interest rates rose to 5%? What if the return fell to 3%? What if both happened? What if lending dried up and you couldn't finance your investment any longer? What then?

(d) So what? The repayment is about €400 a month. It's just like the electricity bill or the groceries. It's just another payment.

It sounds like you are very comfortable with debt, which isn't a healthy situation. I will discuss different types of debt in Chapter 8, but, suffice to say, all debt costs money. Your groceries provide you with nutrition and ultimately keep you alive. Your electricity provides you with light, heat and energy. What does interest bring you? It allows you to enjoy things today that you would usually have to save for and buy tomorrow.

There is 'good debt' and 'bad debt', and a simple rule of thumb exists to differentiate between the two. *Are you still using the things you bought with borrowed money on which you are currently paying interest?* For example, you put €3,000 on the credit card to buy a holiday that you went on last year and there is still a balance of €2,000, on which you are paying the interest monthly. If you're 'comfortable' with this payment, you shouldn't be. The interest on this debt is a useless expense whose sole purpose is to bring profit to a credit-card company.

Another example: you've borrowed €200,000 to buy a house. You'll be paying it off for another twenty-five years and living in it forever. This is 'good debt', as you will gain long term from having taken on this financial commitment.

Perhaps you don't see any problem with 'being okay' with debt, as debt is something that usually has to be paid for years on end anyway. I disagree. If you're uncomfortable with it, you'll try to get rid of it. The harder you work at getting rid of the mortgage, the less interest you'll have to pay on the house, and you'll be paying it for a shorter period of time.

It sounds like your thermostat is 'below zero' and you may possibly be happy 'owing money'. For that reason, I would be concerned about what might happen after the mortgage is paid off – would you consider borrowing again then? I shudder at the thought.

(e) At least when I get that reduced, I can go back to the bank and get another loan to get the conservatory I've been dreaming about.

You're a lender's dream! As soon as they get you in the door, you're a customer for life. You don't see debt as a problem. In fact, you don't even see debt as 'borrowed money that needs to be paid back', but like extra money you got as a Christmas bonus. You've probably wasted thousands of euros over the years constantly 'rolling over' debt (as soon as one loan falls due, you borrow to cover the capital and interest payments). It sounds like you'll never break free from this cycle unless you, first, acknowledge it, and, second, change your habits.

Before you put this book down because you don't want to read any more, let me add one thing: you could actually buy more, spend more and have more things and money, if you simply shifted your money forward. That is, instead of paying to take money in from tomorrow, you could wait a little while and buy the same things – just without paying the interest. In fact, for a lack of patience, you're turning your back on the money you can get for 'being paid to wait' (i.e., the interest payments that you can *keep* in your bank account). Your financial thermostat is well below zero.

Finally, given that debt is such a common (and often necessary) feature of our lives, with the third scenario – the amount you have in the bank cancels out the amount you owe exactly – I want to see how you would react if it was within your reach to eradicate it.

(a) Relief! That's great now, I could pay it all off in the morning.

The jury is out on you. You love knowing that you could pay off all the debt in the morning, but would you actually do it? I have a feeling you've found yourself in situations where you can save very effectively to eradicate debt, but that as soon as this negative pressure wears off, you take your foot off the pedal and find yourself never really getting ahead. Your financial thermostat could be zero – you don't like debt – but that's all.

(b) Why would I not just pay it off, then?

Good point, however, don't jump in so quickly. I didn't specify the amounts. You could have €20,000 in the bank and €20,000 left on the mortgage. You have a regular income, but if anything at all happened along the way, where would you be? Imagine an emergency that required you to eat into those rainy-day savings, or there was a threat to your income . . . You don't like debt, which is good, but don't just think it's possible to 'copy' and 'paste' one against the other.

(c) I wonder what I could borrow and buy?

Ahhhhhhh! What a wasted opportunity! You're no sooner out of debt than you want to get straight back into it. Your financial thermostat is well below freezing – it sounds like you simply do not want to let temperatures climb into warm territory. If you don't realize this, you'll spend a fortune needlessly. Have you ever thought about it in these terms? If this is news to you, and you're prepared to take action right now, you have a financial windfall on its way to you.

(d) OMG! I'm a pay cheque away from being destitute!

This might be a little exaggerated, but you clearly do not like debt in any way, size, shape or form. You have a financial thermostat that is much higher than zero. However, you could be suffering from an acute feeling of financial instability and the resulting anxiety. A greater understanding of your finances, a more thorough knowledge of your income and outgoings, as well as greater self-sufficiency, will all help you to deal with this. We'll address each and every one of these points in the book.

(e) I need to make a lean budget and save, save, save!

I agree. First, your thermostat is in a warm territory, as you want a positive amount of money left when you take away what you owe. If you can save money now, you can pay off the debt and save yourself the interest along the way. Second, it looks like you would continue to be financially fit after the loan is gone and you push your way into the black. This is a healthy attitude to have – long may it continue.

Now, take your temperature. To find your number, look at where the answers you have chosen fall on the thermostat. Also, take a look at the anxiety thermostat to see if you worry about money a lot, or it doesn't concern you enough:

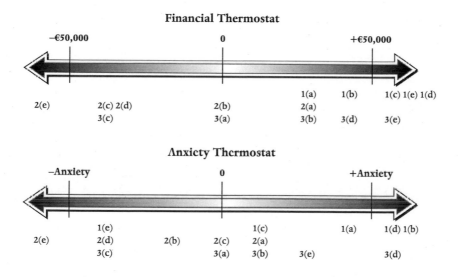

Clearly, €50,000 is going to be too high for some and not high enough for others. Go back and change the figures in the various scenarios I've outlined. Then take the test again: that way, you'll be able to define your own set-point more precisely. If you thought having €50,000 meant you should go out and spend, how about

€15,000? Would you still feel as carefree? Or would you be more careful?

Now, here is a crucial part of the exercise: please take a highlighter pen and write the following sentence. Then take a red pen and underline it. You could also photocopy it, with a 1,000% enlargement. Make copies and put one in each of the rooms of your house. Finally, create a screensaver with it, as well as a daily reminder in your calendar. Yes, it's that important.

Just like a thermostat, your financial thermostat can be reset.

You don't have to be bound by your financial thermostat. You can choose to increase your financial temperature. You can feel as confident with €100,000 in the black as you feel today with €20,000 in the red. And, as you increase the temperature, you can kiss anxiety goodbye. And in the next chapter I will give you a step-by-step guide to increasing your financial temperature – a message that will be reinforced throughout the book.

2

Turning up the heat

I have several strategies to help you increase your financial temperature, and they all have one thing in common: they will permanently reset your thermostat to a higher set-point (that is, until you want to change it again). As a result, you'll be wondering how you could ever have felt comfortable with debt, or with making barely enough to get by.

So just how do you increase your financial temperature? Now that you know where you are, how do you get where you want to be? The first strategy is a very pleasant process that I have used with a lot of success over the years. It's called 'day-dreaming'.

No, I'm not kidding. And yes, you should start to indulge your fantasies. Imagine *you have €100,000 in the bank* . . . imagine *you have paid off the mortgage* . . . imagine *debt is not keeping you awake at night* . . .

I said already that I don't go in for pie-in-the-sky talk and I meant it. There is a saying, 'Goals are dreams that mean business.' Well, if you want to set new goals, the first step is to dream. I promise you that day-dreaming is a proven strategy for improving your finances. It helped me improve my own finances and I'm a financial trainer!

I'm sure you realize that improving your finances will involve making a budget, sticking to it, saving, and inevitably a certain amount of belt-tightening that you may be dreading (I'll try to make it a little more painless). But, for now, while you still dread all the unpleasantness you think is coming up, why not stock up on good feelings with a bit of day-dreaming? It can't hurt.

For me, it starts off when I get up in the morning. I love to do this. As soon as I'm awake, I bolt out of bed, imagining all the wonderful things I would like to welcome into my life. I get this lovely, warm, excited feeling, thinking of all that could be. As a result, I'm never inclined to laze in bed or in any other way procrastinate when I know I have this to look forward to.

After my shower, I might dress up in a suit, or go a bit 'artsy', or just be comfortable. I then put on my make-up and get my accessories. It's like a night out. I like to walk to wherever I'm going, as the fresh air is good to get body and mind moving. This is my ideal set-up for day-dreaming. I settle down in a cosy café and I usually order a large Americano and a scone. Then I start writing. If it's company business, I use our company's headed paper. If it's personal, I write in a journal. If I'm brainstorming, I take the laptop.

By now, I have a number of favourite places to day-dream all over the world. From Java Bay in Dublin, to Gloria Jean's in Cork, to Java's in Galway, to the Citizen M in Amsterdam, to Vinotheque in Malta, to Toast in North Carolina, and airports everywhere. I love to sit and dream in the Phoenix Park or look out at the sea in Salthill. And guess what? If you think I'm rattling off the names of faraway places to show off, keep this in mind: I was able to reach those places as a result of day-dreaming.

At Christmas at home in Cork, I love to sit in the living room with the fairy lights on the tree and my mam bringing me coffee and cake. I dream of Christmases past and think about what the New Year will bring. Sometimes, over coffee with my boyfriend, Ardle, who is also my business partner, no matter where we are, we talk about what we would like to do and he listens to me talk about what our future could look like.

Of course, you may not be able to take a morning to do this or you're a night-person who would be much better suited to a roaring fire and a comfy sofa. Work to your own rhythm and find a bit of space where you can just be relaxed and let your mind wander.

While sipping my coffee, I usually ask myself open questions like, 'Where would I like to be in a year's time?', 'What would life be like if x happened?', 'What is the next impossible thing that we want to achieve?' I write these in the middle of the page.

I then ask myself, 'What's the best that could happen?' A note of warning here: if you're anything like me, doubt will start to kick in. I no sooner have the answer to this question down on paper than negative thoughts pop into my head. I just put them aside – I write them down on one side of the page – and deal with them later.

Keep writing and writing until you can't come up with any more 'best things that could happen'. What exactly does this dream situation look like? How much money will you have? What will the people whom you care about say to you? Who will be inspired by you? How much of your time will you spend in this situation? What will your day look like? What time will you get up in the morning? What doors will it open for you? How will it affect your life positively? How will you feel as you are living that dream? What will be your focus? What things that you worry about now won't be a concern then? What nice types of issues will you have to face . . . ones that when you need to think about them, you'll be delighted?

If you ended up completely oblivious of your surroundings while you were immersed in the exercise, that's fantastic. It's really important that this vision is as strong and as vivid as possible. Now all you need to do is to figure out a way of getting there . . .

But I realize you are quite likely to be thinking that getting there is next to impossible. 'Yeah, right,' you may be thinking, 'double my income! Save 10% of my wages every month! Start a business! Who am I kidding?' I know what that's like. I've heard the same mocking voice of doubt and discouragement challenge my dreams.

Before we begin to work on what next step you can take towards your dreams, we need to address those doubts you wrote down on the side of the paper. We need to bring your current reality into line with your new vision and bridge the gap between the two.

Do you feel uncomfortable facing those doubts and fears? Would you prefer to forget your present situation? This part of the exercise might sound off-putting, but I assure you that it is absolutely necessary. Please do the exercise right through to the end. You may be very, very surprised by what happens afterwards.

What is going on with you currently? What could hold you back?

Why is it that you think you can't achieve what you want? Let's get all this out in the open. Two things can happen here. The first is that the list could be relatively short, which would be a nice surprise. On the other hand, it could be a seemingly never-ending list of reasons why you can't move forward.

It is as much for the list of negatives as positives that I recommend day-dreaming: it is the quickest way to uncover all your invisible barriers and fears. As soon as you say 'Wouldn't it be nice to . . .', you'll be met by a barrage of objections. Before you get disillusioned and give up, believing those objections to be the voice of reason, list them. You're about to gain a priceless insight into what is holding you back.

So anchor yourself in the here and now: all you're doing is sitting in a place where you feel comfortable and thinking about what you would like to achieve. Nobody knows that you're doing this, nobody knows how you're feeling, nobody knows anything! It's safe for you to continue, and it's after this point that the magic happens. The dream you wrote about *can* happen, you just need to stick with me for a while. Finish this list of doubts and fears, then look at that piece of paper and think, 'That's it – that's all that's holding me back.' (Actually, what you're probably thinking at this point is 'Yeah, those 126 reasons are "all" that's holding me back. Piece of cake!')

Once you have your dream vision *and* your list of obstacles, we need to reconcile the two. Have you ever had to take on a huge commitment and felt overwhelmed by it, but you didn't have a choice? Conversely, did you ever start a project thinking it was much smaller than it actually was? Halfway through you found yourself saying, 'If I'd known it was this much work, I would never have started it,' but, as you had committed to the project and couldn't bail out, you ploughed on. And then, suddenly, you arrived at the end. Weren't you delighted that you had achieved something amazing? This is the principle that I'm inviting you to work with here.

Since you've written down each and every thing that's holding you back, you've succeeded in breaking down what was a big, insurmountable mountain of anguish into bits and pieces. (You will find that, as you look back at this sheet of paper over the coming weeks, months and years, the obstacles disappeared, or changed, or weren't as big as you thought, or maybe were too big to get over and instead pushed you in another – and, often, better – direction.) The next step of this process is to pull up your sleeves and to look objectively and openly at each problem on your list. This is where your dream begins to mean business. Take some time to do this. Go through the list and see if you can come up with a strategy for dealing with every item. If you have no idea how to solve an issue, just come up with something helpful that will go some way towards solving it.

You'll find that some of the obstacles on your list behave like vampires: they seem to be sucking out all your energy and your will to improve, but as soon as they're exposed to the light of day they crumble. For example, 'Now that I come to think of it, I wouldn't have to lease a place to start practising my upholstery. There's probably no reason why I couldn't use Dad's shed until I get going.' Others will prove to be more solid, e.g., 'There's nothing I can do about Johnny's new roster and the kids' school timetable,' but at least now you know where you stand. You have determined where the real roadblocks are, and you can devise ways around them. Forewarned is forearmed.

As I write, I've just done this exercise with one of my own goals, and I want to show you how I went through the process. I'd like to take a course that would further my career, build my credibility, enable me to charge more for my services and aid my own personal development, as well as keep me up to date in the industry in which I work. However, the reason that I haven't gone ahead with this course for the past couple of years is because . . .

a. it will require a huge investment of my time, and that's in short supply;

b. I'd have to sit the exam about a year after the course begins and it's going to involve a marathon of study, which will require a lot of self-discipline and sacrifice;

c. if I don't pass the exam, I'd have to go and do it all again
   the following year;
d. I might get bored in the middle;
e. it costs a significant amount of money;
f. if I don't do the exam, I can build the company faster.

Now let's take each of these in turn:

a. This is the biggest barrier, and the one that's the most
   difficult to deal with. I neither want to, nor can, just
   remove existing commitments. I'm not about to let the
   company shut down while I study. Similarly, I'm not going
   to tell my family and friends, who in certain cases need me
   or rely on me, to disappear and I'm certainly not going to
   dishonour commitments that I've already made. On the
   other hand, if push came to shove, I could get up two
   hours earlier two mornings a week for the first six months
   and ask other members of my family to help me out on a
   Saturday morning with my existing commitments. As a
   result, I could probably find a couple of hours a week to
   spend on dedicated study. Also, if I spend the time and
   possibly the money involved in delegating more responsibility to my staff, I'll be able to take more time off as the
   exam date comes closer. In fact, this could be a benefit that
   could outlive the exam.
b. Regarding the self-discipline and sacrifice, there is nothing
   holding me back here. I'm simply going to have to design a
   system whereby I make the study fun (I used to do this a
   lot in my younger days), reward myself regularly to keep
   up my spirits, find a nice, comfortable environment, maybe
   have a study day from time to time with a friend of mine
   and just remember the reasons why I'm doing this course.
   This is all totally doable!
c. The problem around failing certainly won't arise at all if I
   don't take the exam in the first place. I simply can't let the

fear of failure hold me back from going for this exam, as otherwise I've lost before I've even opened a book.

d. The obstacle of 'I might get bored in the middle' is very similar to the self-discipline issue. The same answer applies here; it's just my objection manifested itself twice to make sure I heard it!

e. The cost isn't so high that it's insurmountable. As long as I budget for it, this really shouldn't present a problem. Also, it's immense value for money and much cheaper than if I were to go back to full-time study, which might have to happen in the future if I don't keep up today. However, the cost of taking time out of the company is much higher and brings me back to my responses to the first issue.

f. Indeed, I probably could build the company faster if I didn't take the time to study. However, this is simply a trade-off that I must be willing to make, as the benefits from getting the qualification are that great. Also, I (hopefully) have a long life ahead of me yet in which to grow the company, and anyway I won't be stopping, just easing off the pedal a bit. Although, if I invest in my staff, as I've mentioned in the first point, the company could stay on the same path while using other people's skills more effectively.

The moral of all this is that I've worked out exactly what I need to do to deal with real issues, and I've identified the ones that are just my own fears. In addition, I have short- and medium-term strategies for dealing with the drawbacks, and now I'm ready to get on with enjoying the benefits.

I've been doing this exercise for many years, and just last week I was at a course where they put a name on each of the stages. If you, like me, need a system, think about it this way:

- **G** – Goals: What are my / our goals?
- **R** – Realities: What are my / our realities?

~ **O** – Options: What options have we got to move forward?

~ **W** – What: What are we going to do next (the subject of the next chapter)?

So, 'What are we going to do next?' We have a dream vision and a list of obstacles. Now we know where we're starting from and where we want to go. But we don't know yet how to get there. What we need is a satnav.

Decide your financial destination

3

If I was going there, I wouldn't start from here

If you don't go after what you want, you'll never have it.
If you don't ask, the answer is always no. If you don't step
forward, you're always in the same place.

– Nora Roberts

Once I was in Gorey in Wexford and trying to get to Cork. I followed signs for Cork until they just stopped while I was still in the middle of the town. I took a chance and drove down a road that seemed roughly in the right direction; and when I finally came upon a signpost, a fair way out in the countryside, I saw that not one of the locations mentioned was anywhere near Cork, so I turned around and headed back the way I'd come. I sat in traffic for half an hour going back through the town, only to arrive back exactly where I'd started. I started to panic – where the hell was I going? – so I rang my boyfriend to let off steam and he simply said, 'Just calm down: turn on the satnav and follow the directions.' Yeah, the satnav – it was sitting in there in the car, but I hadn't put it on because I thought I wouldn't need to: Gorey is quite a small town and I assumed I could rely on the signposts. The point of this is that, like many of us in a similar situation, I believed that by just driving I'd at least be making progress and would somehow stumble upon the right road leading to where I wanted to go. But all I did was waste time covering unnecessary ground and end up exactly where I'd begun.

Of course, satnavs aren't infallible. They can't foretell traffic jams. They don't automatically update as soon as a new road is opened. You might set it to take the 'shortest route' and find yourself on back roads where you can only crawl, or run into a flock of sheep, or get stuck behind a tractor. Nonetheless, most of the time they do a great job of getting you where you want to go.

Wouldn't it be great to have a satnav to guide your life? To tell your brain to make €100,000 a year and then sit back while it guided you to your destination? Well, if you think about the exercises you completed in Chapter 1, figuring out your financial temperature, you'll see that actually we do have a sort of internal satnav. As I discussed in that chapter, some people can win money or earn a bonus and then spend it all, until their bank balance is back to where it started. This happens because they can't wait to get back to where they feel most comfortable.

When it comes to getting to a better place financially, you need to programme yourself to get there. My saving grace in Gorey that day was that I knew what to tap into the satnav. In the same way, you need to know your destination. Like setting the device in the car, you need to tell your brain where you want to go and expect it to come up with a route and to guide you as if there were no possible alternative but to get there. Trust me – once you tell your brain that this goal is going to be achieved and that it had better start to work with you in getting there, you'll be amazed at the ways in which things seem to come together to help you succeed.

If you want to discover where you'd like to go with your finances, the first thing that you need to do is figure out your current style of navigation. Let's examine what things look like when you aren't really thinking about where you're heading.

Journey 1

You get your pay cheque, and you promise yourself that this month you're going to be good. You're going to divide it by four and spend only your weekly 'allowance'. The next morning, you get a call from a friend who's just got engaged. You're very happy for your friend, but, inside, you're calculating the cost of the hen night, the gift, the day of the wedding, the day after it, the hotel, the dress, etc.

You think to yourself that as you won't have to spend the money for at least six months, it's not relevant to what happens this week-end . . . except as a reminder of why you need to budget. (I disagree with that way of thinking. This is often how lumpy expenses get on top of us and cause anxiety. Instead, I have a 'wedding/social occasion/fun' fund, which gets x% of my money on a monthly basis. I don't ever need to budget specifically for these occasions, as it's done for me and I can earn interest during the not-so-socially hectic months. Let's talk about this in more detail later!) Your friend invites you out for a celebratory drink on Saturday night. Saturday night comes along and you put €50 into your pocket. That's your limit, you say, and NO stopping at the ATM. You walk into the bar and your friend says, 'Hi, lovely to see you, what are you having?' Straight away you say, 'Thanks, but you stay on your own and I'll get my own.' 'We're all in a round at the table, sure have one anyway.' Willpower is soluble in alcohol and you find yourself at the dreaded ATM at the end of the night in order to get the money for a taxi home. Your sister calls on Sunday and invites you to lunch with herself, her husband and the kids. You haven't seen them in a while and that sounds lovely. 'Where would you like to meet?' you say and your face falls as you know the place she suggests is another €30 down the drain. You check your bank balance online Monday morning at work. One and a half times your 'weekly allowance' is gone already and you don't know how you're going to stick to your plan for the rest of the month.

Journey 2

You get your pay cheque for the month and you want to put away a bit this time for 'back to school' in September. You pay the mortgage. You take a chunk off the credit card. You pay your house insurance, get credit for your phone, get the shopping for the week, pay a fine, buy concert tickets as a birthday present for your brother. You pay the property charge. You have €200 left for the rest of the month. You need to get your eyebrows and legs waxed and the salon only takes cash. After that, you'll have about €150 left to cover the rest of the month. Here we go again, another month of living off the credit card and paying the interest for the privilege. This is such a debilitating spiral. You want to clear the credit card, clear the over-draft and plan to put away some money for the back to school fund, so that it won't overwhelm your bank account completely when the time comes. Instead, you've got a full month before your bank account gets topped up . . . which feels *so* long away. The chunk you paid off the credit card is likely to be borrowed again, so, in effect, you're right back to where you were at this time last month. If only you could get ahead of the bills! Next month, it will be different.

Journey 3

You *promised* yourself this wouldn't happen. You're self-employed and the income-tax deadline is four days away and you have a ball of receipts, bank statements and an income-tax form that you can't remember how to fill out. Nothing for it, only to burn the midnight oil again. You start with the receipts, and, as you're going through them, you reminisce about 'I remember the day we bought that' and 'I can't believe that it's nine months since we did that.' You put them all into nice piles and start to calculate them. Better tot them up again to make sure. This time, you count €100 less than the last time. Start again. Aaargh!

Three days to go. Now, the bank statements. What was that lodge-ment in May? Look at your diary – no idea what that payment for €273 was for. You call the bank and they say all they have is the infor-mation that appears on your statement. They say they can ask the branch to retrieve the specific lodgement and find out if it was a cheque, cash or a combination. You hate putting people to trouble, but you'd better make sure. Next snag, you can't find the bank statement for

October. After a wasted two hours looking everywhere, you find it. The bank calls. The €273 consisted of a €100 cheque lodgement – a present somebody gave you for your birthday; and the rest was a refund of a deposit. All irrelevant for the purposes of the tax calculation.

Two days to go. You start to fill out the form. You have everything you need now – your turnover and your costs. You make a start and everything is going well. You need to find how much you last earned as an employee before you left your job. Now, where is the P60?! Another half an hour gone. You fill in more boxes and flick through those you don't need to fill out. You need to input your capital-gains return from last year! You have a mountain of emails that just have to be dealt with and you spend until 7 p.m. doing them. Retrieve the laptop where you worked out the capital-gains tax return. Spend another hour finding it. A sigh of relief – it's all done now apart from working out the actual tax payable. WHAT??!! That much?!! You don't have enough in your bank account or enough credit on your credit card to pay it, but you do if you add the two together. You go to your online-banking service and transfer enough money to your credit card to pay this tax.

One day to go. You send off the form and call the Revenue to make the payment over the phone. You are put on hold for an hour as they say, 'Your call will be dealt with in rotation . . .' and you wait impatiently to pay this blasted tax. *Next year, it will definitely be different!*

Taking control of your finances – thinking about where you want to go – two separate states of mind with two fantastic benefits. First, taking control means being aware. Instead of being hit by wave after wave of 'unexpected' unavoidable spending, you can be pro-active. Instead of vowing to 'try to be good' each month, failing miserably and convincing yourself that you're 'no good with money', you can sit down *before* you get your wages and work out what your financial month is going to look like. You know what to expect, so you can plan. Instead of paying off all bills and buying presents and making foreseeable annual payments all in one month, with the result that you're left with nothing, you can spread things out evenly. Instead of leaving everything until the last minute and then having to waste days sorting things out, you could set up a system so that it takes less than an hour a month to keep your business or household finances in check.

Second, taking control means being effective. Instead of paying the credit-card company for the privilege of being in debt, you could restructure your finances so as to wean yourself off this expensive form of life support. Instead of paying everything at once, ending up in debt and then stressed out of your mind when the schoolbooks and uniform expenses come along, you could 'spread September throughout the year' and get *paid* interest on the money you're putting by while doing so. Instead of drawing the Revenue's attention every year with a late submission, or having to pay bank charges for recovering lost statements, you could have an efficient system – and getting on top of your tax affairs is beneficial for every aspect of your financial life.

Do you want to continue in a state of disarray or to take control? Do you want to be the worried driver going around in circles not knowing where you're going or do you want to be focused on your destination and confident of reaching it? If the latter, it's time to set the satnav.

'Not worrying about money' is not ideal as a destination. To begin with, the phrase has two negative words: 'not' and 'worrying'. It contains a negative bias, an 'away motivation'. To explain what I mean by that, think of it in terms with which a lot of us are familiar: wanting to lose weight. A couple of years ago, I wanted to lose weight and I knew how to do it too – eat healthier foods and take exercise. However, I could never quite 'get into it'. I had a sea of excuses: *I'm away. It's Friday night. It would be rude to turn down cake with a coffee in somebody else's home. I'm tired.* Basically, I didn't want to not eat the things I liked. On and on it went. Then my brother got me a beautiful Tommy Hilfiger suit as a present, but the trousers were too tight. I really wanted to fit into them, so immediately

I had a positive motivation and found I could turn down any biscuit or cake. It wasn't that I had suddenly developed iron discipline, but that I realized that every single sugary treat was holding me back from wearing those trousers.

So if you're trying 'not to be' something –'not to be fat', 'not to be in debt', 'not to be poor', 'not to be in financial trouble', 'not to be lonely' – this is an 'away' motivation and it's very feeble compared with a 'to' motivation. Applying this to losing weight, a 'to' motivation is thinking about it as wanting 'to be slim', rather than 'not to be fat'. To discourage snacking, dieting professionals encourage slimmers to put a picture of someone with a good figure on the fridge – experience tells them that helping people to work towards slimness is more successful than helping them to work away from fatness. If I aspire to 'not be fat', I can work to the point where I no longer deem myself to be overweight. I have achieved my goal and that's it. Am I fit and healthy? Have I developed a life-style I can maintain? Not necessarily. However, if my goal is 'to be slim', I have something to work towards and I'm more likely to remain that way because I have a clear idea in my head of what the state of being slim requires.

In a similar way, if all you want to do is get out of debt, what then? If you have zero borrowings, but zero money in your account, is that all you want? Have you reached your goal? In fact, if you do get to that point and abandon your efforts to improve your situation, you may have no choice but to fall prey to lenders again. Instead, aspire to 'have €10,000 as savings', 'earn €100,000 per year', 'generate a 5% after-tax return from investments' – all these mean that you can work 'towards' something, and should your savings, earnings or returns dip, you know that you'll need to take corrective action.

Let's take some concrete examples of financial 'away' and 'to' motivations. Do any of these examples ring true to you?

Away: 'Here I am on this cycle of work hard, pay off the mortgage, pay the other bills, worry about money, drain the fun out of my disposable income with anxiety, struggle through another month and then start again. If I just didn't have the mortgage, life would be so much better and my load so much lighter . . .'

To: 'I want to pay off the mortgage.'

Away: 'Another rainy day full of boredom for the kids and frustration for me. I don't want to be wishing the kids' lives away. I don't want to be driving me and them crazy. I feel guilty about just putting on a DVD and allowing them to be zombies in front of it – I don't want their childhood memories to be full of Scooby-Doo and Dora the Explorer – but I can't think of anything to do with them . . . that I can afford.'

To: 'I want to take the kids on holiday each year comfortably.'

Away: As you're looking at your bank statement, you think, 'I hope to God there aren't any emergencies in this family, as I simply will not be able to deal with them. I also hope nobody wants to get married next year, because I can't afford it. As for my husband and his "midlife-crisis" desire to get a Merc next year, he can forget that too!'

To: 'I want to build up an emergency fund of €10,000.'

Away: 'Can I go out tonight? Have to check my account. Can I go on a shopping spree in the January sales? Have to check my account. Can I go on holidays with the girls? Have to check my account. Can I invite my sisters and their husbands over for dinner? Have to check my (larder and my) account. Maybe I should just stop having a social life because I can't seem to enjoy anything without having to check my account!'

To: 'I want to develop an income stream of €100,000 per year.'

Away: 'Imagine my little boy going to college . . . I suppose he'll want to move to Dublin. If he's able to get a job, it certainly won't be enough to keep him throughout the four years. Four years! There will be books too, I suppose, and registration fees. They'll probably go up in the Budget. I know he's only ten now, but I think he's going to have to save money himself between now and then, or else we'll need to remortgage.'

To: 'I want to be able to put my kids through college.'

Away: 'Another year, another waste of time. I got a fantastic 2% on my pension fund. Of course, they tell me that I made 6% gross but after all the fees, commissions, etc., I get a measly 2%. That won't keep up with inflation at all. I would have got a better return by putting it into cash. I'm going to have to give up this idea of using equities in my portfolio and just put away more of my salary; otherwise I'll have to scale back my lifestyle when I retire.'

To: 'I want to learn how to navigate the stock market.'

Away: 'What the hell is he on about? I haven't a clue what APR, ETF, ADR are. How am I supposed to know whether I want to invest in the S&P 500 or the emerging markets? How can the value of bonds fall – sure, aren't they called "fixed income"? Doesn't that mean my income is fixed? This is just complete jargon, I haven't a hope of understanding what he's saying and I don't want to admit it. As usual, I'll just go along with it and hope my money is still there when I want it!'

To: 'I want to be able to converse competently and confidently with my financial adviser.'

Away: 'This is ridiculous! The alarm clock is going off at 5 a.m. again. I have to spend two hours sitting in traffic going to a job that I can't stand. The kids are in bed when I get up and again when I come home. It's dark when I get out of bed and when I get back into it. I finish on a Friday, start relaxing on a Saturday evening and by Sunday afternoon I'm already dreading the "eh, eh, eh" of the alarm clock. It's only April, but at least at Christmas, I'll get a break . . .'

To: 'I want to retire at fifty.'

What all of these examples are designed to show you is that there is always a positive way of perceiving the challenge. Think of what your financial issues are and determine your positive motivation for each. Where are you trying to get to? What is your ideal? What does taking control mean? Let's take the 'to' motivations above.

I want to pay off the mortgage.
I want to take the kids on holiday each year comfortably.
I want to build up an emergency fund of €10,000.
I want to develop an income stream of €100,000 per year.
I want to be able to put my kids through college.

I want to learn how to navigate the stock market.

I want to be able to converse competently and confidently with my financial adviser.

I want to retire at fifty.

In every one of those statements, there is something tangible to work towards; and, if there is one thing you shouldn't do, it's to let doubt enter your mind. This is only something you're putting down on paper. Don't start letting thoughts like 'But sure, that will never happen' into your brain. Remember what I said in the last chapter: let your imagination take hold. If they are shouting for your attention, write them down on the other side of the paper and let them sit there until you're ready to attend to them.

It might be that your doubts are so strong they make it difficult for you to focus on what you consider to be fanciful visions. And it's not as if you can simply switch off that critical voice in your head.

I'm sure you are familiar with the concept of a comfort zone. You contemplate doing something new, something ambitious, something you've never done before. You know it's possible, because others have done it. And then you feel the fear and self-doubt creeping in. That is your comfort zone.

The vision you have conjured up while day-dreaming is outside of your comfort zone, so you feel anxious. You should remember that a comfort zone is simply a particular set of behaviours that has prevailed up to now. You think that your gut reactions about what is and isn't doable are your identity, defining characteristics – like your height or the colour of your eyes. But, in fact, your behaviours are very open to change and your comfort zone can be stretched. Your financial thermostat is one aspect of your comfort zone, and just as it can be reset, so your comfort zone can expand.

Many people confuse their comfort zone – what they are comfortable doing – with 'being realistic'. Yet there is nothing realistic or especially sensible about letting your fears guide you. Fears are, by definition, not real; they are in your mind. If you let fear and doubt dictate what you can or cannot do, you'll live a very constricted life.

There are some things that you've never done before, so you feel scared. You retreat to what you know, even though at times this isn't helpful at all. Say you have a friend who finds it terrifying to go out of a Friday evening: she thinks having to dress up is a huge challenge because she has no interest in fashion, and besides nothing nice fits her, and the thought of mustering the courage to talk to strangers terrifies her. So she prefers to stay home and be depressed because she's alone, telling herself – and you – that she's fat and boring and she'll never find a man. Now, what would you say to her? That's right: you'd tell her she's in a rut, that she's underestimating herself, and that of course if she stays sitting on the sofa every Friday night her prediction may well come true, but it will be because she was too scared to try something new, not because her assessment was correct. You may well use the phrase 'self-fulfilling prophecy'.

If you're thinking that sitting at home on a Friday night is far from being a comfort zone – indeed, it sounds extremely uncomfortable to you – that's because your comfort zone is different. You might relish the thought of getting dressed up to go out on a Friday evening. On the other hand, would you feel just as comfortable going to see your boss about a raise? Maybe not. Maybe that would be totally out of your comfort zone. You would say: 'But I'd never have the nerve to do that!' That's your comfort zone speaking. Others might find it much easier to negotiate for a raise.

It might be that in your field wages are frozen for the moment, but that shouldn't stop you from thinking about how to build your skillset, or working on your confidence, so that when the time comes for things to improve – and it will come – you'll be well positioned to seize the opportunity.

Imagine that you could, one step at a time, expand your comfort zone. What totally non-scary thing could you do now or tomorrow in order to work towards your goal of asking for a raise? You could read a book or two about negotiating. You could type 'negotiate a raise' into Google and see what comes up. You could start asking the people you know who got raises to tell you how they did it. You could start working with a life coach to address your fear of standing up for yourself and asking for what you deserve. In other words, if you're horribly afraid of asking for a raise, don't walk into your boss's office this very minute. You don't have to. But you can still slowly work your way towards getting a raise.

Or, if you're in a business and the prospect of getting a raise feels very remote at present, maybe there's something your employer could do instead that would benefit you both. For example, is there a way that you could get involved in sales, if you aren't already? Let's imagine that you have an idea for an online-marketing campaign or a new sales channel. You could make a deal to split the revenue generated from these efforts between you. Also, I think back to a time when a friend of mine had her salary cut very significantly and it spooked her completely. She went on to pay for further professional education out of her own pocket. If I knew then what I know now, I would have advised her to ask her boss to fund her course in exchange for her acceptance of a pay cut. In hindsight, the company probably would have paid for it, as they would have seen it as an investment in the business. But it never happened, because she never asked.

What I'm saying is, do something, do anything, and don't discount your efforts. Do the smallest thing you can do to get closer to your goal. The smallest thing is sometimes enough, as long as you're always going forward. So, for the time being, acknowledge your doubts, but let your imagination run wild: what will be your 'to' motivation? The reality check will come later, if it needs to come at all.

Every one of us is limited by the unique boundaries of our comfort zone. But if you engage in the day-dreaming exercise I described in the previous chapter, and use it to work out strategies for overcoming real obstacles, you'll be able to identify your 'to' motivations and be in a position to set the satnav on a course towards your financial goals.

4

Getting past the First of January Syndrome

If you've completed the exercises from the previous chapters, by now you'll have a list of financial goals. However, your work has only started, because it's all too easy to set goals and then fall at an early hurdle. If you haven't really thought through how you'll achieve them, or you've said to yourself at the first difficulty 'I'll start tomorrow', all your good intentions will dissolve into the ether. This is what the rest of the book is about – breaking down the process of getting to your goals.

If you're thinking there's still a lot of this book to go, so it must be very complicated, please don't be put off. Think of times when you've made good resolutions in the past – to lose weight, to give up smoking, indeed, to get your finances in order – only to beat yourself up a few months later because nothing happened. You should know that the problem lies not in your willpower or self-discipline, but in the way you set your goals. There are several mistakes that people regularly make when doing this, which means their plans are doomed even as they are conceived. Here are three ways that I failed at achieving goals because I went about things the wrong way.

Having no way to measure success

Like many people, losing weight and getting fit have often been high on my New Year resolutions list. Typically what happens is this: the first of January rolls around and willpower is high. I sign up for a one-year membership at a gym and pat myself on the back for ordering soup for lunch and passing on dessert. By the seventh of

January, I can't find my gym membership card and it's Friday night, so having a bar of chocolate with a cup of tea when watching *The Late Late Show* is surely allowed.

What went wrong?

It's quite simple. In the first few days that you start to instruct your body to lose pounds, it doesn't listen. You don't see any immediate rewards for 'being good' and you lose interest. On top of that, you have no way of measuring if you're doing the right thing: does a thirty-minute walk equal two biscuits? After small lapses, you cast your goal aside until the next opportunity to make a resolution comes along – Lent, going on summer holiday, a wedding invitation . . .

However, it's different when you have a way of measuring success. I joined Weight Watchers and got into its points system (which gives you an individual daily-points allowance, a guide to the points value of individual foods, based on fat and calorie content, and a guide to the points value of individual exercises, based on the number of calories each burns). I could clearly see when I was sticking to my points allowance for the day, and even within the first twenty-four hours I was able to see whether I'd been successful. After that, if I began to flag, I could see, in black on white, my movement towards the slippery slope. Did I really want to go back to the start again? Funnily enough, the weighing scales caught up with me soon afterwards.

It is so important to have small ways of acknowledging your success. This is particularly crucial during the initial stages, when your willpower is strongest. The easier the steps at the beginning, the more successes you can notch up, and the more effectively you'll be grounded when you leap towards where you eventually want to go.

Setting ambitious goals without breaking them down

When I was younger and needed to save for something big, I equated that with 'not spending money'. I decided that from that point onwards I would only 'spend on necessities'. As with losing weight, I would have iron resolve for a couple of days and then it all fell apart.

I recall one time I was on an economy drive that lasted until a college friend rang me to say she had free tickets to go to the *Live Strictly Come Dancing* show in the O2; everyone from our class was meeting in town afterwards. Then, walking by Arnotts one day, I spotted a skirt on sale that was part of a suit that I already had. Next, my boyfriend suggested going out for dinner. Each of these turned out to be 'necessities'. It looked like I would always remain constrained by that overdraft.

Emotions and subjectivity wreak havoc with the best of intents. First, a 'Friday night out in town' was marked down as a necessary expense – right up there with petrol. Second, I was trying to do too much in one go. There are so many products, services and experiences vying for our disposable income, how could I just shun them all overnight? Finally, I didn't give myself any time limit. I could have said, 'I don't have the money to go out this weekend, but instead I will have a great, worry-free weekend next month when my cousin comes home from England.' Instead, I tried to sentence myself to a fun-free life for the foreseeable future.

After that, I changed my ambition and made the decision to save 5% of my salary each month. This was different because, first, I could measure my success. Second, I set up a standing order to take this amount out of my account monthly before I could get at it. Third, removing 5% of my income restricted my spending, but didn't choke it.

The main thing here is that I didn't just say, 'What's the point?' I looked at what went wrong (admittedly, it took a few false starts before I could really see what was happening) and then put in place something realistic that would stop me from making impulsive spending decisions.

Not thinking like somebody who has already achieved their goal

During my second year in school, my beloved grand-uncle died and I became a little disillusioned with the world, as only a fourteen-year-old can! My grades started to slip and I realized it was time to pull myself together. So I began to spend more time on my home-work, doing things like organizing my folders and typing out my notes. At the end of the year I was terribly disappointed to see that the extra effort hadn't made any difference to my results. I had thought that the more time I spent on my homework, the better I would do.

Even at fourteen I saw that the plan had failed because, although I was putting more time into my studies, the only focus for that time was tidier notes. I started to think differently and wonder 'How can I study to pass the exam?', as opposed to 'How can I study more?'

Essentially, I not only started to think like someone who wanted to do well in her exams, I also started to act like that person. I discovered ways to remember more while employing less mem-ory space. I used memory tricks, such as recalling sequences by associating them with landmarks on my way to school. For example, there are four factors of production in economics: land, labour, capital and enterprise. I would associate 'land' with the cross, 'labour' with the pond, 'capital' with the shop and 'enterprise' with the school gate. If I couldn't remember one of them in a test, I simply thought back to my journey to school and usually found the answer.

What my fourteen-year-old self somehow sensed is that success wasn't about working harder, but about working smarter. And working smarter – or SMARTER – is what I'm going to discuss for the rest of this chapter. If you want to achieve your objectives, the key is to break down the process into components:

Specific
Measurable
Attainable
Realistic
Timely
Extending
Rewarding

SMARTER goal-setting in action

For most of 2011, I was working towards a goal that was so huge it seemed unattainable: changing the focus of the business from live-delivered training to blended learning. My business partner and I decided that eLearning – courses delivered over the internet – was a field that we needed to explore and in which we needed to develop a strong competency. We went into Enterprise Ireland and spoke to them about our company, outlining all that we were going to do and the progress we had made towards international expansion. For example, I had gone over to Malta for a week of meetings to see if there was any potential for business there (I'll tell you how that came about a little further along). We had gone to a trade show in New York to connect with similar businesses, to look at what other companies were doing and to identify ways in which we could collaborate with them. We had spoken with a number of government agencies who help start-ups export. My development adviser called me a couple of days later to say that we had secured feasibility funding to investigate the market further and develop a prototype. How feasibility funding works is that, up to a certain level, half the costs of a research stage for a new business or product will be matched by funding from the government. Essentially, you know you'll get back half of whatever you need to spend on a project if approved. So, though we were thrilled to be approved, we still had to spend our own money first. However, that wasn't going to deter us and what was important was to get stuck in.

Both of us had a lot of expertise about the stock market and had been in the financial-education industry for years, but figuring out what to do next was still a big leap. I started the only way I knew how: by day-dreaming and thinking 'Imagine if . . .' Straight away, my mind started to race here, there and everywhere. As a first step, we could digitize the training we already had . . . we just needed people to pay for it. I could put out feelers to current clients about moving their training online. After that I was a bit stumped and did not see a way forward.

I was a member of Plato Ireland a couple of years ago, a networking group that meets monthly to help small- and medium-sized enterprises to develop their businesses, and at one event the SMARTER goal-setting technique was introduced. I immediately took to this way of thinking, as it suited my natural tendency to break things down into individual steps.

One Saturday an organizing mood came over me. I sat down on a cushion on the ground and, like a child at art class, started to cut up coloured bits of paper. I let my mind wander and I wrote down all the baby steps I could think of, without worrying about how hard or easy they were. I wrote down all the contacts I knew of who could help me. I wrote down all the eLearning techniques I could imagine. I wrote down all the experiences I could talk about if I were to go into a sales meeting to discuss my product. I did a ferocious amount of scribbling. After that, it was mostly a matter of imposing some order on it all.

I started to put things together and make *Specific*, concrete goals out of the random bits of paper –'call this person', 'put together an outline for this programme', 'look up what other people are doing', 'compile a list of all the people that could help me', 'join LinkedIn groups', 'research competitors', 'research conferences', and so on.

The next thing I did was to make sure they were *Measurable*. I was hard on myself for this one. I absolutely needed to make sure I could tick the box to say that I had done it. What was the one action, when achieved, or the number, when reached, that would allow me to cross that item off the to-do list?

Most of the things I had listed were very easy, and most of them I could do without having to stretch myself very far – an important ingredient in any plan. It was both *Attainable* and *Realistic*. There was no compunction to 'break the speed of light' or 'move mountains' in there. This was key. These were little things that I could actually accomplish within a reasonable time-frame.

I wrote down deadlines next to all of my actions and goals. I noticed that I kept extending these – I changed them a few weeks later, and then again and again and again. I took a good hard look at the progress I was making and decided the problem wasn't that I was lazy or had become uninterested but that, as happens in life, other unrelated things had cropped up and got in the way. I realized I needed to be a bit harder on myself to make sure that I was moving forward in a *Timely* fashion. After I examined the ways in which I was being distracted, I became tougher with myself about meeting my deadlines.

The *E* in SMARTER is for *Extending*. Even after all I had seen, experienced and done, I still had reservations about reaching beyond where I thought the company could go, in case I was disappointed with the result. However, I forced myself to do this part of the exercise and I'm glad I did. The company's expansion is an ongoing process and I'm getting better at determining the ways that it can stretch, but, even though I'm super-ambitious, I'm never 100% confident. Even as I sit and write this, I'm only now shyly admitting to myself that there are things that I'm striving for in the company that I've not previously acknowledged.

After the challenge of doing the *Extending* part of the exercise, the next, and the most difficult, part was coming up with a list of what would be personally gratifying and *Rewarding* in achieving our expansion. Obviously it would be hugely satisfying and rewarding at a business level to attain our objectives, but how would it be at a more personal level? I'm in that immensely fortunate group of people who spend their life doing what they love, so I find that work is its own reward. After a spa treatment, a lie-in, time with my family, time in front of a fire with a book, hosting a dinner party and a good ol' slap on the back, I was struggling. Now that I think of it, this is an area that I need to work on!

Applying SMARTER goal-setting in your life

Specific

In the last chapter you figured out some of your positive goals when it comes to your money. Now you need to work backwards from these and find out the steps you can take to obtain them. Here are some of the goals you might have along with a ten-step approach to making them more specific.

I want to be in a comfortable position to take the kids on holiday each year.

1. Make a list of the types of holidays that you would like to take the kids on.
2. Research holiday destinations and costs (put pictures in a place you see them often – an image of Mickey Mouse on the fridge door to remind you frequently how wonderful it would be to take the kids to Disney, maybe).
3. Get passports for the kids.
4. Call travel agents / look at websites and ask them if they have any special offers.
5. Work out a budget that will allow you to save €100 per month.
6. Research different banks to find a high-interest account.
7. Find a revenue-generating strategy (see Chapter 18) and make €250 each month.
8. Transfer the €350 per month into the holiday account (you are $x\%$ of the way there).
9. Work out how much you can afford to spend each day on holiday.
10. Book the holiday.

I want to build up an emergency fund of €10,000.

1. Write down the reasons why you would want to build up this fund.
2. Research different banks to find a high-interest account.
3. Organize the identification that you need to set up the account.
4. Make a list of how many ways you could save or make €50.
5. Work out a budget to save €50 per month.
6. Find a revenue-generating strategy (see Chapter 18) and make €150 each month.

7. Transfer €200 into the emergency account – you are 2% of the way there!
8. Make a list of how many ways you can save or make €1,000.
9. Use one of these ten times or use ten of these ways once!
10. Work out how much interest you are making on the €10,000.

I want to learn how to navigate the stock market.

1. Work out the impact it would have on your life if you could make an 8% return on your investment cost free.
2. Research different stock-market training companies.
3. Research different stockbrokers and find the one that would suit your needs the best.
4. Open an account with a stockbroker.
5. Read a book on behavioural finance (find out the mistakes people make in the markets).
6. Work out a budget and identify a lump sum and a regular amount you could invest.
7. Attend a stock-market training course.
8. Find some investment strategies that suit you.
9. Implement these strategies on paper.
10. Make your first transaction!

There is a distinct pattern to every one of these plans.

Step 1. Articulate/calculate how much you want this goal.

Steps 2–5. Easy goals! They don't require you to take any 'monetary' actions. You first need to start living as if you are absolutely going to achieve this objective, when you may still be unsure that it can be a reality. However, there is nothing holding you back from researching, which doesn't cost a cent. If your doubts are making it difficult to take action, you can pretend to yourself you're not actually going to invest in the stock market – for the time being, you're just browsing.

Steps 6–9. Building on the right psychology (that is, avoiding ineffective goal-setting), you forge ahead and take the actions that transform your dream into a reality. They are broken down into small steps that grow incrementally into bigger and more effective strides forward.

Step 10. Enjoying that feeling of achievement and success.

Measurable

Each step of each example above was totally measurable. Anyone following any of the plans would know if they had finished a stage or not. That's key in goal-setting: every single step to a goal must be measurable. It is very important to feel the sense of satisfaction that comes from the achievement of having ticked the 'completed' box. You need to be in no doubt about when you have reached a milestone. This is the feeling that will drive you on when your motivation might flag. So whatever your goal is, go back over your ten steps and check to ensure that each is measurable.

Attainable and Realistic

You might feel that the end result is unattainable at the moment. That's perfectly normal. In fact, if you already knew how to achieve it, you wouldn't be reading this book. The main thing is not to set unobtainable goals right from the beginning. How many times do you decide on a Sunday that tomorrow you're going to start the diet of all diets and never let a piece of chocolate pass your lips again? Or that you're going to get up early every single morning this week to go to a step class in the gym? Why do you think so many New Year's resolutions fail? Because you're trying to achieve too much in too little time!

Again, going back to the examples, the first five out of the ten steps are very simple and easy. They do take a little time, but they are enjoyable. They assume that you're going to reach your final objective – 'when' and not 'if'. You need to achieve the little things first, build your confidence and then go for the later stages, which will be much easier by then anyway because your desire will drive you forward. But don't set yourself up for a fall before you even begin by missing out on these initial steps.

Timely

I frequently come up with a very comprehensive 'to-do' list for the week – full of specific, measured, attainable and realistic objectives – only to look back a week later and see none of them done. There usually isn't any excuse, but the key ingredient missing is that I didn't put a time beside each item. When working towards a timely goal, your actions are more focused and, often, more effective. You are more accountable if you put a time-frame beside each entry and you are less likely to let things distract you.

The important thing is to put down a 'finish-by' date next to each step and to avoid the 'someday' syndrome. This forces you to acknowledge that you will have to make time for this step if you want it to come to fruition, as well as to estimate how long you'll need. More often than not, you'll find, each step can be achieved in a short period of time.

Don't berate yourself if you can't rigidly adhere to your own schedule, but do go back and revisit it to ensure that procrastination isn't setting in. I guarantee that, if you're brave enough (and I mean it – it does require some courage) to put a time beside a step and to hold yourself accountable, you'll find it becomes one of the most effective things ever, because you'll want to avoid that twinge of guilt if you put it off.

Going back to the first example – *I want to be in a comfortable position to take the kids on holiday each year* – this is how you might time each of the ten steps involved.

1. Make a list of the types of holidays that you would like to take the kids on (*Friday night over a bottle of wine with your husband*).

2. Research holiday destinations and costs *(three nights during the week after the kids have gone to bed)*.
3. Get passports for the kids *(gather everything over the next fortnight and send it off by Monday)*.
4. Call travel agents/look at websites and ask them if they have any special offers *(end of next month)*.
5. Work out a budget that will allow you to save €100 per month *(the following Friday night over a bottle of wine with your husband)*.
6. Research different banks to find a high-interest account *(week after)*.
7. Find a revenue-generating strategy and make €250 each month *(end of month two)*.
8. Transfer the €350 per month into the holiday account *(end of month three)*.
9. Work out how much you can afford to spend each day *(end of month four)*.
10. Book the holiday *(sales in January)*.

Extending

Look back over your life. If you were to list all your achievements and send the list back in time to your fifteen-year-old self, how do you think the teenage you would feel? As a student who may have been looking towards her Inter. or Junior Cert., would you be excited about your future? If you can remember what you thought at that age, where did you expect to be by now? Have you done things that you could never have imagined doing? Back then I remember thinking how impossible it would be to have a fifteen-minute conversation in French. Yet one verb and one noun led to hundreds of others, and two years later I was chatting away in my Leaving Cert. oral exam. An early example of stretching my limits!

It is terribly important to stretch yourself all the time. You can't shy away from this aspect of goal-setting. You are in competition only with yourself when going through this exercise. You can choose a goal that is within relatively easy reach or something that you must really push yourself towards. But remember that when you choose ambitious goals, you're stretching your comfort zone and expanding it to encompass even more experiences. (Of course, during hard times, holding your own can be extending yourself without your even knowing it.)

Make sure that your objective is big enough to provide immense satisfaction upon its achievement. Ensure the first half of the journey (the first five steps) is simple, so that your confidence can grow and your brain can become primed to expect the actual achievement of your goals. Make sure that the second half of the journey (the last five steps) to your desired destination seems tough when looked at from where you are now. Imagine how you will feel when you have done it – let your imagination build up a clear picture of what this looks like. If that picture doesn't look exciting enough, aim higher and you will get there . . .

I had the feeling of being daunted by my own dreams in November 2010. We had set up the company in September, and surprisingly we were doing quite well. I don't know why I was surprised but, given the impact of the recession, I thought we would be fighting for every inch of business. However, I just poured in effort and enthusiasm, and day by day it kept getting better. By November I had got past that stage of wondering if I'd made a mistake leaving the safety of paid employment and realized our business really was a runner. I was ready for my next dream, which was to fly all over the world and have operations everywhere.

I still remember sitting at home rubbishing my dream, saying to myself, 'In fairness, how is this going to happen? Business in other countries is exactly that – in other countries. You need to go abroad to find it. You can't just make baby steps with this one – you have to get on a plane. And, on top of that, it's a big world out there – where do you start? And what are you going to sell that's different to what everyone else does? Keep dreaming, but don't hold your breath . . .'

I did keep dreaming and talking to my boyfriend about it, but

I didn't have a clue about how to make it a reality. Then I saw an email from the Dublin Chamber of Commerce about a Maltese trade delegation coming to Dublin. I thought, 'This could be a step in the right direction,' but, again, I didn't really believe it could be. I told the organizer to put me down for as many meetings as they could accommodate.

The day rolled around and I was very stressed. I had lots of places to be and loads to do. My boyfriend suggested that maybe the Chamber event was something I could drop, but I didn't like to withdraw at such short notice. I arrived late, couldn't find parking, went to the wrong place and was in a right state by the time I got there. Luckily they were running slightly late and I was able to have all my meetings, though still with only the haziest idea of what our company could do in their territory. As one meeting followed another, I was becoming increasingly interested by the Maltese perception of the new regulation, the funds industry, etc. I left feeling much calmer, and enlightened by the experience.

A few weeks later, my boyfriend and I were talking about those meetings, about how I wanted the company to be international but without knowing how to get there. Suddenly I said, 'What if I were to go over to Malta and just see how I get on? I have a couple of contacts there now. I could meet with the Chamber of Commerce, do some media interviews, meet the Irish Ambassador and maybe we could look for companies that might be interested in a joint venture.' I got all excited and looked at how much flights would be (€30 return – not a terribly risky investment). I asked Marion Jammet of Dublin Chamber if she could help me and she put me in touch with a woman working for FinanceMalta. Before I knew it I had a full itinerary and an entire sales funnel ready for me, even before I really felt ready to make my dream come true. The Malta story was born and is now worth 5% of our turnover (and growing). However, when I realized I could do it in one country, I then had the confidence to go and do it again and again. At the time of writing, export sales account for 60% of our business revenues.

At the time, the magnitude of the goal struck terror in my heart.

It sounded totally unachievable and outlandish. But, even though I was terribly afraid, I thought there was no harm in taking a small step. And then another, and another . . . one step at a time. Now imagine what I would have missed if I had let self-doubt and 'being realistic' get in the way. What a waste of opportunities.

Episodes such as this have taught me the power of 'What if . . .' When you imagine how it would be if your dream came true, you also begin to think about what you would need to do to accomplish this. It's amazing what happens when you start to say 'Imagine if . . .' and you begin to believe what could really be. And then it's a virtuous circle: one good thing leads to another.

Rewarding

I signed up to do a business-development programme towards the end of 2011. We had training days, homework, a mentor and an executive coach. Prior to this, I thought an executive coach looked through your business plan and worked out margins and strategies for growth. As a result, I gathered all my documents and off I trotted to the meeting. I was about to pull everything out of my bag when the executive coach said, 'Oh, you won't be needing those, this is about you, the person, not the business.' Over the course of those meetings, many ways to make me more productive were uncovered, and along the way I had a couple of soul-searching moments. One of those was when she said, 'You seem to work terribly hard and you achieve a lot – how often do you sit back and enjoy it?'

She had a point. I was very forward-looking, goal-focused and continuously striving. I had a to-do list as long as my arm, and it was always a matter of moving from one item to the next as quickly as possible. It felt like I had reinvented the hamster wheel. What was so urgent? Where was I going so fast? When had I last stopped to smell the flowers?

I often gave presentations on entrepreneurship in which I talked about all the tips, tricks, opportunities and facilities that I had used effectively in my own business; and when I shared my story, I did so with pride. However, as soon as I got into the car afterwards, I was back to reality, the here and now, and looking forward.

On the journey home after my first meeting, I began to look back at my college days. I used to think how much I would love to travel as part of my job and how great it would be to do some touristy things while working. I would take a canal cruise when I went to Amsterdam, visit Gozo when I went to Malta, go to the Atomium when in Brussels. Yet I had been to each of these places numerous times and done none of these things. I darted in and out of countries, soaking up a sliver of the culture, checking my emails all the while.

I also thought about many of the insurmountable things I had done: setting up my own company (and not starving in the process), expanding internationally and taking on staff. If I had known that all this would have been achieved nine months after setting up the company, I would have been delighted. But was I acting like I was delighted? No, I was too busy focusing on the signposts along the road to see the scenery that I had set out to find.

Naturally, I didn't have a personality transformation after that meeting. To be honest, I'm still struggling with the issue she raised, but I'm getting much better at it! Rewarding myself doesn't come naturally, and I think that this can be the case with many women. I punch the air, I ring my boyfriend excitedly, I feel very happy for a while, but I don't 'bank' my successes. I don't think, 'I'll treat myself to a massage now because we got that contract in' or 'I'll take the afternoon off on Friday this week if I have everything finished by 2 p.m.' I just keep going.

However, I am trying to take my own advice, and as a result have given a friend the job of making sure that I take the time to smell those flowers and do other things.

So don't forget to ask yourself the question 'What's it all for if I don't enjoy the process?' The final step in your plan should be to identify the rewards you're going to put in place alongside the little steps you take towards your goal. Obviously, the big reward is the ultimate achievement. However, you'll need to keep yourself motiv-ated between now and then. The best way to do that is to celebrate mini-achievements. Congratulate yourself on reaching all of the milestones and build in some non-monetary gifts on the way.

To return again to the first example – *I want to be in a comfortable position to take the kids on holiday each year* – this is how you might reward yourself for achieving each of the ten steps on time:

1. Make a list of the types of holidays that you would like to take the kids on *(a lie-in on Saturday)*.
2. Research holiday destinations and costs *(invite a friend round to talk excitedly about your plans)*.
3. Get passports for the kids *(a lovely warm bath)*.
4. Call travel agents/look at websites and ask them if they have any special offers *(a free hair treatment at your local hairdressing school)*.
5. Work out a budget that will allow you to save €100 per month *(an agreement with your husband that, on achievement, he'll clean the bathroom next week)*.
6. Research different banks to find a high-interest account *(a trip to the library to borrow that book you've been meaning to read for ages)*.
7. Find a revenue-generating strategy and make €250 each month *(go to a clothes-swapping outlet and have a mini-shopping spree)*.
8. Transfer the €350 per month into the holiday account *(spend time making a collage of pictures, words and other things that will form that holiday, i.e., print brochures of the tourist attractions, read reviews on TripAdvisor, look on Google Maps to see how far the local amenities are from the accommodation that you have picked out)*.
9. Work out how much you can afford to spend each day *(put together a list of things that you'll be bringing with you on holiday)*.
10. Book the holiday.

Now you really are ready to absolutely smash that goal. Before you turn this page, write down your first step in your diary. This may sound so simple, but writing it down is essential. It's not good enough if it's just in your head: make that first commitment by writing it with a deadline next to it. As a result, you'll know if you're procrastinating. On the other hand, if you take the action and achieve that first step, you can feel the reward of ticking that measurable box and seeing your dream beginning to turn into reality.

Remember, we're setting the satnav. After all, if the satnav tells you to 'Turn right at the next intersection', you don't say, 'Oh, yeah, that sure is a good idea, I'll get around to it sometime. For now I'll just drive on, though.' No, you turn right. This is the difference between looking at a map in your kitchen to prepare for a journey, and sitting in the car, behind the wheel. In the first instance you're not actually moving in space, you're just getting a feel for the route; and in the second, you're in the driver's seat, taking actual steps to reach your destination. You can read this book like a map, or follow the instructions as you do with a satnav. The former won't get you to your destination, while the latter definitely will . . .

So put that first step into your diary. This should be your sole focus between now and then. Don't think any further ahead than this first step. It's in your diary, it's in your head, and it's written in your future. Go for it.

STEP THREE

Learn to love budgeting

Putting the boring stuff on automatic so you can get to stuff that really makes a difference

Some time ago I attended a business course, once a month over six months. Each session involved a day's training in one aspect of business. Everybody was fired up to start, and I particularly remember one participant. He seemed terribly excited the first day and said the energy, enthusiasm and motivation in the room made him think about the importance of having a bigger vision than he'd ever had before. We all left in high spirits and spoke of how much we were looking forward to the next session.

The following month, when I asked how he was doing, he said, 'Oh, I was much too busy over the last month to be thinking about this.' The trainer questioned him about various aspects of the vision he had had the first day, but the details were very sketchy. The trainer was curious: 'This is your business and it appears that you don't know a lot about it. Why do your customers come to you?' He replied, 'I wasn't talking about my current business; this is going to be my future one.' If I heard that once in the six months, I heard it a million times. It was like a mantra – 'I wasn't talking about my current business; this is going to be my future one.'

At the end of the six months, he was no closer to achieving any of his business goals, future or otherwise. In fact, as time went on, he would leave earlier and earlier, and even when he was there all he did was spend his time on emails. The last session was to be a summing-up of how far we had come in the six months since the course had begun, and we all had to present aspects of both our personal and business development. Just as everyone got up to shake hands and wish each other well, he stuck his head in the door. Somebody asked where he had been all day and he said, 'I was five minutes away in my office – I was far too busy to be coming in here.' I imagine that if I were to call him up today and ask how his business was doing, he would tell me: 'I'm far too busy to be working on my business.' He was always too busy to improve his own business and, by extension, his own life. Please don't make the same mistake. Don't let the motivation you felt at the end of the last chapter be forgotten – don't let that wish-list wither and die. Do whatever is necessary to make sure you take action, the sooner the better.

In this chapter and the next I'm going to give you some tools that will help you to get further along the way to a better life.

Running your financial life on automatic

We all rely on systems in some shape or form. You set an alarm clock to wake you up at a certain time, so you don't have to keep waking up all night to check the time. You set the oven timer so that you don't have to get up every five minutes to see if the cake is baked. When you're on leave from work, you set an autoresponder on your email so that people won't get frustrated when you don't reply to messages. You set up a standing order for the mortgage so that you don't have to depend on your memory to pay it every month. Each of these systems allows you to relax; knowing that you have automated something means you don't have to worry about it and can focus on other things.

Systems also provide a trail of evidence if something goes wrong. Baking is a classic example: recipes are systems that set out very precise instructions, and if the outcome isn't what you expected, retracing your steps will enable you to find out what happened.

Systems are transferable, that is, they can be taught to other people. We see this all the time in work: someone new joins your company and in no time at all they're reporting in a like a pro. That's because in well-run businesses there are clear systems for core tasks that a person with the right skillset can be quickly trained to use.

Finally, systems are constants. You can automate mundane stuff that, however necessary, doesn't add a lot of value, so that more time and energy are left for the good stuff. So, for example, when you use an alarm clock to outsource the job of waking up, you can relax and sleep better. In the same way, I would prefer to budget when it comes to my essentials and be strategic about how to spend my disposable income, rather than worry the whole way through the month about the routine stuff.

A good system consists of five building blocks:

1. Identify your desired output – i.e., what result do you want to achieve with this system? What concrete, tangible form will this result take?
2. Identify your inputs – i.e., what are the things that will feed into this system? What do you need to set up, what do you need to feed the system for it to output the result you desire?
3. Figure out whether the inputs need to be processed – i.e., do inputs need to be changed before they can move towards output?
4. Decide if anything needs to be added to the system to get to the desired output.
5. Decide on the best tool to run the system, e.g., a spreadsheet, a process documented in a step-by-step guide, a productivity app, another tool?

The point of all this talk about systems is to get you to think a bit more deeply about how you're going to achieve your financial goals. Wouldn't it be wonderful to be able to set your financial satnav and then to sit back and relax, knowing you're going to arrive at the correct destination? Well, you can do that, but first, as ever, there's a bit of homework involved before you can put the right systems into place. A good satnav relies on complex positioning programmes to tell you where you are, to ensure you're on target or to tell you if you need to correct course. You can construct your own financial satnav to do all the same things when it comes to your financial goals. That's what this chapter and the next are about: building the systems that will guide your progression to your financial goals.

Before you build your financial satnav, you need to know where you're starting from – to track exactly how much you're earning and spending. To make this easier, I've built a smart budget spreadsheet that you can use to log your revenue and expenses. You can download it for free from my website: www.savvywomenonline. com. There is an explanatory video on the site that shows you how to use it. It's the same spreadsheet I use in my own budgeting, and I'm quite proud of all its bells and whistles! It will save you a ton of work and is your treasure map, guiding you to your goal. In the next chapter I'll explain its features in a little more detail.

At this juncture, I want to talk about the word 'budget'. To many people, it's a constraint, something they have to work within. It's often not large enough and it holds them back from doing all they want to do. But there is another way of looking at it: you could see it as a type of control. If you know how much you have to spend, you're in a position to evaluate your options and make the best choices. Similarly, each of us has a time budget – and we can choose to use our time well or to waste it. What I'm saying is that the idea of a 'budget' is going to be a positive or negative for you, depending on how much you feel in control. Systems, knowledge and action can ensure it's the former.

This is how I would approach building a very basic budget, using the building blocks of a system outlined above, as well as the budget spreadsheet.

1. *Identify output.* The output here is a full, smart, compre-hensive report of how much money I'm spending, and on

what, on a monthly basis, in comparison with projections. Being in a position to decide in advance how much I'm going to spend, and on what, could be considered another kind of output.

2. *Identify input.* The inputs are my known or projected revenues and expenditure: all the information I can gather about how much I earn and how I spend this money: receipts, bank statements, pay slips, etc.

3. *Figure out whether the inputs need to be processed.* I would like to automate the following instead of having to do it manually: every time I add an expense, I would like the budget to automatically deduct that amount from my revenues and give me a balance; if I have subcategories (i.e., fixed, variable, discretionary and savings), I would like my system to calculate their total; I would like my system to calculate the percentage that each subcategory of expenditure represents in my total budget.

4. *Decide if anything needs to be added to the system.* I would like to turn my monthly totals into an annual budget.
I would like my system to be colour-coordinated so that I can easily see which expenses belong to which category at a glance.

5. *Decide on the best tool.* Excel fits the bill perfectly.

After going through this exercise, you'll see why using a spreadsheet such as the one I've devised is a key tool in helping you to gain control of your finances.

As you know, I use the SMARTER technique all the time to make sure that I'm moving forward with my goals. I give myself daily, weekly, monthly and annual targets for achieving certain things.

Even with these techniques, I find that I sometimes get stuck and can't pinpoint exactly where I want to go and what needs to happen next. Whenever that occurs, I have an array of other strategies to get me unstuck, one of which is writing a letter from my future self. This sounds crazy, but every now and then I write a letter that starts off: *Dear Susan, It's the year 20xx and you are . . .* I write about what my dream life will look like at that point and then I work backwards from there, identifying all the steps that separate me from my dream vision.

I also use action brainstorms. When I'm at a complete loss and don't know how to move forward towards my goal, I simply write down a list of steps that I could take: big things, little things, impossible things (or so they might seem at the time), people I could call, websites I could research, emails I could send, things I could buy, anything and everything that could possibly help me. And when I make to-do lists, I always put a time-frame next to each item.

Once I've listed all those actions, I ensure that I make them happen. I take a 'solely achieving my goals' day once a week (which I built up from once a month) when I focus only on ticking things off my list, and I don't let any distractions get in the way.

Another strategy, and a tremendously effective one, is to hold review and accountability meetings. I have a range of people – my boyfriend, various friends – with whom I share my goals, and I commit to giving them a full report on my progress on specified dates. I call them my accountability partners. With my boyfriend, it's once a week – on a Friday night over dinner. I call these our weekly board meetings, which is a cause of some hilarity to everyone who knows us.

Finding the time to take control of your finances

All the techniques listed so far tell me what I have to do. But that sometimes makes for an overwhelming to-do list. I sometimes have so much to do that I don't know where to start or how to categorize everything I have to do. So I have two simple but highly effective models that help me prioritize. If it's a long list, numbering items gets ridiculous after a while so I take my tasks and put them into the following grid, along two scales of urgency and importance.

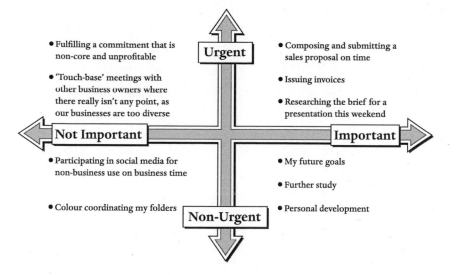

- Fulfilling a commitment that is non-core and unprofitable
- 'Touch-base' meetings with other business owners where there really isn't any point, as our businesses are too diverse

Urgent

- Composing and submitting a sales proposal on time
- Issuing invoices
- Researching the brief for a presentation this weekend

Not Important

Important

- Participating in social media for non-business use on business time
- Colour coordinating my folders

Non-Urgent

- My future goals
- Further study
- Personal development

Keeping in mind that important but non-urgent items will ensure you thrive, while day-to-day items will only ensure that you survive, will certainly focus your thinking from now on. The things that are important yet not urgent are often those that do make a difference in our lives, but that come without any deadline attached. Of course, the high achievers in this world set up self-imposed deadlines and make certain that key milestones in all aspects of their lives aren't forgotten. Let's take a leaf out of their book and also make certain that these 'important but not urgent' items don't fall by the wayside as we rush to put out fires, because they are the really momentous things that will make a huge difference in the long term. Personal development is an obvious one. Colour co-ordinating our folders, on the other hand, seldom has the same impact!

The things that need to be done right now are both important and urgent. However, we can often be in a state of mild (or severe) panic when we are under pressure. This can detract from the quality of our work and particularly our enjoyment of the task. Whenever I see something popping up on my 'important and urgent' radar, I do my best to tackle it early on, before it becomes 'very urgent'.

Funnily enough, the things that are urgent but not important are often the things that stress us out the most. We don't find them worthwhile or useful, yet they pit us against the clock and take us away from those things that we need to do in order to achieve real growth. So it's good if we can find a way to delegate them or delete them, or to make sure they're limited to certain times of the day or the week. We shouldn't feel as if they're taking over our lives.

Things that are neither important nor urgent shouldn't be taking up any of our day. After all, if they are neither of the above, they don't add anything. In fact, they could simply be described as time-wasters. If we're not in a productive frame of mind, we usually turn to these things to convince ourselves that we're 'working'. Indeed, these things are not likely to be on our to-do list, but we will do them spontaneously, in order to procrastinate or take a break.

Your time budget is the same as your money budget. You should observe where your time goes – what are the things that you must make time for (commuting, working, eating, sleeping), as well as what else happens to be taking up your time. If you find that, for example, spending time on Facebook is something you do on a regular basis, you can respond to this information by moving Facebook to your leisure time (if it's taking up 'urgent/important' business time), cutting it down, or finding some other, less time-consuming and more recharging break activity.

So this is my time-management and productivity system. As you can see, although it's a very basic system, it follows the five-step process that I showed you earlier.

1. The outcome I want is a very structured to-do list.
2. My inputs are each of my tasks.
3. I need to process my inputs by assigning them to the correct quadrant and by analysing each quadrant with a view to producing my desired outcome.
4. The only additional resource that I need is one that I'm going to describe a little further along – my Six-Task Technique, which is the perfect complement to this model.
5. The tool employed is the 'Important and Urgent' grid.

The next thing to do is to edit your to-do list so that you eliminate tasks that are urgent but not important along with things that are neither important nor urgent. That will allow you to focus on the really substantial stuff. When it comes to the tasks that are urgent but not important, think of the following:

- Could you delegate them? Could it be that paying somebody to do the task would cost less than the money you could be earning in the same time?
- Could you draw on past experience? If you have a presentation to give, did you do something similar before so that you could at least have something to build on, rather than starting from scratch?
- Could you cancel – is there time to change your mind about the task?
- Could you turn the experience into something useful – could you mould what you're doing into an experience that has a useful learning outcome?
- Is there any way you could save time, for example, by having a conversation on the phone rather than a face-to-face meeting?

And it's self-evident what you need to do about unimportant and non-urgent tasks – have a complete rethink:

- Why are these items on the list at all? Do they need to be done? If they were left undone, what would happen?
- Could you clear them out of your working day and into your leisure time? For example, could you have phonecalls with friends and family only after 7 p.m.? Or could you give yourself the treat of sitting down with a cup of tea after the kids have gone to bed and then research holiday packages, as opposed to doing that during valuable working time?

Now that you've cleared the non-essential urgent tasks out of your life, you're free to move in the direction of your goal. To the tasks that remain on your list, I suggest that you apply the additional resource I mentioned at Step 4 above – my Six-Task Technique. This is a way of working that prevents jumping from one project to the next without ever finishing any of them, and feeling overwhelmed and endlessly busy. It's an organizing trick that allows you to get things done on time and to prevent tasks from incessantly migrating into the 'urgent' category.

A. Write down the top most important six tasks that you need to complete.
B. Do not do anything else (outside of real, absolute emergencies) until they are all done.
C. Repeat A.

Even if you've struggled in the past, I promise you that if you use this technique, you'll have laser-like focus, because you simply cut out distractions. After all, are you likely to put 'Spend an hour on Facebook', 'Call my friend for a chat', 'Check out cheap holidays', 'Google where to go this weekend', 'See who I know on LinkedIn' on this list?

This also is the perfect 'buckle-down' tool. When the going gets tough and you don't know where to begin, this narrows down your focus to what must really be done. You choose only six things (or fewer if you prefer) and for a while you forget everything that isn't those things. So you stop churning to-do items in your mind and clear the decks. Don't worry, all the other things you need to do won't be forgotten; they'll simply be waiting for you when you're done with the six most important ones.

One last tip: the first item on that list should be strategizing how you'll complete your entire to-do list.

By taking a little time to plan and think smartly like this, you can do everything, cut out the distractions, feel less panicked and more organized, be very effective with your time and ensure that nothing falls through the cracks.

Getting your head in the right place

Now I'm going to talk about your head (and your heart) because your attitude is vital to successfully using all these techniques and ultimately making the kinds of changes that will bring you financial freedom. If you've downloaded the spreadsheet, drawn up your SMARTER list and spent time working on your to-do list, by now you might be feeling a bit overwhelmed. A lot of this may be new to you – or maybe you'd heard of some of these techniques, but never applied them before – so therefore it's both time-consuming and energy-sapping. Come to think of it, maybe you've only read through the last section and you're daunted and already exhausted! But, if you bear with me, in the next chapter I'll give you an example of someone using all of these techniques effectively without getting bogged down. Before that, though, let's look at why you might have found it difficult to make changes in the past. This is the psychology bit.

Changing a habit is simply performing a process repeatedly, over and over, until it becomes, well, habitual. The trick is to stick to the process for as long as it actually takes to become habitual. But all too often we don't plan habit change properly. We suffer from First of January Syndrome: we're bursting with enthusiasm to achieve something, only to find that that something fades out of sight after a couple of days. We also get emotionally attached to our habits. People who smoke, for example, connect cigarettes with relaxation. How often do we eat because we're bored, lonely, feeling down or feeling that we deserve a treat?

And one of the biggest snares is that short-term frustration looms larger, much larger, in our minds than long-term results. You walk past a spa and pine for the facial you're not getting, while not thinking of the much improved financial situation you'll be in ten years from now, when you've paid off your mortgage early. As a result, we become convinced that, well, this is just the way it has to be.

After several failed attempts, we settle for the way things are and think that we just don't have it in us to succeed.

But all these obstacles can be conquered. People have stopped smoking, lost weight, eaten less and exercised more, saved money and generally improved their lives in countless ways. And all this without feeling miserable because they're forcing themselves to 'be good'.

I think you too can successfully change. Let's focus on the main objective of this book: taking control of your finances. To reach it, you need to get into the following habits:

Spending an hour per week managing your finances

If I were to advertise a mentoring service that promised to organize a client's finances with just one hour per week for ten weeks, I would find plenty of takers at a four-figure sum. Instead of putting out a four-figure sum, you can do the same for yourself for the cost of this book. If you take the time each week to organize yourself, reflect on the week, seek out and take action towards the direction of your dreams, you will get there. I'm not asking for an impossible weekly time commitment, only for the equivalent of two episodes of a soap on TV, or sitting in traffic for twelve minutes for five days, or the time it would take to clean up after three meals in a typical family household. That's all. So you should really make time for it.

Schedule this hour as you would an appointment with a highly paid financial consultant. After all, this single hour per week is actually worth a lot more than four figures in the long run. Don't try to squeeze it in at any old time during the day. Your lunch break is not a quality-time hour, nor is any hour during the day when you're likely to be disturbed. Settle into it when you know that you'll have a full hour without interruption.

In the next chapter I'll go into more detail about how to use this hour most effectively.

Keeping an efficient system

An efficient system is easy to keep when it's frequently maintained. If you set up the spreadsheet discussed in this chapter, pick a start date and spend a couple of minutes each day or a couple of days filling it in, it will be very easy to keep. However, if you start off with gusto and a fortnight later are trying to figure out if you spent €5 on ice-cream for the kids (Or was that coffee and a scone for yourself? Or parking? Can't remember!), you'll probably end up starting all over again the month after and will have lost information that you should have gathered.

You do need to take the time to fill in that spreadsheet, which you can do at the beginning of the hour that you have set aside for your finances every week. The document has been set up to process the information for you. Alternatively, you could log each expenditure daily. For example, you might buy your lunch at work, put petrol in the car, have to pay a bill and pick up something for the dinner on the way home. This might take three whole minutes to log.

Schedule a time during your day to log in your expenses. After dinner? During commercial breaks as you're watching TV in the evening? Whatever works for you. During your 'weekly finance hour', you can then take a look at your credit card and debit-card statements to make sure that nothing has been left out. That's simply all that's needed to maintain an efficient system.

Again, in the next chapter, I'm going to explain how to use the spreadsheet creatively to give you a fantastically detailed and responsive tool that could change your life. It changed mine.

Replacing 'comfort spending' with another form of emotional nourishment

I've been working hard all week and I deserve a new outfit. I'm so angry with my boss that I'm going to get a manicure! I don't know anybody in this new town that I've moved to – I feel so lonely, but maybe some new make-up might help? We've all had these moments when we're feeling down, and we think a little bit of retail therapy might cheer us up. But the only thing it does is force money out of our pockets. When was the last time you actually, really, lastingly felt cheered up by a manicure or a random pair of shoes?

I call this 'comfort spending' – we try to address the feeling of wanting love and self-care by spending money. Instead, it's very important to find other ways of rewarding yourself. Ways that really nourish you, instead of depleting your energy, self-esteem and money. Spending time with loved ones, a film with a cup of tea, a walk that you enjoy, a lie-in, reading a book that your friend lent to you, singing along to a favourite tune at the top of your lungs, a Skype call with a trusted friend whom you can confide in, looking through the contents of your kitchen and trying out a new recipe, watching funny videos on YouTube, going to a free event in an area near you, taking a break from your normal routine – these can all be ways of taking care of yourself that don't involve money.

It's not that you shouldn't buy nice things, enjoy fantastic experiences and spend money on making your home beautiful. In fact, the purpose of this book is to show you exactly how to do more of all of these. However, if you're feeling down, lonely, depressed or sad, buying a top that you will never wear costing €50 won't make you feel any better. Spending money to numb your negative feelings doesn't address the underlying situation and chips away at your pocket. If you find cost-free ways to nourish yourself when you're feeling down, spending money in the right frame of mind can be so much more enjoyable!

Replacing negative self-doubts with positive dreams and language

It's important to check the messages that you are sending to yourself – something that I talk about later on in more detail. Would you say 'I'm not where I want to be' or, rather, 'I'm on my way there'? Do you see the difference between the two? Do you see hardship, difficulty and struggle at every turn, or can you find the adventure, the learning and the silver lining in each experience? I must confess that I'm of the latter persuasion. I choose to see what can be done now instead of what went wrong. I know it's easier said than done, but I really do try to see the positivity in each situation. No doubt, each of us has had to learn some of life's lessons the hard and unpleasant way. On the other hand, there are wonderful days, warm friendships and little as well as large successes along the way.

There are times when even I need help to see the bright side. I turn to other people to buoy me up when I'm feeling down. I turn to governmental organizations, business mentors and colleagues if I feel that I just can't move my business forward. I sometimes down tools when things aren't going according to plan and take time to regroup and meditate over a solitary coffee. The main thing is that I always assume that it will pass, that creativity or success will flow again, and that it will all be okay. So far, I have always been right.

Instead of thinking 'It can never happen', can you think 'It hasn't happened yet'? Can you focus on what you can change, rather than becoming frustrated with what you can't? If you need reminding that something can be achieved, ask yourself if others have blazed that trail before you. This will show you that it can be done, and that you can not only follow their lead but also leave your own track.

Equating spending with opportunity cost

Opportunity cost is when by spending money on one thing, you eliminate the possibility of spending it on another. Thinking in terms of opportunity cost means that, every time you feel like spending on something you know you shouldn't, you don't have to feel depressed because you're denying yourself something. Instead, you can think of what the same amount of money would buy you, if you chose something that gave you better value. Let's take two scenarios.

Anne-Marie goes out every weekend and pays €100 to be sick and miserable all day on Sunday (some call it a hangover). She burns €60 per week in nicotine (and tar, and a host of other nasty chemicals) and never spends more than €20 on any piece of clothing, because she would rather have quantity than quality. She never bothers to cook and instead spends €30 per night buying processed take-away food. Sometimes she feels bad about her lifestyle and gets a manicure and pedicure to make herself feel better. She has been known to survive on bread and milk during the last week of the month, as she often has rather too much month left at the end of her money. Yet she can't figure out why.

Dervla sits down on a Saturday morning after a luxurious lie-in to plan her budget for the week over a cup of tea. She spends €100 on shopping for the week and loves to try out new recipes. She loves her social life and often hosts dinner parties in her own home. She always gets public transport into town on a night out and never gets into rounds. She bought a set of light weights recently and creates her own mini-gym by running with these a couple of nights a week. She would love to own her own home some day and has worked out a plan to get there. She always thinks of the dream home that she will have rather than the short-term expense that she sacrifices for her bigger dream. Her wardrobe consists of a modest number of quality clothes that can be mixed and matched in so many ways. She gets a lot of value out of each accessory, because she can create whole new outfits with patterned tights or a silk scarf.

Ah, perfect Dervla. Perhaps you already hate her for being so perfect! But, clearly, Dervla gets so much more value out of her money than Anne-Marie, although she probably spends less. She doesn't spread her income thinly across low-value items, but instead takes the time to plan. That way, she can get some real value for money: from the food she eats, to the social life she enjoys, to the clothes that she buys. And, as you can imagine, Dervla generally feels better, healthier and happier than Anne-Marie.

In order to make the switch from an 'Anne-Marie' lifestyle to a 'Dervla', think about what you could buy with the same money that you're spending right now. Discipline doesn't mean being miserable. I could go out to my local pub every weekend for a month or I could go somewhere abroad for a weekend. I could buy a fabulous new jacket if I brought my lunch to work each day. I could buy a new pair of boots with the money that I would save in a month if I stopped some useless standing orders coming out of my account.

I want to give you an example of a useless standing order that I cancelled some time ago. For as long as I've been buying mobile phones, I've always ticked the box for the monthly insurance payment. After all, these days my phone is like an extension of my anatomy; hence, if I did lose it, wouldn't I be very happy that I'd spent 'the couple of euro' on it each month? However, one day, on reviewing my budget, I actually considered exactly what it was I was paying for.

I called the company that had sold me the phone and asked if I was eligible for an upgrade, and they confirmed that I could have a vast array of new phones at zero cost due to my spend in the previous eighteen months. Whilst on that call, I asked about what would happen if I lost my SIM card. They replied by telling me that, first, there wouldn't be any cost involved in assigning a new card to my existing number; and, second, that it could be done on the spot.

Of course, I was also concerned about my contact numbers, so I put that question to the company too. They told me that there was a SIM backup option on my account, which cost €2 and could be set up in a few simple steps.

Therefore, if I regularly transferred my photos, etc., on to my laptop, there would actually be very few consequences if my phone were to be lost, and certainly none worth the €100-plus that I was paying for insurance each year. Needless to say, my next phone call was to the insurance provider to stop the payment immediately.

If I hadn't taken those five minutes to mull over my bank statement and budget, money would still be flowing out of my account for absolutely zero return.

6

Knowledge is power . . .

While in college, I worked in a supermarket, and if I had a euro for every time I heard 'I only came in for bread and milk and now I'm after spending €50!', I could have funded a year of registration fees. I was surprised to hear that they were surprised – didn't they know that millions of euros of research have gone into making just that happen? In fact, it's not uncommon for people to go into a shop three times to get what they had originally intended to buy, but something else catches their attention, and they leave money on the counter every single time.

Think of what happens when you go shopping without a list. You meander through the aisles, a captive audience for the supermarket's marketing and product positioning, going exactly in the direction that they want you to go. Supermarkets are optimized to make you buy, buy, buy, in clever ways you can't even begin to fathom. You walk past the shelves and think, 'Oh, yeah, I could do with that', 'That's on special offer, I must get some of that', 'I'm not sure if I have that at home or not', and walk straight past the pasta, which was what you went in for in the first place.

And it's not just supermarkets that trip you up financially. It might surprise you to learn that:

~ 49% of our 'food spend' consists of cigarettes and alcohol.[1]

1. http://followthefoodlink.wordpress.com/2011/10/16/what-do-irish-people-spend-their-money-on-world-food-day-october-16th-2011/

~ The average Irish household spends €520 on presents, €258 on food and €165 on socializing at Christmas (four times the spend of Dutch households).[2]

~ 33% of all food bought is thrown out.[3]

~ '81% of consumer-foodservice spend is in channels such as Quick Service restaurants and pubs/coffee shops, where convenience, cost and informality are the key magnets attracting customers.'[4] Clearly, a lack of planning is what feeds this industry – literally.

~ People in Britain spend more money on coffee than on electricity.[5] And, let's face it, when it comes to spending, we tend to be similar to our nearest neighbours.

~ The more Americans make, the less they spend on groceries. The bottom fifth of earners spend a whopping 12% of their yearly budget on food at home, compared to 9% for the middle fifth, and 6% for the top fifth.[6]

~ Dry-cleaners estimate that business people may spend between $500 and $1,500 annually on dry-cleaning.[7]

Going back to the supermarket, you could think of an unplanned meander up and down the aisles as a metaphor for how you conduct your financial life: many of us wander through with a vague sense of purpose, but end up making what seem like random choices and

2. http://www.irishtimes.com/newspaper/weekend/2011/1210/1224308851762.html
3. http://www.stopfoodwaste.ie/index.php?id=59&menu=
4. http://www.bordbia.ie/industryservices/information/publications/bbreports/FoodserviceReports/2011%20Irish%20Foodservice%20Channel%20Insights%20report.pdf
5. http://www.dailymail.co.uk/news/article-2027256/Heavy-Starbucks-Costa-Coffee-drinkers-spend-2k-year-More-electricity.html
6. http://www.forbes.com/2006/07/19/spending-income-level_cx_lh_de_0719spending.html
7. http://www.edsuite.com/proposals/proposals_169/85_3_intel-_dry_cleaner_and_laundry.pdf

forgetting what was important to us in the first place. The best way of managing a trip to the supermarket is to go with a shopping list in hand; and the best of way of managing your financial life is to draw up a budget.

Yes, I'm saying that a budget is essentially a very large shopping list. It's an opportunity for you to plan your spending so that you make sure that you're taking advantage of the best special offers and don't get sucked into wasting your money on things you don't really need. Instead of buying two litres of milk when you already have some at home, you can focus on spending your money on that delicious gourmet cheese.

The benefits of using a budget spreadsheet

Could you answer these questions?

- How much of your budget is spent on discretionary items?
- How many pay cheques away are you from being destitute? Do you know how long you could 'hold on in there' if you lost your job?
- How much does attending a wedding cost you?
- If you could shave 10% off your utility bills, how long would it take you to save the equivalent of a holiday (all expenses paid)?
- In terms of the sources of income that you have outside of your fixed salary, if you have one, how far away from your financial goal are you? If your goal is to save €10,000, do you know how long it will take you? 20 months? 36 months? 100 months? You couldn't possibly imagine?
- Can you take advantage of an opportunity of a lifetime right now? Can you afford to invest in a money-making idea? Or will you have to let it pass because you can't afford it, even though you know you'll be kicking yourself later? If a friend called you up and said, 'I just won two round-the-world

plane tickets, but I have to begin using them in the next three months. Want to come with me?', could you take that trip around the world?

∼ How much do you spend on greetings cards or birthday presents in a year?

I doubt that many people can answer each of these questions straight off the bat. However, it would take about five seconds to find this information in a well-structured budget. There is real information contained in this document. It could safeguard your family's financial security if you have been living beyond your means and haven't realized it. It could give you the confidence to actually start that business you've always been dreaming of. It might allow you to make an informed decision about whether you can afford to go to your friend's wedding in Thailand, which you really don't want to miss.

A budget isn't about painfully reminding you of how much you spend and how little you have at the end of the month. It's about giving you real, concrete information about your life. It's about highlighting your budgetary blind-spots. For example, I went through my credit-card statement one morning and realized that I no longer used a piece of software that I'd signed up for six months before. It's cost me €7.71 a month, times six. I would prefer to spend that €40 on petrol or getting a haircut than on something I haven't used in six months. Also, should I fail to clear the credit-card balance every month because of that small expense, I'm paying interest on *not* using the software.

A budget is also about letting you check whether your financial thermostat is at the proper level. You'll see exactly where the money goes. If you have an extra €500 this month and your subconscious is uncomfortable with that, you'll see the additional spending on clothes, beauty treatments, taking others to lunch, taking a taxi instead of waiting for the bus, etc. On the other hand, it can show you just how you brought your credit card back from the brink. The numbers will praise the way you planned so that you didn't have to eat out, asked friends to pop over to your house for a cup of tea instead of meeting for dinner, were more inventive about getting presents, shopped around to cut your utility bills and chose a less expensive hobby than retail therapy.

A budget will enable you to play around with your money and think about the impact a decision will have before you actually take it. For example, you can slot in a manicure and pedicure and then see if you can afford it before making the appointment. A budget will show very clearly how choosing a night out at the cinema instead of dinner and drinks will bring you that top you've been admiring. You'd see, black on white, that if you ate breakfast at home on weekend mornings instead of at a café, got up half an hour earlier to get the bus instead of taking the car, cancelled your gym membership and used the (free) road instead of a treadmill to keep fit, you could absolutely go to London for your cousin's hen weekend and comfortably enjoy it. On the other hand, you'd see the impact of a 3% pay rise on your life, which might give you the courage to approach your boss about such a proposition. You'd see how a 5% rise in the turnover of your business could affect your dreams for the future. This might be just what you need to inspire you to look for inventive ways of creating that 5%. As a result, this spreadsheet could be the carrot (and a little bit of stick) that you need to spur you into action.

In essence, if you could write your dream financial life on one spreadsheet and compare it to your current budget, you could see exactly how close you are. The distance could be big or small, but now you can measure it. If you earn €500 per week and you would like to earn €750, 52 times a year we have to find a way of getting another €250. If you have €3,000 in savings and would like €20,000 instead, we simply have to work out a strategy to squirrel €17,000 out of your earnings to hit your goal. This may seem impossible now, but bear with me. It only seems impossible because you haven't read the whole book yet . . .

Do you know of anybody else who earns €750 a week? Is there

anybody in the world who has €20,000 in savings? Yes, millions of people. It can certainly be done; you just need to work out the road-map between here and there and then start your journey. However, to do this your budget is absolutely key, because it can, in an instant, calculate the distance between the two locations. It will give you crucial information about how fast you can get there, and from a safe (non-scary) distance will show you the impact of turbo-charging your engine.

Why a spreadsheet is the key to telling your financial story

Let's say you already collect all your receipts and you have a pretty accurate, but still rough, idea of how much you're spending. Why should you go to the trouble of copying the exact same information that's on your receipts? What will you gain by just copying this information?

Well, there are lots of people who have their receipts in a box somewhere, but this doesn't mean they have the same information as that contained in a budget. Getting the information into a smart spreadsheet like the one I've designed for you to download makes all the difference, as it's a way of identifying spending patterns and extracting real, actionable information from those receipts.

The spreadsheet I have built for you uses all the resources of Excel: when you're copying the information on each receipt into the spreadsheet, an inbuilt algorithm will calculate totals and per-centages, so that you don't have to do it manually. In one fell swoop, you'll have a wealth of information you would never have been able to glean by just looking at one receipt after another.

And honestly – who looks at one receipt after another anyway? It's just not usable information. What difference does it make if I know that, on a weekly basis, I spend €100 on groceries, €60 on petrol and €60 on a night out? Not a lot, as I probably knew that already. However, that's €220, and yet I seem to get through €500 per week – where does the rest of it go? A budget will force me to find that answer and look it in the face.

Also, if all I'm doing is looking at my paper receipts, I'm not looking at my standing orders, direct debits or my online purchases. And what about all those things that we don't get a receipt for? A take-away coffee? A newspaper? A couple of things at a corner shop? Have you ever looked in your purse to see €5 and said to yourself, 'Imagine, I had €50 in there this morning and now it's mostly gone. What happened?' Have you ever decided you were going to try to cut down on spending, only to get to the end of the month with the same result as last month . . . and the one before that . . . and the one before that? Again, you can't figure out where the money went, so you just decide that you're 'no good with money' and hence you'll always have to make do with less than you would like to have. Not true. A budget will show you exactly where the money goes.

Let's say I keep all my receipts and have a good idea where my money is going. I set myself a goal of saving €3,000 this year. Where do I start? I tell myself that I'll begin to shop around when I buy petrol rather than just going to the first station I see. I follow through – fast-forward a couple of weeks – how do I measure my success? I think that I used to spend around €60 per week and now I spend about €55. I find this paltry and not worth the effort, really. However, contrast this with a person who knows that they spend €60 per week on petrol, as laid out in their budget. They spend an hour on a Saturday morning going through their finances. First, they can see the impact of saving €5 every week on petrol on their weekly, monthly and annual budget. Second, they want to think about how they could actually do this with minimal effort. They download a free app on to their smartphone that picks up their location via GPS and directs them to the cheapest petrol station near them. Now, fast-forward a couple of weeks and they're going through their expenditure. They see that they saved €5 each week and that there's an extra €2 expense – that was an ice-cream for the kids, as it was a hot day. They feel in control and now move to their other revenues and expenses to see how they can optimize other areas. The point is that they take the time to identify a saving, as well as a clear path on how to do so, which then allows them to actually quantify their success. A smart budget takes out all the guesswork and rough estimates that blur your vision.

One more scenario. I always hold on to my receipts and I have a 'rough idea' that I spend €60 each week on petrol. It comes to the end of the year and I'm thinking of changing the car to diesel, as I know that in general the costs of diesel are lower. However, the car dealer wants an extra €1,000 to make this switch. I estimate that I could save 5% weekly by switching to diesel, so I do the following quick calculation in my head. The annual saving of €156 (€60 × 52 × 5% = €156) is much smaller than €1,000, so is it really worth it? Probably not, and as a result I choose a petrol car.

Contrast this against the person who has the information at her fingertips to make this decision. First, she realizes that she actually spent €3,500 on petrol last year, as opposed to a rough estimate of €3,120 (€60 × 52 weeks). Her petrol costs were high because she had some relations home from America during the summer and she drove them around sight-seeing. Also, some weeks were busier than others and she made three purchases of €60 in a single fortnight sometimes, but she didn't really think about it as she was busy. Luckily, her budget is there to remind her.

Now a 5% saving on a €3,500 spend actually amounts to €175. However, she thinks about the other factors that are relevant to this decision. Her daughter is becoming interested in every hobby under the sun, and no doubt her son won't be far behind. As a result, she'll be covering a lot more ground over the coming years. She also does some research and discovers that, since a diesel car is more efficient in terms of CO_2 emissions, she'll be able to cut her car tax. On top of that, she also knows that oil prices could easily rise. Finally, she plans to hold on to this car for three years, and even then her next car will be a diesel one, so she's likely to save the 'petrol price premium' for many years to come. In fact, using a diesel car could bring about a 10% saving when all things are taken into account. She can now make the decision from a much more informed place and she puts the following information into her spreadsheet:

Annual cost	€3,500
Rise in petrol cost over three years	5%
Annual cost with rise	€3,675
Petrol price premium including tax saving	10%
Annual saving using a diesel car	€367.50
Saving across three years	€1,102.50

Now, even during the life of this car, the savings made have paid for the upfront cost.

From this example we can see that the difference between a collection of receipts and an Excel spreadsheet is that the spreadsheet gives you that most precious thing of all: perspective informed by deep knowledge. I speak at entrepreneurship events all the time and when I ask questions like 'Who is your biggest customer?', there are lots of people who stare at me blankly, even though they're intimately aware of every euro that goes through their accounts. Wouldn't you think that a business owner would know that information? Well, this is how we sometimes fail to be aware of what's staring us in the face.

Have you ever looked at the clock and said, 'I don't know where the time went'? Have you ever met somebody after not seeing them for a while, and, in answer to their question 'How have you been?', were a little surprised at how much had happened since you'd last seen each other? While our brains are amazing things, they can't be fully conscious of every single thing that happens. Essentially, this budget spreadsheet is a monitoring system that gives you another view of what's going on, one that provides concrete information about how to improve your life in general.

If I were to ask you how much you spend on your shopping each year, could you tell me? After all, you do the shopping each week and always take a look at the receipt as you put it away, so could you hazard a guess at the answer? Also, if I were to ask you how much money you throw into the bin every week, could you tell me that? As you read earlier, a lot of the contents of our shopping basket are on a one-way ticket to the bin. And still we willingly pay for them, each and every week. Again, you're the person handing over the cash and then putting these things directly into the bin – how much money does this add up to? Would you be able to tell? Looking at this in terms of lost opportunity, what amount do you actually throw away? Does it correspond to the price of the entire electricity bill for the year, a designer outfit, a weekend away, a family holiday or the cost of an extension?

Using your spreadsheet

If you download the spreadsheet and then leave it at that, you still haven't got anywhere. The information in your budget is revealed only when you start to fill it in. I spend an hour on a Saturday morning checking through everything. I keep a note of my cash payments throughout the week and go through my online statements at the weekend for everything else. I type these into the main budget and Excel automatically processes them. At the beginning, you'll need to spend a little time inserting new categories, but after a while everything will have been covered.

After I've done my updates, I simulate what would happen should I add a new item of expenditure – say, that I want to get my hair done that week or the possibility of a holiday has arisen. I can plan in advance for the cost of larger items so that my budget doesn't have to get painfully lumpy. If, for example, I think that I can comfortably put away €150 a month, based on a couple of months of data, I'll contact my mortgage provider about increasing my monthly payments to pay off that mortgage early. On the other hand, if I see that my percentage of disposable or variable expenditure is much higher than in previous months, I'll take steps to address that.

This hour with my budget also gives me the time to do things that can often get on the 'I must do that some day' list. I send emails or make phonecalls to research some projected expense and gather data to simulate that expense accurately. It's a fair point that a lot of services still don't open on Saturdays. However, I can email them or I can put a note in my diary to make the call. The important thing is that I've considered how to take the action related to furthering my financial success, and then either taken it or made a time-specific plan related to it. I cancel payments (like the software subscription mentioned above) by logging into my account and communicating that I want to cancel the standing order. I take the time to review my mobile-phone package regularly, so that my usage is reflected in my payment options. Think about it: if you've been procrastinating a review of your mobile-phone package, it might be because you intuitively know that you don't have the data needed to take an informed decision about whether it's right for your current usage. And you have no idea how to actually calculate what package would be best. Whereas if you had a budget, you wouldn't need to fish out those phone bills and think back to how much you used your phone in the last six months (who can remember that in detail anyway?). Your budget lays it all out for you, and there you have your answer, at a glance.

If I'm over-budget, I move things around until order is restored: I always know where I have some money left over, which can be used to cover any unexpected expenses, or I'll devise some other strategy to avoid being in the red. If I'm under-budget, I decide whether to spend or save what's left – or both. Before making that decision, I take a look into the future. Is there a payment that I know is coming and for which I can earmark the funds? Is there a holiday, a wedding or 'something nice' on the immediate horizon or can I happily transfer the money into my savings account to better prepare me for any unexpected events?

The next thing I do is to look back over my budget and see if this 'under-budgetness' is a one-off or regular. If this is an irregular occurrence, I unpick what happened to cause it, with the hope that it can be repeated. However, if I succeed at this and hence have some extra money each month, I can then see if I want to increase my savings standing order, increase debt repayments or look for a new financial opportunity. However, I can do none of the above with an adequate level of financial confidence if I don't have the information that is provided for me by my budget.

Remember what I said in the last chapter about the importance of turning all these new money-management systems into habits. Well, to get into using your spreadsheet regularly, you need a reminder system. Reminder systems are what carry us through from initial enthusiasm to actually making something part of daily life. In order to integrate a new habit into your life, you must do it over and over and over again, so that your body and mind treat it as second nature.

For example, you might spend a couple of hours gathering all your receipts, credit-card statements, bank statements, etc., and then forget about inputting the data each day as life gets busy. You could then get disillusioned and think it's all too much hassle to try to think back to each euro that you spent. Instead, if you had a daily reminder, you wouldn't forget to spend a few minutes filling in your spreadsheet. In addition, the more often that you repeat an action, the more mechanical it becomes. After a while, you won't need the reminder and then your goal is almost on autopilot.

I like having the luxury of being able to rely on a reminder system. Because there's so much going on in my life and taking up space in my memory, I'm all in favour of a piece of technology that can take on the responsibility. I use three reminder systems:

A reminder tool on my phone or computer. There are lots of software programs – from Microsoft Outlook, to productivity apps on smartphones, to the old-style traditional alarm clock – that you can use to remind yourself to do something on a regular basis. The snazzier the technology, the more it will allow you to do – you can practically run your own and other people's lives if you pick something that's sophisticated enough! That may suit you, or you may prefer something simpler – just decide what you will actually use.

Leaving things ready to go. Here's a low-tech but fantastic technique I learned from my maths teacher in school, Mr Hanley. He told us one day that it was far easier to get into studying if your desk was 'ready to go' rather than neat and tidy. If you don't have to start opening books and retrieving pencils and notebooks, it's easier to avoid the trap of wasting time and becoming distracted getting yourself set-up. Instead, if the book is open, you simply pick up where you left off. Similarly, I never shut down my computer but instead put it into 'sleep' mode. I have all of the things that I need to remember there in front of me as soon as I open it up and I don't have to wait for the laptop to boot. If I need to send an email tomorrow, instead of expending mental energy trying to remember it, I simply create a new email, type in the name of the person and just leave it there. If I have to do a proposal for a client, but I don't have time at a particular moment, I create a Word document, start it and leave it there to be finished later. If I need to remember to book a train ticket, I open the appropriate website and then 'refresh' it when I look at it again tomorrow. It's very simple, but highly effective, because it's great to begin the day with a 'quick win'. I don't have to say to myself, 'I'll just finish that now and then leave the office,' but rather, 'It will take only twenty minutes to finish that in the morning and I'll have a great start to the day!' You don't have to get yourself into the state of mind necessary to start a presentation from scratch; things are much easier when you're a couple of slides in!

The random-object technique. My mam has a great way of remembering things to do – and there isn't an app for this. You might arrive at our house to find the hall spotlessly clean but with a random object like an apple in the middle of the floor. The first time I noticed this, I asked her what, in the name of God, was she doing? She said that the apple was there to remind her, for example, to bring a tablecloth up to Chrissie's (our next-door neighbour). I said,

'Could you not put the apple somewhere other than in everybody's way?' She said, 'That's the point. Every time I walk up and down the hall, I'm reminded of the tablecloth. In fact, if it's bothering you so much, why don't you take the tablecloth up to Chrissie's and save me the job? You can do what you like with the apple then.' I laughed at the time, but I often do the same thing now myself, like leaving a cookery book outside the bathroom door (to remind me about my shopping list) or a carton of orange juice beside the keys of the car (to remember to reply to a voicemail from yesterday). These are totally out-of-place places to find these things and it works like a dream!

One word of warning about habit change and reminder systems – don't try to do everything at the same time. I once downloaded an app on my phone to remind me to build five new habits. I lost interest because I couldn't keep up with any of them. I became completely annoyed by that green light on my phone reminding me of one thing all the time – my failure to keep up five new habits simultaneously. So I uninstalled it. Instead, focus on one thing at a time and keep at it. Praise yourself for each day that you stick to your new process and remember that the longer you can do it, the more likely it is to really become a habit.

Your financial satnav in action

So you should have it all together now. The previous chapter and this one will have given you quite an extensive 'master system': you know about habit changes, monitoring systems, reminder systems and what-not. You have tools to play with and make an integral part of your life. How do you fit it all in? How do you implement that system?

In the last chapter I told you I would give you an example of someone applying all of this to her life without becoming overwhelmed, and here it is. Jenny wants to improve her financial situation and has already decided on a SMARTER goal and a list of steps to take. She built her budget spreadsheet and just needs to remember to fill it in. Other than that, she wants to cut costs by bringing her lunch to work rather than eating out, and she needs to look out for occasions when her financial thermostat is trying to get her back down to her previous temperature. This is Jenny's account of what happened during eight days of using all the resources, tools and techniques thus far in the book and putting some enthusiastic action behind them!

Saturday

11 a.m. Got dressed and put on my make-up. I went to my favourite coffee shop and used the GROW model (see Chapter 2) to articulate the goals and realities of one element of my financial dream (earning more revenue). I then examined my options and whittled down my list of 'What will I do next?' to what I can do next week. Out of this list, I put SMARTER actions into my diary for the week and I'm really looking forward to hosting a dinner party next Saturday night as my reward.

Sunday

8 p.m. I worked on my budget today. I inputted my expenditure over the weekend and worked out how much I need to spend each day until Friday in order to remain on target, and then I factored in what I would like to spend on areas that are 'wants' rather than 'needs'.

Monday

8 a.m. I got to my office early so that I could have an hour before my working day to implement my first SMARTER action of the week. Full of the joys of spring today so it was easy to get up.
8 p.m. My alarm rang, reminding me to take five minutes to write my daily expenditure into my diary . . . and I left the diary open as a

document on my laptop so that it wouldn't be far from my mind. I like it when I make my own life easier . . .

Tuesday

8 a.m. I got to my office early so that I could have an hour before my working day to implement my second SMARTER action of the week. I can't believe my enthusiasm is waning already, but it was a little hard to get out of bed this morning.

8 p.m. Like yesterday, my alarm rang, reminding me to take five minutes to write my daily expenditure into my diary . . . and I left the diary open as a document on my laptop so that I wouldn't forget it.

Wednesday

8.30 a.m. I got to my office early so that I could have half an hour before my working day to implement my third SMARTER action of the week. It was so hard to get out of bed this morning. I'm kicking myself for having lapsed slightly – I'm going to do better tomorrow. The funny thing is that I actually woke on my own this morning without needing the alarm clock, but I gave in to rolling over for a second sleep. On the other hand, I'm proud of the fact that I was so tempted to not bother making my lunch for work today, and just get something in town. However, I thought about the 'opportunity cost' and told myself that the 'laziness' premium that I would pay for lunch in town could be equivalent to the cost of the dessert ingredients for the dinner party at the weekend, so I was inspired to take the ten minutes to make that lunch.

2 p.m. I was so tempted today to go shopping at lunchtime. I've just been told that I'm getting the pay rise that I plucked up the courage to ask for a month ago. However, I didn't want my financial thermostat going back to its old level, even though I'll be earning more. I wouldn't want the amount of money that I have at the end of the month to be the same as now. Otherwise, why take the trouble to ask for a pay rise at all? Anyway, I haven't even got the money yet.

Instead, I called my friend who works in the building across the road and we met for a celebratory coffee.

8 p.m. My alarm rang, reminding me to take five minutes to write my daily expenditure into my diary . . . and I left the diary open as a document on my laptop.

Thursday

8 a.m. I got to my office early so that I'd have an hour before my working day to implement my fourth SMARTER action of the week. I had to drag myself out of bed at first, but when I actually looked at the progress I'd made with four action steps, I began to feel quite proud.

11 a.m. I couldn't seem to get on top of things today: everybody shouting for my attention, the phone always ringing, and I had to have a big important project ready for the next day – there were so many urgent things to do that my head was spinning. I took five minutes in the middle of the madness and used the 'important and urgent' quadrant to find my way out. I used the Six-Task Technique, put an autoresponder on my email to say that I wasn't available, turned my office phone to 'busy' and concentrated on being highly effective.

8 p.m. My alarm rang, reminding me to take five minutes to write my daily expenditure into my diary . . . and I left the diary open as a document on my laptop.

Friday

8 a.m. I got to my office early so that I had an hour before my working day to implement my fifth SMARTER action of the week. I bounded out of bed today – it's Friday and I'm cruising towards my goal.

8 p.m. My alarm rang, reminding me to take five minutes to write my daily expenditure into my diary . . . and I left the diary open as a document on my laptop.

Saturday

10 a.m. I brought a cup of tea up to bed and did my shopping list for the dinner party. I put a cookery book outside my bedroom door to remind me to get some red napkins to go with my 'theme'.

11 a.m. I got all 'dolled up' and headed for the coffee shop again for my weekly check-in with myself. I was looking forward to reading what I wrote last weekend and to ticking the boxes. I saw that, after having taken a small number of actions this week, there was actually some progress towards my 'impossible idea'. However, as I had a better vantage point from which to view my goal, I could see a ~~problem~~ issue (remember: positive language!). I thought about it over my coffee and told myself that I could dedicate Monday morning's action to coming up with a solution – maybe I could call Marie or Darren about that, they might be able to help me. After all, it doesn't mean that I can't reach my goal, it's just that I'm not there yet.

Sunday

8 p.m. Keeping a weekly spending diary has shown me how much the 'lunch at work' was costing me – I hadn't realized that I could pay both my phone bill and my electricity bill by simply making my lunch at home. Also, I saw how I could save €250 per month, which would come from my pay rise as well as just getting better value for money on certain items. I finally saw how €20 can walk out of my purse without my even noticing; a bottle of water, a taxi and a magazine – all needless expenses – can just make it go 'poof'. I genuinely thought that I didn't have places to cut costs, and that, even if I did, it would drain the life out of me. But it's actually quite interesting that I can be richer in more ways than one by doing this. I'm looking forward to what I can learn next week.

STEP FOUR

Curb your spending

If you think cost-cutting takes the fun out of spending . . . think again!

Thinking about tightening your belt isn't much fun. You're cutting back, denying yourself things, staying in instead of going out, not going shopping and yearning for the day when you will have more money.

That's certainly one way of looking at it, but another is to think of cost-cutting not as skimping, but as exploring the ways you can increase the value of the money you do spend. What things, what companies, what providers, give you enough value and enjoyment to really deserve a share of your hard-earned money? What other things don't? It's all about planning.

Before we get to that, though, think about how you're spending your money at present. Imagine this. You're running extremely late, the traffic is really heavy and you're trying to make a very important meeting. It looks like there's nothing for it but to park the car and get a taxi to the meeting. Do you sit in the car and nervously watch the clock or hand over the money? In the interests of keeping the appointment, it's probably worthwhile spending the money, and you do.

Or this. You're going to a wedding and have nothing to wear. It's the first of February, but the wedding isn't until the twenty-fourth, so you'll think about it later. It would be lovely to have a nice shopping outing – you think you'll ask your niece to look after the baby for the day, bring a friend and make a day of it. Fast-forward to Thursday, the twenty-second of February, and you're absolutely up to your eyes in work. You've booked the next day as holiday, and nobody is going to take that from you. You need to get your hair done, take the baby to your mother's, pack the car and drive the

200 kilometres to the night-before dinner of the wedding. And you still don't have an outfit. There's a window of one hour at 10 a.m. tomorrow and if you don't find anything then, you'll have to wear a pair of jeans! You flit into the shopping centre and head straight for your favourite brand. You almost breathlessly tell the sales assistant that you have forty-five minutes left to buy something for a wedding tomorrow. The result of this is that you've bought something kind of okay that costs €120 when you had intended to spend €80.

Or, finally, this. You're on a diet and you started the day really well. You had a bowl of muesli, low-fat milk and took an apple to work in case you were tempted to snack. Off you went on your day, and started to feel a little hungry around noon. You say to yourself: 'I'll just get this email sent, report done and three voicemails answered, and then get something healthy and filling.' At 3 p.m., you're still finishing things off and about to get your super-healthy lunch. Your boss pops his head in the door and asks you to sit in on an emergency meeting. It lasts longer than you had anticipated. At 5 p.m., your stomach is screaming at you to put something in it *right now!* Your boss phones the local bakery and asks for coffee and pastries. Two croissants later, you promise yourself that you'll start again tomorrow . . .

In each case, you needed to get something done in a very short space of time. As a result, you were happy to pay a premium for whatever it is you wanted to do. You paid for the parking and a taxi in exchange for avoiding the stress of sitting powerlessly in traffic and for getting to your appointment on time. You paid €40 more than you wanted to and sacrificed the possibility of finding an outfit you really liked, as well as that pleasurable day of shopping you had planned, in exchange for doing everything else that got in the way. You paid the price of extra calories and the feeling of having let yourself down again in exchange for working non-stop at urgent tasks.

The main lesson here is that when you don't have a plan, it's so easy to be driven off course. In the first case, if you had Google

Mapped the location first and allowed twice as much time to get there, you probably wouldn't have run into such difficulties (or expense). If you had scheduled your shopping trip for the week after you initially thought about it, you probably would have got an outfit that you loved within your budget. If you had taken your lunch at the right time, brought it in with you or had it delivered, you would have had enough in your tummy to support willpower. Each of these three separate scenes arose out of a lack of planning.

I have learned the high price of bad or no planning the hard way. A couple of years ago, my business was going very well, or so I thought. My diary was spilling over with mentoring appointments all over the country. They were all happy to pay, and when I sat down to calculate the revenue I would take in the next week, sometimes it equated to a month's wages from my previous job. It would have been perfect, had it not been the case that by the end of the week I was exhausted, running behind on my administration and with little, if any, profit at all. In fact, when I looked back on it, even though I took in a month's salary in a week, I ended up with a month's salary at the end of the month but after having put in significantly more hours. What was going on?

There were two problems. First, as in the example above, I was so busy that I was getting taxis if I was mentoring people in Dublin. If it was outside the Pale, I would either drive or get a train and then another taxi the other side of my destination. On top of that, I didn't have the time to cook for myself either, so I was always eating out.

I can imagine you reading this and saying to yourself, surely she copped on to herself, saw what was going on and stopped it straight away. I'm afraid it took a while for me to see what was happening. I saw lots of money coming in and I had an attitude to costs that went something like this: 'I have lots of money, a €10 taxi here and a €20 train ticket there is well worth it because I can honour all of my commitments and work on the move at the same time.' I got a serious reality check one rainy afternoon, in Ballyliffin, Co. Donegal, when I was stuck in a hotel room with hours to kill before a party that night. I happened to be in an organizing kind of mood so I turned on the laptop, filled in an Excel spreadsheet and, just as I showed you in Chapter 6, started to peel back the layers of my revenue. I went through all my sources of revenue and did a short profit-and-loss (P&L) exercise with them. For example, if I earned €150 from a meeting, I would then take away the cost of transport, food, printing, phonecalls, etc., to get the actual profit of the meeting. I also applied a key litmus test: if my own company were to hire me as a consultant at a high rate, could my company afford me?

Effectively, this was a totally non-sugar-coated way of looking at the numbers in my business and identifying whether it was sustainable or – and this is a hard thing to admit – whether I was actually running it the best way for me, those around me and the health of the company in general.

Up until then, I had customers ranked on my spreadsheet in terms of revenue: depending on turnover, I would call them 'my best client', 'my second best', etc. I rearranged my customers by profit. As the rain pounded against the window, my jaw dropped as I saw the result. First, my view of my best customers changed utterly; and second, I couldn't believe that I was actually making a loss with my second-best revenue stream. *A loss!* I hadn't been trying to change it either. After all, as far as I was concerned, up until that point the more money I was taking in the better. I was completely blind to the fact that I was actually losing money by undertaking the activity into which I was putting so much energy. I'll show you how I turned this around later in the book, as you may find this technique very useful in many ways.

As the saying goes, 'Everything changes when you give a little attention to it.' That's exactly what happened. With a change of attitude, a sharpened vision and exactly the same amount of effort as before, the spreadsheet changed out of all recognition, and in the right direction. This chapter and the next are designed to show you how to pay attention to how you're spending your money. You may be surprised at the results!

Question: Which is heavier? A ton of coal or a ton of feathers?

Say you are looking at two cartons of milk, both costing €1. One is just your normal, average bottle of milk, while the other is calcium enriched and has added Vitamin D and other good things. You pick up the first one because it's closer to you. You hand over €1 and miss out on the extra nutrients. What would it have cost to research what you were handing over money for? A couple of seconds to scan the calcium content. If you knew that you would be getting more value for the same money – what would you do? Of course, you would buy the better product.

Now, let's change this analogy slightly. There are two cartons of milk – exactly the same apart from the packaging. You pick up the one closer to you and pay for it. The next time you go to pick up milk, you actually take a second to compare the prices of the two brands and you see that the one you left behind last time costs 50c less. What would be the rational thing to do? Given that they are identical apart from the packaging, you'd get the cheaper one of course.

You may be reading this and thinking that life is too short to get excited over 50c. Let's change the product, then – take a flatscreen TV, a sofa, a holiday, a car, a house. The bigger we go, the more difference it will make. Would you get excited over a €50 saving on a flatscreen TV? Maybe. You're certainly going to be more interested in that than in a 50c saving on a carton of milk. Does your household consume 100 cartons of milk in the year? If so, multiply 50c by 100. That is €50.

To go back to my riddle, feathers or coal – they both weigh a ton. And €50 and 50c x 100 are also the same. It's not just about the individual saving that you make, but the number of times that you make it.

I heard the consumer journalist Conor Pope on radio one day saying that 40% of our groceries get thrown away. I thought this was an inordinate amount of wasted money, i.e., out of every €100 we spend in the supermarket, we could just as easily put €40 into the same bin as the receipt *every week*. After that, any time I poured sour milk down the drain or threw a shrivelled-up half-lemon into the compost heap, I could almost hear him saying, 'See what I mean?'

I was determined to tackle the waste and did it using two very simple techniques. I sat down and wrote a schedule of meals for the week. I didn't make it too elaborate – just an outline. For example, 'I'm at home for dinner three evenings this week. I'm going to a workshop Thursday evening, a board meeting on Friday night, my mam's on Saturday night and my boyfriend's mam's on Sunday night. I'm going to cook shepherd's pie on Monday night and freeze half of it. I can have some on Tuesday night also. I'll try out that new pasta recipe in Rachel Allen's book on Wednesday night.' I then built my shopping list around that, and if I saw, for example, vegetables on special offer I walked past them, as I would only have ended up throwing them out because of their use-by dates.

This is all fine when everything goes to plan or when you can buy exactly the quantity of food that you need. But it doesn't always work out like this. I made a beautiful chicken salad the other day with mint and basil. I was left with half a packet of mint, which on another day would have gone straight into the compost heap. Instead, I searched in my cookery books for recipes with mint. I ended up making pea and mint soup from Jamie Oliver's *Ministry of Food*. A similar thing happened when I was looking in the fridge for ideas on a sandwich. I saw a half-used packet of brie that I had bought a while back– another potential candidate for the rubbish bin. I thought about sandwich-bar menus with brie in them and ended up putting it in a ciabatta with garlic, ham and relish, which were all in the cupboard anyway. It was delicious.

Neither of these approaches takes the fun out of spending, and, if anything, there is the additional pleasure of discovering a new recipe. In addition, you can also put an ionizer into your fridge, which prolongs the life of your perishable food, thus giving you a bigger window in which to use it.

Let's say you spend €50 per week on groceries and you waste €20 of it. That is €80–€100 per month. Does this equate to the payments you're making on the car? The heating bill? The annual amount wasted is about €1,000. Could you book a holiday with this amount? Could you take a month off the mortgage? Better yet, if you took €1,000 off the capital of the mortgage each year, you could take years (and thousands in interest) off the full payment of your house. The more money you spend on groceries, the more exaggerated this effect becomes.

Think about it. If you want to cut costs, which makes more sense? Continuing to spend the way you are now, with possibly a small, significant or large amount of waste built in? Or using your money to give yourself more of the things that you want? Again, I'm not talking about being mean or eating bread and water for a month. I'm simply talking about revising your current expenditure so that you get more out of it.

There is a term in basic accounting called 'gross profit margin'. Let's say I run a business that sells bags of crisps. I calculate the cost of every single thing that I need to spend on getting the crisps made, packaged and delivered to the buyer (e.g., 60c per bag). I divide this number by the amount that I receive from the buyer (e.g., €1 per bag). As a result, my 'gross profit' would be 40c per bag and my gross profit margin would be 40%.

Let's say that I sell a million bags of crisps in a year: my gross profit would be €1,000,000 × 40% = €400,000. Now, let's say that I'm really ambitious next year and I want to double my revenue. I figure out a way of doing it and it comes to pass. I sell two million bags of crisps and then my gross profit is €2,000,000 × 40% = €800,000.

Gross profit	Revenue	Gross profit percentage
€400,000	€1,000,000	40%
€800,000	€2,000,000	40%

That's great, isn't it? However, let's think about two scenarios here:

1. The company cuts its costs by 20% – to get to the same level of profit, how many bags will it need to sell to get to a profit of €800,000?

Recall: it costs 60c to make the bag of crisps and to deliver it. If you cut that by 20%, it would now cost 48c per bag and the company would be making 52c profit per bag (i.e., a gross profit margin of 52%). Now, if 52% of the revenue is profit, then if we divide €800,000 by 0.52, we get to 100% of the revenue that the company needs to generate in order to get to that profit level.

Gross profit	Revenue	Gross profit percentage
€800,000	€1,538,461	52%

If this company were to cut costs by 20%, it would need to sell (2,000,000 − 1,538,461) 461,539 fewer bags of crisps – almost half a million – to get to the same profit level.

2. The company cuts its costs by 20% – how much extra profit would it have made had it gone ahead and reached the target of selling two million bags of crisps?

Recall: it costs 60c to make the bag of crisps and to deliver it. If you cut that by 20%, it would now cost 48c per bag and the company would be making 52c profit per bag (i.e., a gross profit margin of 52%). Now, the profit is €2,000,000 multiplied by 52%.

Gross profit	Revenue	Gross profit percentage
€1,040,000	€2,000,000	52%

So the company would have made €240,000 extra in profit.

The reason that I wanted to talk through this example is that I'll be showing you many ways to generate revenue later on in the book – and everybody loves to make more money – but it could have a much greater impact on your life, if you start cutting costs first.

Can you calculate the gross profit margin on your household? How much does it cost for your household to do what it does (i.e., how much does it cost to run your household on a weekly, monthly or annual basis)? How much is that relative to the amount of revenue that you generate? What is the profit margin, then?

Is this figure negative, i.e., do you spend more than you earn? As a result, if you earn more, will you spend more? If so, there isn't any point in earning more, because you'll only find yourself back in the same spot.

If this figure is positive, that is, you spend less than you earn, what is the percentage of your 'profit'? Let's say it's 10%: that means that you have €10 left over out of every €100 that you earn. Does this mean that if you earn an extra €1,000 next year, you'll only have €100 left out of it at the end of the year? That's your choice – but I can show you how to increase that percentage.

Thinking more carefully about your spending is not just important for you; it can also have an impact on society in general. I was in college during the boom years. One spring day, my friend and I were discussing the best options for how to spend the summer. We were joined by someone she knew who said something that I'll never forget: 'Don't worry too much about getting a job. Get into debt. When you're working, three or four grand will be like, "Oh sure I will just transfer it across there out of my wages and I won't even notice it."' Do I consider what that girl said to be wrong? Yes. Do I blame her? No. I blame society at large, because at that point in time those were the lessons that were being passed on by everyone around us.

You have an incredible influence on the attitudes that your children and those who look up to you have about money. When your kids are young, you have a unique opportunity to sit down with them and to teach them about budgeting. It is also an immense responsibility.

You can convey the idea that managing money well is an uncomfortable, boring business that leads to a life 'without' and is only for mean people. Alternatively, you can teach them a lot about this life skill and how to enjoy using it, which will be helpful to them for the rest of their lives. Let's say they get €10 from their granny for their birthday. You could make a point of sitting down with them and saying, 'What could we do with this money? You could spend it on sweets and it will be gone right away. You could spend it on a new toy or a book, and get a lot of fun out of it. You could put it into your savings account and spend it on a big day out with your auntie when you go shopping with her at Christmas as a treat.'

Imagine the impact it could have on their lives when they earn their first money from a part-time job (and keep their gross profit margin high), when they move from home, when they go to college, when they buy their first house . . .

That summer I ended up living in Edinburgh, sharing a flat with two fabulous Australian girls with whom I've remained friends ever since. The three of us were finding it difficult to manage financially, because we were trying to pay rent in advance, while working in arrears, and coping with all that comes with starting in a new place. I remember one day Vanessa Jan said that, in order to save £2.20 on the bus, she walked all the way into Princes St. Instead of complaining about it, she said, 'I saw so many things that I never even bothered to notice any time I went on the bus,' and she went on to regale us with her stories of the day.

Similarly, if I hadn't looked for a way to use up the packet of mint, I wouldn't have come across the recipe. Of course, you can have fun with money too! However, when you do think differently about cost-cutting, it becomes a means by which you can:

- get better value for money for what you do buy;
- buy things that you enjoy with the money you would usually waste;
- get better use in general out of the money you earn;
- come across things you normally wouldn't; and
- teach children healthier lessons about money.

It's a good skill to learn, isn't it? See it as an adventure in which you achieve all these things from the comfort of your own home.

When you think about cost-cutting, I want you to banish – right now – ideas about 'being tight', 'penny pinching' or 'draining the fun out' of your money. That's not the type of person that I am, and anyway, I don't think that's the correct path to rounded, happy, financial security. But you can go about this totally the wrong way. Let's look at how . . .

Saving a couple of cents and rewarding yourself with a much bigger expense

Let's take the example of somebody who gets up fifteen minutes earlier in the morning to take the bus to work rather than get a taxi. They save €9 and feel very proud of themselves. They take a walk through town during their lunch break and reward themselves for their efforts that morning with a €20 manicure on special offer (which they typically would only ever get for a special occasion). In fact, if they had stayed in bed, got the taxi and hence never needed to reward themselves, they would have saved €11 instead.

I know that I have said it a million times by now, but it's crucially important that you find other ways of treating yourself that don't involve money. Of course, you can buy nice things as a way of giving yourself a bonus treatment for an achievement. But it becomes an issue when you always spend money as a way of doing so – you can be nice to yourself without putting your hand in your pocket.

Saving pennies that cost pounds

You're going on holiday for the weekend. You have the choice of two hotels – one is central and another is a little bit out. The first costs €50 more than the other and the facilities that they offer are much the same. Without giving it any further consideration, you choose the cheaper one. Fast-forward to the date of your arrival in your chosen city. You walk up to the information desk at the airport and ask, 'What's the best way of getting to my hotel?' You get a train into the centre, and, since it's late, you get a taxi to your hotel, costing €15. The next day you want to do a tour of the city at 10 a.m., but you're tired after the journey so instead of getting up early for the bus, you order a taxi. Another €15. You get the bus back to your hotel after your day, which costs €2. You go shopping in the centre the next day and spend €2 travelling to the centre of the city. Again, you're exhausted after the day and simply want to feel the comfort of your bed for a while. The sum of €15 for a taxi seems a small price for the pleasure, so you hail a cab. You have just one more day and you want to go home refreshed, so you take it easy and go for lunch and a walk around the area of the hotel. That night, you want to experience the city nightlife, so you get the bus in and a taxi home, which costs another €17. You need to get to the airport relatively early the next morning, so instead of getting up at the crack of dawn to get the bus into the city and the train to the airport, you simply order a taxi to take you straight there, costing €35. Now, let's look at how much you 'saved' over the weekend on getting a cheaper hotel. You spent €15 + €15 + €2 + €2 + €15 + €17 + €35 = €101. So you spent double the amount you saved on expenditure completely and solely related to the fact that you stayed outside the city.

If you had spent more money from the outset, you would have enjoyed your holiday more, having been able to spend more time in the city rather than going to and fro. This approach is one that enables you to save in the long run. Could it be the case that your life calls for the opposite of penny-pinching? You need to shift your thinking from looking at each individual 'micro' expense to the 'macro' picture. This is what's known as a 'false economy'.

Looking at cutting the amount that you spend rather than increasing value

Imagine that somebody takes an axe to their expenditure with only one aim – and that it is to cut as much cost out of their lives as possible. They have total tunnel vision and will not listen to anybody who tries to talk them out of their view. They search for low-cost house insurance on the internet and find a company which can offer cover for half the price of their existing supplier. Without another thought, they move company and are happy that they achieved their aim. Disaster strikes a couple of months later and they need to make a claim. To their horror, they realize the reason the cover was so cheap was because it involved a €2,000 excess (excess is the amount of money you would have to pay in the event of a claim). The company has a reputation for claims taking three months, and it dragged its feet completely, taking advantage of some grey areas in the contract. Between the hardship, the stress and the cost, that person would have actually saved 100 times the actual 'saving' they got from having made the change. The problem here was that the person focused on price, rather than on value. Even though this is an extreme example, I'm sure you have witnessed such examples of lower cost turning out to be more expensive many, many times. Whereas it's possible to have a better standard of living simply by being savvier with your spending.

In the next chapter, I'm going to show you how to focus on value, rather than on price, and how to get the best use out of the money that you have in order to bring you closer to where you want to be.

8

Savvier women think smarter . . .

Enough of the theory. Let's push up our sleeves and get to work. Take a moment to answer this question: which approach would you like to take to cost-cutting?

~ The one that will have the greatest impact on my finances.
~ The one that requires the least effort.
~ The one that affects my lifestyle the least.

I hope that you answered honestly, because I think each would be a natural and totally understandable approach for someone embarking on a cost-cutting journey. Let's consider the road ahead from each of these viewpoints.

The approach that will have the greatest impact on my finances

In essence, you genuinely want to get to your goal in the fastest possible way and are willing to do what it takes to get there. There are lots of things that you can do, but you're likely to start with those things that, once in motion, will have an effect that automatically repeats itself over and over again. In addition, if you can put the right systems in place and check on them regularly, you really could develop a very healthy habit that will last a lifetime, prompting others whom you know to emulate you.

The approach that requires the least effort

I would invite you to step back for a moment and revisit the goal you settled on at the beginning of this book. It doesn't sound like it's that burning. Isn't it worth striving for? If not, why not? Effort doesn't mean blood, sweat and tears; it means taking the time to care for yourself and push your life in the direction that you want it to go. On the other hand, it may be that you're perfectly content with your life already, but if any handy money were to come floating around, you wouldn't say no. Do you know the funny thing? The 'least-effort' ways to cost-cuts are those very same things that have the greatest impact on your lifestyle. Think about it. There is absolutely no effort involved in not shopping, not going out, not eating out, etc. In fact, if you were to just stop spending your discretionary expenditure (i.e., your 'fun' money), the requirements of your approach would be met. By comparison, it involves much more effort to pick up the phone and call your electricity provider for a better deal. Personally, I would prefer to save on my electricity (which would have zero impact on lifestyle) than to cut out the money involved in having a social life. However, it's up to you.

The approach that affects my lifestyle the least

You like having your cake and eating it. Why wouldn't you? Everybody does. I would be interested to know how far we can push this, in seeing whether your life can be more financially sound without your even noticing the cost savings. However, before you start to think that I have a magic wand, I invite you to question your attitude. Is your lifestyle so perfect that you wouldn't want to change it at all? Are you open to new things and new experiences? What would happen if I challenged the way you do things, with a view to your making slight changes that may actually be better for your pocket as well as in many other ways? Stick with me and let's see what happens.

With those thoughts in mind, let's see what you can do. I'm going to start with an easy one to get you going. There is one set of costs that you really won't miss. You absolutely will not notice any change in your lifestyle whatsoever and yet you'll have more money in your pocket. There is a small degree of effort involved, however. I'm going to ask you one more question – how long would it take you to earn €120 in your job, business or on benefits? Let's say that it would take you three hours. May I take it, then, that you would, correspondingly, spend three hours on a task that would save you €120? If I could double it, treble it, quadruple it, would you spend the corresponding time? Right, let's go. In preparation, pull up your bank and credit-card statements for the last three months.

The easiest money to save is that which you don't realize you're spending. This exercise is about shining a light around your expenditure to find 'invisible money'. First, look at your standing orders and direct debits. Do you actually use each and every one of them to their full capacity? If you've signed up for a gym membership, do you actually go? If you have a TV channels package, do you pay for movies and never have the time to watch them? Have you signed up to pay a minimum amount each month for cosmetics or entertainment, and the only time you think of it is when you look at your credit-card statement and say 'I must cancel that'? Remember the piece of software that I told you about that I stopped using? I cancelled it and it hasn't affected me in any way apart from a better credit-card balance. Make a list of each and every 'invisible hole' in your accounts.

Next, decide on the action you're going to take to remedy it and write it down beside each entry. For example, do you need to make a call, send an email, log into your online account?

Finally, if these things can be done right now, just go and do them. If not, put an entry in your diary for each item that needs to be followed up.

We aren't finished yet. Next, take out your spending diary. If you haven't started one yet, hopefully the next activity will motivate you to do so. Take a look back over the month, and, as you run your eye over each entry, ask yourself, 'Which of these would I not really have missed?' and 'With a little effort or planning, which of these could I have eliminated?'

The first time I did this, I was shocked by how much I was spending on eating out. I actually love to cook – but only when I have time to put all the love I feel for the process into it. I'm a busy person, and when it comes to shopping, cooking a dinner and cleaning up afterwards, I used to think I could save myself all that in exchange for just a tenner. When I gave it a bit of thought, I saw that, as I already have a routine of cooking for my boyfriend's family on a Sunday night, I could simply start doing an extra bit of chopping and prep work then, double-up on quantities of whatever I was cooking, bring the prepped veg and leftovers home, and have most of the work done for the week. For example, I use the salads for lunches over the next two days and the cooked meat as the start of another dinner; I freeze the soup; and I bake a batch of easy (healthy) wholemeal muffins for breakfasts on the go. Each is used up according to how quickly it goes off: say, a natural yoghurt dressing on Monday and defrosted soup on Friday. I saved an absolute fortune, by taking the time to do some highly enjoyable planning around my hobby.

Take a good look at the things you spend your money on and see how you could get the same enjoyment for the same money. Afterwards, take a sheet of paper and work out how much you might save on a monthly basis, multiply it by twelve and then give yourself a pat on the back. What are you going to do to treat yourself? Only please don't say something that involves spending much money, which totally defeats the purpose. Could you go to visit a friend that you haven't seen in a while? Could you dedicate an evening to 'me-time'? Could you go to the park with a 'mini-picnic' and read that book you've been promising yourself?

I said earlier that when it comes to cost-cutting, the impact doesn't have to equate to pain, loss or doing without. Looking at the direct debits, standing orders, etc., that you don't actually use may have already made this clear to you, but I'm going to focus on financial services now. In preparation for this, write down a list of your loans, mortgages, insurance, service providers, savings and investments. First, I'm going to discuss debt, insurance, utilities, accommodation costs, discretionary expenditure, etc., in detail, and will deal with savings and investments later in the chapter.

If you're in debt, you need to review your credit provider. Write down a list of every single cent that you owe and who you owe it to – from your mortgage to your credit card to the fiver you borrowed from a friend because you couldn't find an ATM. Beside each entry, write down the interest rate that you're paying and the terms of the loan. If you don't know any of that information, find it out immediately. Order that list by interest rate, as the higher the rate, the more your own money is being used to build the profits of other companies.

Apply two strategies to the list. First, move the higher-interest-rate loans to a lower rate. For example, if you have a large credit-card debt, you could go to your credit union, or some lower-cost interest-rate facility, and get a medium-term loan to pay it off. In order to avoid the same thing happening again in the future, I suggest that you work out a way to remain strictly within your budget and use only a debit card or buy a prepaid credit card to do your shopping. Second, if you move your debt to a provider with a lower rate of interest, keep your repayments to the level they were at previously, so that you can pay down the principal of the loan faster and clear yourself of this weight on your shoulders.

Alternatively, if the above isn't feasible, put all your energy into paying down the most expensive debt first. For example, you could move to a new (lower-interest) credit-card provider and cut down your spending to the absolute bone for a few months. In addition, if you have other (lower-interest) loan commitments, could you decrease the amount you're paying back there and increase the higher-interest repayments? When the higher-interest loan has been paid back, you could then apply the same monthly repayment to your original loan – which you'll eat through quickly because of the lower rate. I passionately believe it's important to move this short-term, expensive debt out of your life, because this is the obstacle that prevents people from getting out of a debilitating debt spiral. This money that you used to roll over short-term debt and its accompanying interest can then be redeployed in making a real dent in your long-term debt – and this will see you much more likely to achieve financial freedom.

Here are the steps that you need to take:

- Develop your strategy to cut through this debt – moving to lower interest rates and/or using more of your current income to get rid of it.
- Research your credit provider's competitors and see what they're offering.
- Examine your budget to see how much you can actually afford in payments each month. Give yourself some leeway for times when the kids go back to school, one-off payments throughout the year and seasonal charges (e.g., car tax).
- Contact the provider that you would like to work with and ask them what's involved in signing up with them.
- Contact your existing service provider and ask what's involved in moving your account elsewhere. It's quite likely they have an account-retention department with the power to match competitors' offers, and you'll be offered a better deal to stay with them. You will have already done your research, so you'll instantly be able to make the decision to stay or leave.
- Set up a standing order to take these new amounts out of your account. This is crucial, as it will automatically leave your account before you can spend it. Once it's automated, you don't have to think about it again, and the amount that's left in your account reflects your actual disposable income much more accurately. This may seem a hard, crude way of dealing with the issue, as you may have to

live very leanly, depending on the level of debt that you are currently in, but this is the definitive way out of the situation.

Now let's take a look at your insurance contracts. This is an area where some focused research and a few phonecalls might end up saving you quite a bit of money. How can you make sure you're paying the right price for the insurance you already have? What should you look out for when doing your research? When should you cancel your existing contract?

The first thing that you need to do is evaluate your existing service. The old saying is true that 'you get what you pay for', but I would invite you to ask: what are you getting, and do you actually need all of it? Look at your financial products and write down the characteristics of each package. For example, there are various sorts of car insurance that you can avail of, a raft of different benefits that come with them and an adjustable level of excess that you can pay (excess is the amount of money you would have to pay in the event of a claim). Answering the following questions will help you to make a list of the main attributes of your car-insurance policy:

- What is my premium?
- What is the value of the car that I'm insuring?
- Is the cover third party, fire and theft, or fully comprehensive?
- Does this policy insure me to drive other people's cars?
- Do I pay a regular amount throughout the year or a one-off payment when due?
- What is the excess on the policy?
- What is my annual mileage on the policy – is this accurate?
- Is somebody else insured to drive the car?
- How quickly will a claim be processed and the money sent to me or the car-repair company?
- If my car needs repair or is written off, have I access to another car in the interim and, if so, for how long?

- If I claim and have to go to court, are my legal expenses covered?
- Am I paying for personal-injury cover as well as car insurance?
- Have I paid for gap-insurance protection, if I have insured a relatively new car? (If I buy a car and then damage it to a point where it needs significant repair, the value of the car will fall simply because it has been crashed. Gap-insurance protection pays out on the gap between the market value of the car before and after the crash.)
- How many years of no-claims bonus have I got and is this protected?
- In the event of a breakdown, have I paid for breakdown cover from the insurer and/or roadside assistance from a private body; and/or is it included in the guarantee from my car dealer; or would I be left entirely to my own devices?
- Does this policy insure me to drive abroad?

This is a long list of questions and you need an efficient way of processing the answers, so I have created a spreadsheet and checklist especially for you that will come in very handy. You can download this at www.savvywomenonline.com.

Next, take some time to call several car-insurance companies and ask them for a quote. Go through each of the items on the checklist to make your research super-effective. For every company, put a tick if the answer is yes or fill in the appropriate details (e.g., the euro amount of the premium). At the end of this exercise, you'll be in a supremely good position to decide how to whittle down your list. The next thing you need to do is to evaluate what attributes you need or don't need. Perhaps you don't need breakdown cover, as you have a guarantee from your car dealer already? Perhaps you have very comprehensive accident cover which actually duplicates personal-injury cover? Perhaps you would be very seriously incapacitated without a car if anything happened to it, so you would absolutely need a replacement vehicle? Perhaps you could afford a higher excess than is currently on your policy? Perhaps your mileage has fallen significantly since you changed jobs?

Take the time to go through each line of this spreadsheet and strip away what's irrelevant to your circumstances. Now, which insurance companies are offering the best deals? Call them back and say that, having reviewed your needs, you won't need each of the items that you struck off your list. What is their quote based on that information? Write down the revised rates; these should give you a very good idea of who is offering the best value, based on your actual requirements. Indeed, it's easy to convince people to pay more for a product that has more, does more, offers more – however, do you need that 'more'?

If it turns out that the best-value option is not your existing supplier, you need to cancel the contract. However, if you tell them that you've found a policy that offers all that you need for a more competitive price and you're going to move, they may tell you that they can match it. This will save you the trouble of moving your account, and the exercise has had the additional benefit of making you more informed as well as saving you money.

If they can't compete with the quote you've discovered through your research, ask your existing company about the procedure involved in changing supplier. If there are any snags in the small print, they will surface quickly at this point and you can react accordingly. They may try to keep your custom by offering additional extras, and, if so, refer back to your list. Are these things of value to you? If not, they don't count. If they do, re-evaluate from your current informed, learned position. And, should your existing supplier drag their feet or try to manipulate you into staying, you have even more reason to go, as you can tell them that this type of customer service is simply not what you want to pay for.

Let us now move to the next area of your budget where we can increase your value for money. You'll need your budget for this step. Take a look at the 'variable expenditure' column, primarily the section that consists of the household's utilities – the electricity, the heating, the phone, the groceries, the car expenditure, etc. You need to look at each of these and ask yourself two questions:

- Can I change to a cheaper provider?
- Can I decrease my consumption?

Let's take your heating bill. Spend some time researching your existing service provider's competitors based on your particular requirements and follow the same step-by-step process that was outlined in the insurance example. Next, what could you actually do to reduce your consumption of heat?

- Insulate the house (are there any 'green grants' available for this?).
- Turn down the thermostat by a couple of degrees.
- Decrease the amount of time that the heating is turned on.
- Turn off the radiators in uninhabited rooms.
- Keep doors closed and seal as many gaps as possible.
- Change your heating system so that the heat goes off after the room reaches a certain temperature rather than after a certain period of time.
- Invest in some solar panels to collect 'free' energy (check out the Sustainable Energy Authority of Ireland website for a list of grants available and registered contractors).

Let's take your phone bill — spend some time researching your existing service provider's competitors based on your particular requirements and follow the same step-by-step process as I outlined in the insurance example. You can often get some really good 'introductory' deals offered by telecommunications companies because competition is rife. In addition, if a supplier signs you up with a direct debit, most people simply 'won't bother' changing over. You may have wondered why a supplier is happy to offer a loss-making deal to get you on to their books: it's done on the assumption that you probably won't change provider when the introductory offer runs out. Consequently, the supplier will make that loss back several times over when your direct debit increases to the standard charge, which you pay automatically month after month.

Next, after having found the best-value provider, look at how you could spend less:

- Ask the phone company to review your usage and recommend the best package for your needs (do this periodically, as this can change regularly).
- Can you make certain calls at a certain time of the day for free? If so, make non-time-sensitive calls during those hours.
- Can you send texts for free from the internet? If so, and you have a smartphone, it's going to take the same time to go online and send them as doing so from the text button on your phone.
- In order to keep your roaming costs down, call your provider before you go abroad and ask them which company is the cheapest.
- Are there other ways of communicating with people rather than on the phone – could you Skype them, send them a message using a social network, email them or meet in person?
- If you have a mobile phone as well as a landline, do you need both? Why not consider getting rid of the landline totally if you, and all the people in your house, have mobile phones?

Apply the very same sort of logic to each and every one of your variable expenses. Take some time, make a few calls and you may be amazed at what you can do.

Next, move to your fixed-expenditure list. Since you pay a certain amount each month/quarter/year, if you change your consumption levels, it's not going to make any difference whatsoever, unless you change the actual amount that you're paying. As a result, the only question that you need to ask is: could you get better value?

Typically, the largest expense that people will incur in their lives apart from tax is their accommodation expense. If you're paying a mortgage, does your contract allow you to move and, if so, have you looked into whether this would save you money? Could you afford to pay a higher amount of money than you are currently, in order to eradicate the loan more quickly? Let's go further and ask if your current house is bigger than you might need. Could you downsize and reduce the mortgage accordingly? Alternatively, there are ways for your house to make you money, which I discuss in Chapter 19. On the other hand, if you're renting, have you ever discussed a decrease in the price of your rent with your landlord? Have you considered moving to bring down cost? Have you looked at the price of commuting to your place of work in conjunction with your rental costs and looked into bringing down both by moving closer to work? Or by moving to cheaper accommodation that allows you to take public transport instead of your car?

Look at the utilities that are on that fixed-expenditure list and examine them in the same way as above. Are you paying the right amount for your services, relative to what you need? For example, if you have a smartphone and wired broadband at home, do you need a mobile dongle as well?

Finally, let's tackle the one you don't want me to talk about: your discretionary expenditure. Before we take a look at this, first make sure to look hard at *all* other expenses, since 'fun money' is the last one you want to cut. Essentially, this part of your budget is spent on your hobbies. I'm not going to ask you to change your hobbies, so, once you're certain that you really do need to cut costs here as well, we'll look instead at how you can get the same enjoyment out of less money: put simply, how to get you better value for money.

Do you think you could make the following changes?

If you buy rounds when out for a few drinks, think about stopping that right now. It puts people under pressure; and it's totally unfair on those who drink less expensive drinks and on those who get caught at the beginning. Also, if you're in a round, you typically find that you drink more, as people tend to buy their round as soon as the fastest drinker arrives at the bottom of their glass, which speeds up everybody else. People have said to me, 'Surely if you can't afford to be in a round, you should simply not go out.' I disagree completely – why shouldn't you be able to go out and spend the money that you want to spend, at the pace that you want to spend it? Why should you subsidize somebody else's night out, or vice versa? If you think that other people will consider you 'tight' because you choose to stick on your own, believe me, they may well thank you for having the courage to refuse, as it's something they wished they'd done themselves a long time ago. Which would you prefer – having more money in your pocket or paying for other people's hangovers? You choose.

If you're going out for dinner and you can take the initiative on where, take a look on the internet for deals or coupons. You could save everybody money as a result and have just as good a night as you would have had in a restaurant that isn't running any special offers.

If retail therapy is a hobby, I suggest thinking about finding an activity to complement that. In any case, have you considered going to a charity shop or a clothes exchange? I've picked up many great bargains in charity shops; and, in turn, I've sent some of my own very good-quality clothes that cost a lot into these shops for one reason or another. We all have 'previously loved' garments that just don't fit, are no longer our style or we've got fed up wearing. However, they could be 'future loved', if we bring them to a clothes exchange to freshen up our wardrobe without spending a penny.

If you enjoy meeting friends for a coffee, what is it that you enjoy? The coffee? The excuse for cake? The chat? If you invite him/her/them over to your own house, wouldn't you still have all of the above?

If you love your beauty treatments, take a look around for a beauty-therapy college. I used to get a blow-dry each week at a salon where one lady practised on my hair for a whole year. If you'd like a free or cheap massage, wax treatment or facial, look out for a willing student who would love to practise on you under the watchful eye of their supervisor.

If you'd like to learn a language, join a local library where you can find texts or audio books with which to make a start. Next, look for a conversation group where you can get some 'free' training and meet some new people too. Some websites also offer to pair you up with a native speaker of your target language for free.

In essence, all that you need to do is think smarter. What do you love about the things on which you spend your discretionary expenditure? Can you re-create those in other ways? Are there any special offers that you and those around you would gladly avail of, in order to enjoy all the attributes of your existing expenditure, but for less money?

At this stage, I really hope that your head is swirling with ideas of what to do and when. Cost-cutting doesn't have to be doing without; it can be a life-affirming skill to ensure that you get the best value for your money now and always.

Finally, once you've thoroughly examined all your expenditure, it's time to take a look at your savings. Write down a list of every single cent that you own, the interest rate that you're getting on it and, finally, how long it's locked away for, if at all. If you don't have these answers, find them out immediately, as something can be done about them only if you know what you're dealing with. There are three categories of savings into which you can separate your money.

Current-account money. You should have a certain amount covering all your needs for each and every month. This should come wholly from your regular income stream: your salary, self-employed revenues, investment returns and social-welfare benefits. If you are dipping into your savings or relying on credit cards and other forms of debt to fund your lifestyle, you are simply living beyond your means, need to face that fact and react accordingly by cost-cutting and/or increasing the amount you earn. On the other hand, if you have more than enough money in your current account, it's unlikely that it's earning any money for you, so you need to move that into the next category.

Emergency money. We all face expenses from time to time that require more than our monthly income can sustain. In some cases, these expenses can be for wonderful things – travelling abroad for a special occasion, changing the car or taking advantage of a good investment opportunity. However, they can also be for ill-health, sudden loss in income or any other unwelcome and involuntary occurrences. On these occasions, you need to focus on capital security (the knowledge that the full amount will be there) and easy access to the money, which is essential to your peace of mind as you deal with the emergency. However, any or all of these events might be months or years apart, and hence you might very well have a large block of time in which to generate a return. Once that emergency fund has reached a satisfactory level (that is for you to define), move any money left over to the next category.

Investment money. Many people earn enough money to sustain a suitable lifestyle while also being able to put away a reasonable amount in case of (good or bad) emergencies. The remainder can be used to generate a return with as much risk attached as you want to take on. We call this 'investment'.

Can you separate your money into each category? It's important that there's enough in your current account before building up an emergency fund; and it's important that there's enough in your emergency fund before building up an investment portfolio. The categories should be viewed as building blocks, as opposed to three distinct pots.

Now, let's look at a step-by-step process to build your savings and investment balances.

- Evaluate how much money could be put into each category currently and how much you would like to be in each one, ideally.
- Research your savings and investment provider's competitors to see what they're offering.
- Examine your budget to see how much you can actually afford to put away in savings and/or investments each month. Remember to give yourself some leeway for times

when the kids go back to school, one-off payments throughout the year and seasonal charges (e.g., car tax).

∽ Contact the vendor that you would like to work with and
ask them what's involved in signing up with them.

∽ Contact your existing service provider and ask them what's
involved in moving your account elsewhere. They might
offer you a better deal to stay with them. You will already
have your research done so that you can make the decision
to stay or leave on the spot.

∽ Set up a standing order to take these new amounts out of
your account. You'll now have a realistic disposable income
while at the same time building more and more financial
security into the future.

Talk to the experts

9

Let others help you on the way towards financial freedom

If you don't communicate about money, it's like being stuck in a dark hallway that you're struggling to get out of. There may be doors with windows of light here and there. At other times the walls close in and the windows disappear. You occupy this space alone, because, although you can see people through the glass in the doors, it doesn't occur to you that you can get their attention. Though the hallway is dark, it might feel safe – while you're in it you're not exposed. If you walk outside it, you may feel vulnerable and have to forsake the pretence of 'knowing it all'. You may fear that you'll lose your cover and give somebody else ammunition to use against you.

This image may seem a bit stark, and some of your fears may be valid, but approaching your money issues in this fearful way prevents you from taking up all the wonderful things that are waiting for you outside – all of the people and resources with time, energy and money that are there to help you. And when you approach money like this, you're not giving yourself credit for your capacity to arm yourself emotionally, mentally and practically against all your fears.

If this sounds like you, and you want to open a door to the right kind of support to help to reach your financial goals, take some time to think who you would like to be on the other side of the door. I have already told you about times when I've found myself in situations where I was starting from scratch. There wasn't any defined path in front of me, and I had absolutely no choice but to take it one step at a time. The challenge was figuring out what that step was. The key question that I asked myself was: 'What resources are available around me?' In other words, 'How can I find help?'

Remember in Chapter 4, when I told you about the time I was trying to figure out how to expand my business and I sat on the floor cutting up scraps of paper on which I'd written every single angle I could think of? Well, I recommend that's where you start this exercise. Write down a list of each and every thing that is within your power to do in order to move towards your goal. I mean literally everything, any little and apparently insignificant thing. Let me give you a suggestion – in answer to the question 'Who can help me?' you might write some of the following:

- The people who work in the Revenue office could help me find out if there are any ways that I could save money on taxes (No, really. They *can* actually help you do that.)
- A friend of mine is in business and I could ask her about how I might start something myself.
- My son is a whizz at Excel. I could ask him to help me set up some budget spreadsheets.
- I could call up different utility companies and ask what package they could offer me if I switched.
- I could go to meet my bank manager and ask if she has any suggestions for meeting financial goals.
- I could sign up to social-media outlets to find ways of saving money (LinkedIn groups, Facebook pages, personal finance blogs, etc.).
- I could go to my local Toastmasters and build up my confidence through public speaking (this could help in many aspects of your life e.g., selling, bargaining, coaching others, increasing your employability, etc.).
- I could call my travel agent and ask her to look out for some special offers for me.
- I could go to training events around money, finance and business. For example, the County Enterprise Boards and Skillnets offer lots of subsidized training. I could then send the trainers and attendees on the course a LinkedIn invitation and add them to my network (and follow up regularly).

- I could ask a person I met recently, and with whom I get on well, whether they would consider becoming an accountability partner – and whether they'd be interested in my doing the same for them.
- I could go to the Careers Advice service where I went to college to get some advice on moving forward in my career. Also, I could join the University Alumni and become an active member in that network; this would help me to meet new people and identify opportunities.
- I could ask my boss out to lunch to discuss how I could get a promotion or pay rise, or what I could do in order to add more value to my work (and thus make those things happen).
- I could arrange to meet all my clients, both past and present, over the next three months to see if there was any new business that I could do.
- I could look into doing a house swap this year and have cost-free accommodation to help with the holiday budget.
- I could use the services of those discount companies that offer beauty treatments at knock-down prices.
- I could talk to my friends about any money ideas they have and any strategies they found helpful.
- I could talk to my neighbour who has started minding my friend's child. Perhaps this would be a cheaper option than the crèche that I'm currently using.
- I could look at TripAdvisor and pick up useful info about a place that I'm visiting soon. (I was in Copenhagen last weekend and I had a quick read on TripAdvisor about the hotel I was staying in. A number of reviewers mentioned the free shuttle they provided to and from the airport. I saved two taxi fares, just because I 'asked' other people for the benefit of their experience and they had no idea they were even helping me!)
- I can look up the national contacts to help me apply for European funding.

∽ I could have a fun night in with a few of my friends. Send them a text offering wine and Pringles in exchange for their opinions. For example, 'I'm thinking that I would like to set up a business, and you might just be my target market: a mobile manicure service for mums. What types of things would make you buy or not buy?'

∽ I could look up any networking events that are happening close by, where I could meet new people and contacts as well as simply chat to people who are in a similar situation.

∽ In a light-hearted way, I could just 'put the question out there' over dinner or drinks: 'If you were to save €x in the most innovative way, what would it be?' or 'If you were to start a business with zero money, what's the craziest way to do it?' You never know what might come out of it.

Look at the people in your team. Each and every one of them has the goal of serving you as best they can. Reach out and take advantage of what they have to offer.

Next you could ask yourself: 'What information could I access for nothing?'

∽ I could sign up for the newsletter from the National Consumer Agency, which contains money-saving ideas.

∽ I could download the budget from www.savvywomenonline. com and download some apps to keep a check on my spending.

∽ I could borrow books from the library about budgeting, setting up an online business, etc.

∽ I could read articles online about money-saving, investing, setting up an online business or entrepreneurship in general.

∽ I could sign up for email newsletters from companies offering special deals on restaurants, holidays, beauty treatments in my local area.

~ I could find inspirational stories and quotes in books, TV programmes and on the internet to 'keep myself going' when I'm not feeling motivated.

When you've come up with as many solutions as you can manage, pick up a project planner at a stationery shop; or, if you're feeling creative, you could make your own colourful one with Excel or good ol' paper and pens. Write down all the things you can do and all the people you can contact. Put them into categories such as Budgeting, Money-Saving, Inspiration and Goal Development, Earning More Revenue. Then tease out even more possible activities for each category. For example, under Earning More Revenue, the following could be included:

~ Read stories about other entrepreneurs in the library.
~ Open up some conversations with people about setting up a business.
~ Attend a 'start-your-own-business' course.
~ Organize a 'focus group' with your target market (that's the wine and Pringles idea!).
~ Look for a business mentor.
~ Ask a close friend to simulate some sales meetings with you so that you can practise explaining your product and over-coming objections.
~ Join a local networking group.
~ Watch a YouTube video every day about your business area.
~ Ask people if they know somebody who might benefit from your service.

Devote some time to developing your own list, and within a short while you'll have lots and lots and lots of actions that you can take, as you make the best of other people's abilities, contacts and experience, which they will willingly want to share with you. Out of this list will arise a very concrete step forward, with many straightforward actions.

In keeping with the SMARTER theme, put a time-frame beside each one, so that you won't let procrastination set it. Before you know it, you'll have made huge strides in the direction of your goal. I hope you see all of the doors that communication can open up for you and why you don't have to be on your own in that enclosed space in your head that I mentioned earlier.

The whole point of communicating is that it makes progress faster and much easier. Just by asking – asking for information, asking for help – you can shorten the time it takes you to get where you want to be. Remember, if you don't ask, the answer is always no. Just by communicating your goals, you'll connect with important people and resources. Don't be afraid that, by asking a question, you'll make a fool of yourself. What is more embarrassing? Thinking that you might be perceived as an amateur or a fool because you don't know? (And, yes, I am saying 'Thinking that you might be perceived' because it's all in your head.) Or being left stranded with no way forward, just because you were too proud to ask?

Of course it's always very rewarding to solve a problem single-handedly and come out the hero or heroine. And I'm not saying you shouldn't try to solve problems on your own, but sometimes it's much, much more efficient and effective to ask.

There are many ways to solve a problem. Finding a solution can come through hard work, or being clever, or knowing the right people. It can also come, very simply, from stating your 'problem' or block or obstacle. Just say it out loud: 'At the moment, I'm running into this issue.' And – lo and behold – soon you have to field answers left, right and centre from people who have solved this issue themselves, or people who know someone who knows someone who might be able to help – and would you like to be put in touch? So, when it comes to dealing with some obstacle, I'd always put out a question first. It might save me, oh, let's see, several years and thousands of euros in wasted effort.

I can give you an example of this from my own business that occurred a couple of years ago. A public-sector company had put out a job to tender, and I knew that, because our company had the technical know-how, we were in a very good place to make an offer. However, two rules prevented me from moving forward with a proposal.

Now, I believe that it is the duty of entrepreneurs, innovators and leaders to question rules and change them for better ones. Everybody from Alexander Graham Bell to Steve Jobs to Moya Doherty came up with game-changing products by questioning the prevailing orthodoxies – about how sound travels, about the mutability of devices, about the appropriate way to present Irish dancing, respectively. I think that, when rules come at the expense of a better process or outcome, you can find ways to deal with them.

The two rules that were proving to be a thorn in my side actually make a lot of sense. The first is that you need three years of accounts before you can apply for a tender with a public-sector company; and, second, that the contract must be within a certain percentage of your revenue. (Let's say that percentage was 30%. If the contract was worth €100,000, you would need to show that your turnover was €300,000 at least.) Both of these rules have a lot of merit. The first establishes that a company has been in business for a certain length of time, that it's not a fly-by-night operation; and the second ensures the winner of the business is big enough to handle it. In this case, I believed that we could do a really good job based on our experience, but these were two rules I couldn't find a way around, as the company wasn't old enough or big enough at that time.

One day I was at a networking meeting at the Guinness Storehouse, and we were invited to put forward any issues that we were having. I explained my problem – our company hadn't been in business long enough and last year's revenue figure was proportionately too small for it to qualify – and said surely there's still a way to apply for this contract?

One member of the group said, 'You haven't a hope of going for it alone. You need to team up with a bigger company which has these attributes and can strengthen your case.'

As the meeting went on, my mind started to whirr into action.

The contract was indeed big enough for more than just our company and I mentally went through my network. I called my boyfriend, who is also my business partner, and told him of the advice I had received. What did he think of my approaching a particular company that I had in mind? We both agreed it was the way forward and I met with them the following day.

They came on board, and that was when I could see the full benefit of the rules that had so stymied me. Indeed, our new partners did bring strength to the case, but they also brought the vision, language, pricing, connections, resources and experience of a bigger company. They could easily absorb the contract as it stood, and extend their resources to meet it if the contract expanded. We may have been able to do this on our own, but not as easily, effectively or efficiently at that stage. Hence the rules stood everybody in good stead. We went on to win the contract and it worked out well for all parties concerned.

I see two morals to this story. First, if you put your issue on the table, you can be absolutely sure that another person at some stage in their lives has come across this problem and can give you a nugget of learning, advice or help. Did I feel that I came across as amateur by asking? Perhaps a little, but that only hurt my ego. The business networking event was a platform for me to voice what might, after all, be a very common business issue. All I needed was the benefit of someone else's experience – which I could now share, because it had become a part of my own experience. I could have kept schtum, trying to appear to know it all – and I would have lost out on the business. Also, there may well have been people in the room that day who had experienced a similar issue and gained some benefit from my question and the forthcoming answer.

I don't recommend stopping people in the supermarket to ask how they get on with their significant other regarding their finances, because you've been having lots of rows about it lately, but I do recommend finding the right environment in which to ask for help, receive it and put it into practice.

The second moral is to question the rules that you think govern your life, rather than simply accepting that they constrain your efforts. If you search for a way around what may appear as an obstacle, you may be surprised to find a path that leads straight through those rules. I didn't have to figure out how to bend a rule; all I did was to ask how I should deal with it and the end result was what I had originally set out to achieve: our company was now dealing with a public-sector organization on a tender contract. It just so happened that I needed another party to team up with me, but that would never have happened had I not communicated my problem. In the end I was very happy to have a slice of the cake, rather than the whole lot at a time when I wasn't ready for it.

This is why I think it's so important to communicate, especially when you can't see a way through (or around). Instead of hitting your head against that wall again and again and again, instead of wringing your hands and giving up, you can, by asking for help, achieve something through teamwork that you wouldn't have been able to conquer on your own.

Bringing in other people will also help you to achieve something that I find crucial: a change of perspective. Perspective is very important to me. I believe that the perspective we adopt daily has a huge influence on our frame of mind – and on the way we act. You might have noticed that this book is about financial strategies on the surface, but that it's also about changing perspectives. Changing perspective is what will help you expand your comfort zone, raise your financial thermostat and turn around your financial situation.

Sticking to a budget is not 'tightening your belt', but 'getting closer to your goal'.

Cutting costs is not 'doing without', but 'choosing who deserves your money'.

I typically choose to use positive language rather than negative words. I think it alters your way of thinking and provides a better outlook, which often becomes a self-fulfilling prophecy. I choose to say 'I'm not as early as I thought I was' instead of 'I'm late.' I prefer to say 'Things aren't quite as good as I expected' rather than 'It's bad.' I prefer to say I'm 'actively making my life better' rather than 'My life is deficient in some aspect.' I prefer to say 'I haven't seen that place yet' rather than 'Never been.' It's just my way. I actually didn't even notice I did this until somebody picked me up on it.

And in this chapter about communication, I want to address a particular choice of word that I find really important. I'd rather talk about 'issues' than 'problems'. I find that thinking of something as a 'problem' doesn't put me in a useful frame of mind. As soon as I write that word, I think of discomfort, negativity, pain, something that isn't enjoyable. It makes me shift in my chair. I don't like it. I think of a distressing phonecall that I have to make, expecting only disappointment on both ends of the line. I think of a situation when the means of transport I was counting on doesn't show up or is late or somehow doesn't work out and it throws everything off. I think of a task that needed to be done yesterday and I can't find a way to slow down time. I think of things that are difficult to solve without hurting somebody and having to sustain huge stress.

An 'issue', on the other hand, is something that is to be ticked off on a 'to-do' list. I know of a way of dealing with it, and I'm comfortable with that way. It's just something that has to be done, and I have every intention of doing it without stressing. I think of a phonecall that will be a huge weight off my shoulders when it's done. I think of Googling to find a taxi company, calling them and getting where I need to go, even if I'm not there as early as I had wanted to be. I think of calling the person or company imposing the deadline, explaining my situation, delegating what I can, prioritizing what is of paramount importance and putting everything else on a to-do list, so it's not taking up space in my brain. The main thing here is that problems are debilitating, but issues can spur you into formulating a strategy with which to deal with them.

I don't know anybody who likes dealing with problems, but very few people have an issue about dealing with issues. You might say, 'That doesn't take away the fact that I have a problem.' I understand that, and maybe it won't make any difference to you, but it does to me. I find that using the word 'issue' puts me in a different frame of mind. It's something to be resolved calmly rather than getting upset about. If you find that just changing the word is a poultice on a wooden leg, well, I would say, in a way it is, but, again, it's a question of perspective. I choose to think that the way you describe things has some bearing upon the thing itself: by improving the word, you improve the thing somehow. On the other hand, I can see that you may find that irritating and childish. I would still recommend that maybe you just give it a try. You don't have to wholeheartedly believe in it, but do try changing a negative word for a more positive one, and see whether you like the outcome. Or it might be that 'issue' is not the right choice for you. Maybe some other word will do better? How about 'this thing I need help with' or 'I need a solution' instead of 'I have a problem'? I'm sure you can come up with your own phrases, those that will help you reframe the issue, without their sounding ridiculous to you.

I think perspective plays a big role in both the issue itself as well as its outcome. Let me give you an example.

Scenario A

Karen sees a job advertised at €41,500 per year. That's quite a nice salary and one that she feels she could live on comfortably. She meets someone that she went to college with and they just drop that they're 'on upwards of €100k' into the conversation. Karen thinks that now is the right time to buy a house and she takes a look at some properties in the window of an estate agent. She makes a quick calculation in her head; at the most, she could get a mortgage of €120,000; but, after every cent of the €20,000 savings that she has is added to that, she would still only have €140,000. Not quite enough for that house by the Salthill prom she's been dreaming about. Her friend asks her to be a bridesmaid . . . in Australia. There are five more of her friends getting married this year. She realizes what the tax man is going to take off her and she wonders – how is she going to save at all?

Scenario B

Sinead sees a job advertised at €41,500 per year. That's quite a nice salary and one that she feels she could live on comfortably. Her last job was €25,000 a year, so this is a massive jump. She survived on the salary from her previous job and now she calculates that she'll have just over an extra €400 per month (she works this out very crudely by taking out 40% for tax from the larger amount, 20% from the smaller amount and dividing what's left by the number of months in the year). If she saves €300 a month, she would still have an extra €100 of disposable income with which to enjoy life. In fact, if she could find a bank account offering 4% on her savings, she could get a few weeks' salary 'for free'. She now has both a financial cushion as well as more money to spend on having fun.

The two scenarios above are for the same situation, showing how two people could approach it from different angles. Karen was on €25,000 a year previously, but she neglected to mention the increase in the first scenario; whereas Sinead was delighted. Karen spoke about all the money the taxman was going to take off her; Sinead simply factored the tax into the calculation of her net pay to ascertain how it was going to affect her life. Karen got stressed out by the fact that she had been invited to so many weddings and particularly one in Australia; Sinead simply pointed out that she had more money to spend on having fun. She didn't even mention her friends' weddings, as they weren't a source of stress. Karen focused on what she couldn't do regarding the house she wanted; Sinead made a plan about how to get started in the direction of her future dreams and was savvy about how to accelerate it. She focused on what she could do right now. Karen hasn't even applied for the job yet and it's all doom and gloom already. Everything is a struggle and a sacrifice, as all she sees is that she's going to have to 'do without'. Sinead has a measured response and doesn't let her financial thermostat draw her back to a place where the extra money is nice for a while, only for her then to wonder how she ever lived without that pay rise.

You might well consider the perspective of Sinead to be delusional. *After all, she hasn't even applied for the job yet, let alone got it. All her plans depend on the job interview going extremely well, and that is not something she can control 100%, can she?* Indeed, you have a point. But which of the two women do you think is going to go for that job interview well prepared, doing everything she can to stack the odds in her favour, as if the job were hers already? Which of them do you think might feel so depressed and crushed by negative thoughts that she ends up thinking, 'Why bother at all? I won't get that job anyway'? Who do you think might say to herself, 'Indeed, €41,500 a year would be very comfortable. In the event that I don't get the job, are there any other jobs with the same pay that I might apply for? Or perhaps I could make an extra €15,000 a year while staying in my old job?'

As a final point on perspective, I want to share something that a neighbour said to me at home over Christmas: 'You can have a lot of money or a little, and I've found myself in both situations. In either case, however, you can have a lot of fun.' I have to agree with that. If you need to save or budget, that's not to say that fun can't be had. I love to spend time with my loved ones, cook, drink coffee and write. None of these costs much. My goddaughter and I can put together a Peppa Pig jigsaw and laugh our hearts out, and it doesn't cost anything. My best friend and I can sit and chat in Stephen's Green for zip. You can borrow books from the library for free and a fiver can go a long way towards some creative soup out of a cookbook. I can buy a jar of coffee for €2 and a notebook for another €2. It costs nothing to sit on the rocks in Salthill or on the grass in the Phoenix Park or in the sitting room at home in Cork (I spent the day there today and it was wonderful). Indeed, I love my spa breaks, dinners out with my boyfriend, conferences abroad and going out with my family and friends. Do I enjoy the latter more than the former? Not particularly. The money side of life shouldn't dictate the fun side of life. Fun and living shouldn't be in proportion to how much money you have, but how much imagination you have when it comes to using that money.

So is it worth thinking about how you can do an activity more cheaply? I haven't got the money at the moment to spend on buying books; I could go to the library instead. I haven't got the money to go to the cinema and I fancy seeing a movie; I could go to the shop for popcorn, get my duvet off my bed, turn off the lights and watch one that's on TV. I don't even have to walk out into the cold. I feel like buying a new outfit, but my bank balance doesn't agree; I could go to my local charity shop to see what I can find. Alternatively, I can get a new pair of tights, a belt or some accessory to give a well-loved outfit a makeover. I want to go on a holiday next year, but my budget is zero. Could I sign up as a mystery shopper and be 'sent' on one? Could I save on accommodation by registering on Couch-Surfing.org? Could I find a temp job abroad?

Take a wedding, for example. So, you're going to a wedding and you come out in a rash at the thought of the cost. You don't want to compromise your enjoyment of it, but you do want to keep the amount you spend to a minimum. First, what are the costs that you need to think about?

- The outfit
- The hotel
- The childcare (possibly)
- The present
- The transport
- The grooming – hair, make-up and perhaps nail and tan treatments

How might we deal with these costs, throwing some communication into the mix? Could you ask for help, for ideas?

The outfit

There is something lovely about wearing a new outfit to a wedding that has a value of its own. Also, no one wants to wear the same thing to two weddings where many of the guests will be the same. Taking this into consideration, you could:

Rent an outfit. I know of a dress-hire company that provides not just the dress, but also the shoes, bag, accessories and alterations all for one all-inclusive price. You could look at this two ways. You're spending money on getting just a single wear out of a dress. Maybe you would rather invest in buying the dress, and then at least you could wear it again. On the other hand, it could save you a lot of money (and time) if you were to take the shoes, etc., into account. In addition, it will help you avoid the 'I spent €100 on those shoes because they were just fabulous with the dress, but then they gathered dust until I brought them to the charity shop two years later' syndrome.

Borrow an outfit. You could ask your sister, friend, colleague, etc., if you could do an 'outfit swap'. You're of a similar size and you both have functions to go to where you really need to be wearing something new. Why not solve both your problems at once, and for free? Also, neither of you is asking a favour of the other, so it's not too embarrassing.

Have you considered 'swap shopping'? You bring a garment or two to a swap shop and then get a currency to spend on the previously loved (and sometimes never worn) clothes of others. You could neatly pick up something that suits you now in exchange for something that did a couple of months back . . . but not quite today.

Update a current outfit. I was at a lady's house one day working on a contract, and while I was there, she brought a skirt that she had 'five years forward'. She got the idea in a magazine and all it involved was simply cutting triangles out of the hem and replacing them with a material in a fashionable colour; it all went wonderfully well with a top she had of the same shade. If you have a particular skirt, blouse, shirt, jacket, dress, etc., that you love – build a new outfit around it. Get creative and see what you can do. If you don't think you have the skills, you could ask somebody who does, or take a sewing course yourself.

The hotel

Unless you live close by or are staying in somebody's house, the first thing that you'll probably do in preparation for the wedding is make a reservation at the hotel where it's taking place, so that you'll be 'close to the action' and able to pop upstairs before the reception to freshen up. Taking this into consideration:

Ask around for lower-cost accommodation in the area. Are there any B&Bs or hotels with lower prices in the environs? It's likely that you'll get the same sleep wherever the pillow is located. You can still party with everybody else but at a much lower cost.

If you're going with a number of people that you know, you could rent a house and significantly cut the cost. The more people, the better. In fact, this could add to the whole experience immensely. Also, you can save a lot on the cost of hotel food, as everybody can put €20 into a 'kitty' and fill the fridge for those midnight snacks, breakfast and 'just because we're on holiday' meals across the weekend.

The childcare

Unless you're going to bring your kids to the wedding or go to only a part of it, you're going to have to think about this one.

Family. The best thing to do is leave them with a trusted family member while you're away. You may need to return the favour at a later date.

Bring a babysitter. The other thing you can do is ask a trusted friend or relation to go with you. I was fourteen when my cousin Marie asked me to go to Killarney to look after her new baby boy while she and her husband went to a wedding. I did that many times, as a teenager, for my cousins when they had babies and young children. I got to see some new parts of the country and was delighted with my weekends away.

Club together for a babysitter. If none of these are options, how about asking the hosts if other guests might be in the same situation as you? You could hire a babysitter (or two) for the duration of the event, and share the cost with other relieved parents.

The present

As Ireland got wealthier, the wedding-present amount rose up to pressure-cooker levels. If you ask any shop assistant in Brown Thomas, they'll tell you that the starting point for a couple was €150. In line with the recession, the number has fallen to €100. Of course, you will have people close to you for whom you might like to spend more. It's a lot of money, if you have a couple of weddings in a year. I think communication can help a lot with this one. Why don't you talk to the other people that you know going to the wedding? Suggest that you form a group of four, with each contributing €75; with that, you could buy a very big present for €300, for example. If you get a wedding list, rest assured there won't be too many individuals or couples who'll be able to afford the really big items, whereas together you can get something that will have a great impact. Everybody is happy.

The transport

The journey to a wedding of a friend or relative is always filled with anticipation, as you're looking forward to enjoying the day, catching up with people you may not have seen for a while and leaving daily life at home. The trip back is often full of tiredness, smiling at the memories and the thoughts of getting everything organized for the week ahead. If the wedding is in the country, do you really have to drive there and back?

Carpool. With a carpool, the fun of the journey can be shared among friends, and if everybody pitches in money for the fuel, it could be far more cost-effective than everybody driving there and back on their own.

Public transport. Could you look at a way of getting public transport?

Wouldn't it be lovely to relax all the way home, as opposed to having to keep your tired eyes focused on the headlights and signposts in front of you for a couple of hours?

Killing two birds with one stone. If travel costs are at a premium around the time of the wedding, could you look at taking a mini-break for yourself? Why not combine the wedding with a holiday that you would usually take anyway? At first, you might think this may actually add to the cost of the wedding, but think about the additional costs of having a whole other holiday. You would still have to book transport, accommodation, etc. On top of that, at the beginning of a holiday, a 'settling in' period is often needed. People need to destress and become less attached to what's going on in work and at home. A wedding certainly takes care of that. As a result, you could ease your way into the holiday by 'starting off with a bang' at the wedding. Or, alternatively, you could have a relaxing couple of days, with the wedding to look forward to at the end of your holiday. People often do this if a wedding is abroad. But why only do it when you hop on a plane? Why not look into renting a house for a couple of days beforehand, near the area where the wedding is taking place? You can prolong that wonderful feeling and be fully relaxed and refreshed when everybody gathers for the big day.

The grooming

There is a lot of fun in getting pampered for a wedding and looking fabulous for those pictures that will last forever. However, there can often be a lot of expense, which people feel under pressure to bear because it's the done thing. I have the following suggestion. I'm sure you remember the days when you were a teenager and you and your friends went to each other's houses to get ready to go out. Re-create that with lots of fun and laughter. Is there a friend that can do a fantastic blow-dry? Is there another that is secretly an aspiring make-up artist? Could you pool your nail-varnish collections and give each other manicures? (Remember to bring lots of remover for when giddiness takes over!) Could you get a tanning glove and take turns working on each other – particularly useful for those hard-to-reach areas? I have always gone to my best friend Gráinne when I have a big presentation or a function. She can do 'smoky eyes' like I never could. My cousin Fiona can do a blow-dry that makes you look as if you just walked out of a salon. My friend Trudie has every (and I mean *every*) colour of nail varnish under the sun. It's always lovely to visit a friend and get a relaxing treatment done while having a chat before you go somewhere exciting.

So, in summary, my top-five tips for budget-friendly weddings:

- Build a holiday around the wedding.
- Rent a house with friends or family instead of staying in the hotel.
- Swap outfits.
- Club together with other guests to buy one really substantial present – at less cost to each of you.
- To make yourself beautiful for the big day, go back to your slumber-party days.

The example of the wedding shows that costs can be cut, thanks to a little planning beforehand and – you guessed it – communication. So, how do you like the idea of talking about money now? I hope that you've come to think it might be a great thing after all, and not as scary or as unpleasant as you might have thought at first. But how about talking to your bank manager? Do you shudder at the thought? Believe it or not, talking to people who make a career out of your financial success can be both extremely effective and pleasant. That is the subject of the next chapter.

10

Getting along with the bank manager (and everyone else in your financial world)

What would you think of a school that called you only if your kids started to misbehave? If, throughout their eight years in primary school and five or six years in secondary school, you didn't get a report, an invitation to a parent–teacher meeting or a letter? Would you be happy with this? Do you think that companies hold meetings internally among managers, staff, clients and suppliers only when there is a crisis looming? Would you think it wise for the Dáil to convene only in times of trouble? Of course not.

Reflect on times of trouble in your life. How did you survive? I would imagine that in many cases there was somebody there who helped you to pull through – a friend, a colleague, a neighbour. You know the feeling of needing to turn to somebody at a time when you're stressed and anxious. It's great to be able to call somebody and say, 'I'm really in a pickle at the moment and I'm seriously stuck. Could you . . .' Indeed, I'm sure that you've been on the receiving end of those phonecalls too. Women are very resourceful in times of panic; however, what if you didn't know that person well enough to call?

Similarly, you need to be able to communicate with the finance professionals that you deal with. I call your accountant, bank manager, suppliers of income (i.e., your employer or clients), service providers, etc., the 'stakeholders' in your finances, as they all have an influence on your situation. I think it's very important to meet with the stakeholders in your finances regularly. Regular communication achieves a lot, and helps you build rapport when things are good, so that you have an ally to talk to when things are otherwise.

Regular communication isn't about ticking a box and saying, 'That's sorted for another couple of months.' It's about building a relationship. If you are going through a period of success, it's a great feeling to tell them. From their perspective, they can be happy that they have a good, stable, reliable customer or that the services they give you bring you value – and that you'll keep buying from them. And, very simply, they are happy for you that things are going well in your life. In addition, you can pick up a lot of intelligence about things that might affect you directly.

I was at a marketing course given by a fantastic presenter who was a lecturer at NUI Galway. He told us an interesting story. At one time he used to travel a lot and always booked through a particular travel agency. After a while, he stopped using their services and changed to another service provider. One day he was at an event where he met the original service provider, who said, 'Ah, hello and how are things?' They exchanged small talk, concluded their conversation and went their separate ways. Clearly the man had had absolutely no idea that he had lost a very good customer, because he had never checked in with his clientele. Had he been aware of this, he would have taken that golden opportunity to regain this custom. Because of his lack of awareness, he didn't even know it was there to be seized.

In the course of a conversation with my accountant, I told him that I was going to implement a particular process in the company over the following week. He put his head in his hands and said, 'Have you any idea of the paperwork, time and expense that you're bringing on yourself?' I hadn't a clue. As an accountant he had been sitting down with businesses for years, going through their plans and problems – and also been the director of a company himself. No doubt, somebody else had made the mistake I was about to make, but a simple conversation with him was enough for me to benefit from his experience and to avert a minor disaster. I was only too happy that I had made an appointment to meet with him that day.

I was getting a beauty treatment done at the salon I always go to, and the beautician said to me, 'Did you know that I run special offers on a Thursday?' I hadn't. She said, 'I've just started that recently, so if it suits you to come on a Thursday instead of at the weekend, there's a discount on offer.' It didn't make any difference to me what day of the week I went to her, so just by having that chat with her, I found a way to save money and make her order book more time-efficient.

Communication doesn't just help you gather intelligence; it's also key for those times in life when you need to lean on people. Contrast these two situations.

Rebecca has been running a successful business for a number of years. Every quarter she pops in for a half an hour to see her bank manager. Rebecca gives her a general sense of how things are going, the changes that have happened since they last spoke, what the company is thinking of doing in the future; and she gets an update on the bank's services. The bank manager gives her some ideas for things she might need to look out for in the long term, and they have an opportunity to tease out various 'what if' scenarios. Rebecca has decided to expand, because she feels the market, as well as her own business, is ready. However, she needs the bank to back her by giving her a loan with some flexible repayment options for the initial period.

Bridget has also been running a successful business for a number of years. She only goes into the bank to lodge her cheques and to do whatever she can't do online. The bank manager wouldn't recognize her, even though she has been a loyal customer for years. Bridget has decided to expand as she feels the market, as well as her own business, is ready. However, she needs the bank to back her by giving her a loan with some flexible repayment options for the initial period.

Each one calls the bank manager on a Tuesday morning. What do you think might happen from here? This is what I think.

The bank manager says 'Hi, Rebecca. Sure, call in any time tomorrow. You might bring in all the documents that you can and let's have a chat. I would be delighted to hear about your plans.' Rebecca goes in prepared, because she knows what she needs in order to make the decision as easy as possible for the bank manager, through her knowledge of how she operates. Of course, this doesn't mean that she will get precisely what she's looking for, but she can stack the odds in her favour.

Bridget calls and the bank manager says, 'Hello. You have your account here – oh, that's great. Let me just check my diary. Would Thursday at 2 p.m. suit? Could you bring any documents that you have, please?' Bridget arrives with her one-page summary and begins to pitch her idea. The bank manager says, 'Before you start, could you just give me an idea about your business, please?' As Bridget is talking, the bank manager is thinking, 'I have some sort of an idea of what her business is now' and 'I'm not quite seeing how this business is different from the rest' and 'Could I ratify this loan comfortably?' and 'What is the margin I could make on the deal?'

Bridget starts to pitch her idea again and the bank manager says, 'That sounds interesting. Can you bring me the accounts for the last three years, a ledger of your debtors and creditors, your projections for the next three years for the company taking the expansion into account, as well as details on any other sources of funding that you might have? Why don't you give me a call as soon as you're ready and we can have a more detailed discussion?' Bridget's first reaction is to be completely deflated. Where is she going to get all that stuff? That will take ages to do. Is it worth it? She wants to persevere, so she spends the next three weeks gathering all the data and gets an appointment with the bank manager a month afterwards. She is now in a position to go back to the bank, prepared with all she needs, and pitch the idea again.

At this stage, Bridget is beginning where Rebecca was a month ago . . . minus the rapport. She's a month further down the road than she had planned and she might be getting stressed, because builders and suppliers have been lined up and she may need to pay deposits to lock in those prices. She is worried that the whole thing might fall through unless she can get the finance. The bank manager senses that feeling of panic and she becomes even more vigilant, asking for more data.

The differences between the two scenarios are self-evident. The bank manager knew a lot about Rebecca's business from their quarterly meetings over the years, and she had a good foundation on which to start, whereas Bridget had to begin from scratch. Rebecca was able to use her time to explain anything the bank was unsure about in previous meetings, as opposed to Bridget, who had to deal with all the uncertainties about her business model while also fielding queries about her expansion plans. Rebecca was well equipped with all she needed when she went to the bank, her knowledge informed by her previous discussions with the bank manager. Bridget thought that 'having something on paper' was enough. Rebecca had built up a rapport with the bank manager over the years by spending two hours a year talking to her. Bridget had only a couple of seconds to establish a rapport, before having to launch into her pitch. Rebecca was on time with her plan and Bridget was a month behind. Bridget is now getting worried and her stress levels are rising, while her chances of getting the finance are falling. Rebecca, who has been much more realistic with her timings, is driving forward.

In certain situations, of course, Rebecca wouldn't have got the finance she was looking for, even if she had moved into the bank and served the staff champagne and caviar. This can occur when someone has unrealistic ideas (in the eyes of the bank) or because of highly restrictive policies regarding lending. In the recent past, banks may have had their doors open, but some acted as though they were essentially closed for business. In such cases, a client could threaten to move her account, bring the denial of credit to an appeals committee or seek outside counsel in the form of a paid professional, an association, a government body, etc., to articulate her case. However, a good relationship with your bank in good times and in bad can serve you well in most scenarios – it certainly doesn't hurt.

Now, I hope you see the benefit of having regular communication with the stakeholders in your finances so that their trust in you can grow during the good times and will be there when you need it.

I'm not recommending you meet with your bank manager just because it would be nice. I'm recommending it because I know for a fact how much it has helped me and my business. Typically, I call or email and ask to meet with my own bank manager. She slots me in whenever it suits us both. Of course, it would be easier to have the chat over the phone, but I think it's worth it to call in. I treat it as a 'free meeting with a bank finance consultant'. She talks to businesses each day and is familiar with the changes coming down the line in terms of regulatory requirements, new products or some other nugget of information that I don't have. I don't go in with any formal agenda, but just for an informal chat that might cover:

- The developments the business has made since our last chat.
- The new avenues that we, as a company, would like to pursue.
- I invite her to look at our accounts and see the changes in our cashflow, usage of products, etc.
- Is there anything new coming down the track that we aren't aware of?
- Is there a way of looking at our new plans for the future that we haven't thought of?

I always leave the meeting (and all our other communication meetings, by the way) feeling that it was worth it. As a tiny example, I was in a rush one day to get something done at the bank. I arrived there just as they were about to close. I said to the woman shutting the door that this would just take one minute, I really needed it and my business account was in that particular branch. The bank manager happened to be passing behind her and said, 'Oh, hi, Susan.

Come on in, we're just finishing up here but what can we do for you?' At the time, that meant a lot, because I really needed to get an issue sorted. If the bank manager hadn't recognized me, the woman closing up might well have just said, 'Sorry, we're open at 10 a.m. tomorrow,' which would have been too late for me. Another time, we had a quick chat about the best type of company credit card for the business; and on a different occasion we spoke about the best way to deal with exchange rates when I started exporting. Most recently, when I was opening a bank account in the UK to accept payments in sterling, she could certify all the documentation needed to set up the account. And because she was so completely up to date, I found that the amount of admin I had to do was greatly reduced.

You might be thinking, 'Isn't it humiliating to have to report back to them every quarter?' But I don't think it's humiliating at all. I'm taking the lead. I ask for the meeting and I know the value that we can get from it. I'm not going to them for their sole benefit; I'm going for the benefit of our company. I don't feel that I need to defend our position when I get there – I tell it like it is. I ask *them* to add value. Many thousands of people are happy to pay charges for all sorts of things, while I want 'bang for my buck'. I feel that 'reporting to our service provider' enables them to provide a good, comprehensive and timely service tailored to our needs. If they don't know about the specifics of our business, how can we expect to get the best from them?

But, you say, 'Why would I discuss my finances with my bank manager? They'll try to sell me more of the bank's products. And, also, what if they're simply not interested in meeting with me? I'm "small fry".' Or 'My finances are in a shambles and I'm ashamed to discuss them with a finance pro, like my bank manager. What if they lecture me?'

To which I want to say, you may well have a point there. They could try to sell you some of the bank's products. However, make it a cast-iron rule that you're not going to leave the meeting having signed up to anything. You are simply on a fact-finding mission in order to:

- Develop a rapport with a stakeholder in your financial situation.
- Learn about the requirements for gaining finance from them in the future.
- Establish a dialogue regarding where you stand with them and how you can move forward.
- Ascertain if there is any way that you could achieve what you want to in less time or with less money.
- Benefit from their expertise – this is a 'meeting with a finance consultant', which you have paid for with bank charges.

If you get a whiff of 'Thank you for coming in here today and let me show you our latest range of products', cut that out from the outset and stick to your objectives. If you don't feel comfortable saying an outright 'no' to their offers, you might let them know in advance, when you book the meeting, that you're not interested in buying new products, but that you simply want to discuss your situation. You've asked for this meeting and you can take control of it. Alternatively, you could ask them in earnest, 'How, precisely, is this going to help? Can you show me, calculator in hand, how this will improve my situation?' If the product they recommend does seem to make a difference to your bottom line, ask to think about it before you agree to buy it. Indeed, there may be a high-interest account or a cheaper package of bank charges that could be of use to you, and that your account manager is recommending in good faith, because she thinks it will serve your purposes. Take the information away and discuss it with an independent party (e.g., your partner, accountability partner (see Chapter 11), business partner, financial adviser or even yourself when you have the time) but do *not* leave your signature on anything during that meeting.

So far I've focused on a business as a case study, but the very same might be applied to somebody who wants to speed up paying off their mortgage. Let's take the example of Anne, who wants to shorten the life of her home loan by five years. She makes an appointment to meet with the bank manager the following week. What is she seeking to achieve in this meeting?

Develop a rapport with a stakeholder in your financial situation. By taking the initiative, Anne is separating herself from the crowd; most people never approach the bank about such issues. She's helping her account manager to attach a face to that bank-account number.

Learn about the requirements for gaining finance from them in the future. Anne may be unsure what exactly is involved in changing the terms of her mortgage, the contractual agreements and the subsequent consequences she might be signing up to, e.g., the net increase in her monthly repayments, etc., so these are all questions she wants to ask.

Establish a dialogue regarding where you stand and how you can move forward. Anne now has an opportunity to ask all the questions that may have been churning in the back of her mind. Similarly, the bank manager has an opportunity to speak directly with one of her clients about anything that might be concerning her.

Ascertain if there is any way that you could achieve what you want to achieve in less time or with less money. Anne will find out exactly how much more she'll be paying in exchange for the years taken off her mortgage, as well as how much she'll be saving in interest. She won't need to rely on 'mortgage calculators' on the internet, but will get the information directly from the provider. Perhaps the bank is in a position to offer her a deal, or to point out that the extra amount she was considering paying was too high, or too low, or that she hadn't actually factored in the timeline of future payments. In any case, she leaves the meeting better informed than she was.

Benefit from their expertise – this is a meeting with a finance consultant, which you have paid for with bank charges. Anne gets somebody who works in this industry to sit down and focus on her and her finances, one on one.

If you approach your bank and they are simply not interested in meeting with you, I suggest that you carry out the exercise outlined above for examining the differences between service providers in order to choose a new one. I once closed an account with a bank and moved to another. They gave me about five reasons to stay and, had I been in any way interested in remaining with them, those offers would have been a significant improvement on what I was getting. However, I was going and that was that. If the bank isn't interested in meeting with you periodically throughout the year, they don't deserve your business.

It's in the bank's interest that you handle your finances well, because:

- This decreases the chance of your defaulting on your loans.
- The faster you lift a heavy financial burden like a mortgage, the sooner you may want to do something else, like extend the house, take a holiday, upgrade the car, etc. These types of loans are more expensive than a mortgage, so the bank will make a better margin on these products. I am *not* advocating that you do any of this, by the way. I'm just looking at the prospect of this conversation through the bank's eyes.
- You are more likely to build up your savings, which gives them more capital to lend out.

Say your finances are in a shambles and you're ashamed to discuss them with a finance pro – that is exactly when you need to speak to somebody. Your bank manager has access to your account anyway, so she can see your balances and transactions any time she likes. If your situation gets too far into the red, you'll appear on her radar, and she may be the one to request a meeting with you. As a result, you're better off taking the initiative by seeking out this appointment to address the situation. They'll appreciate that you're not burying your head in the sand.

Think of it as if it were – as you might see it – an embarrassing medical problem. You go to your doctor and go scarlet the minute you start to describe it. He or she doesn't even flinch, as they deal with this all the time. Similarly, your bank manager has seen accounts in all shapes and sizes too.

In my mentoring sessions, people often share with me things that are quite difficult for them to ask. If I had €1 for every time I heard 'Sorry, this might be a stupid question now, but how do I . . .', I would be very rich. To me, the only stupid question is the one that isn't asked. Why should someone be intimidated by the fact that I might have the answer to their question? After all, they are paying me to address the gaps in their knowledge – it's what I'm there for. I've never had any issue with anyone who asked a question about the financial markets. I'm only too glad to be able to give them value and deliver a good service. And I'm only too happy to shine too.

Think of it: where are you supposed to learn about managing money? The only lessons we get are those attitudes passed on to us by our family, friends and society. Financial management wasn't taught in schools when we were all on the junior side of a classroom table (and this is something I hope to change). You might think you should 'just know', but that's not a reasonable expectation. You only know by reaching out, by getting help and information and by building up your knowledge, sometimes the hard way.

If your finances are a mess, seek all the guidance you can from other people. If you can get their assistance without paying any additional fees, so much the better. I very much doubt that the bank manager is going to lecture you. After all, you're a client. In any case, if she does, turn it around and ask for advice: 'Now that you know my situation, what do you recommend that I do?' Enlist the assistance of people whom you're already paying – in this case, through bank charges – to help you whip those finances into shape.

Now let's get ready for that meeting with your bank manager – preparation is key. What are the questions that your bank manager is most likely to ask? What kind of answers are they expecting?

What kind of data will they want to see to be convinced? If you're meeting them in order to obtain something, the data-gathering techniques covered in the previous chapters will come in very handy now. If you're going for a simple review, have as much data collated as possible, so that you can get the most out of it.

So, let's have a look at a possible script – feel free to reuse parts of this in your actual conversation. For each question, I've given a 'translation' to show you what is going on in your bank manager's mind, along with the answer that's likely to have the most impact.

What can we do for you at the moment?

Translation. You've scheduled an hour of my time. You're a client and I'm happy with that, but I presume you have a reason for coming in to see me. When you tell me what the issue is, we can work towards solving it. Given that I have an opportunity to speak with you directly, I might also see if we have something to sell you . . .

Answer. I'm here to discuss with you how I can reach my financial goal, e.g., pay off the mortgage early, save for my retirement, save for my kids' education, ask about your high-interest savings accounts, etc.

Why do you want to make that change in your life at the moment?/ Do you really think that it's possible?

Translation. Uh oh. Have you really thought about this?

Answer. I have put a lot of thought into this and it's something that I would like to do, because I think it would have an immense impact on my life for the better . . . in many ways. I have the following plan in mind [produce the plan]. Of course, it's not final and that's why I'm here. I've been a customer here for *x* years, and I can imagine that you have lots of people coming in to see you with the same ideas. As a result, I thought why not get the benefit of your experience before pursuing it further? I'm sure you have a lot of advice to offer on this matter, based on what I've shown you and my account balances/records?

What changes have you made to adapt to that situation?

Translation. Do you have any idea how you're going to implement the plan that you've put on paper?'

Answer. Well, I have outlined a number of steps I could take. I've thought about the way to tackle each one.

In order to pay an extra €50 per month off the mortgage, I'll need to increase the standing order. As you can see from my statements, that is possible and has been for the last x months.

Or . . . If I were to save €250 per month, I'd have x amount of disposable income left over. I've put together a budget [produce it] and I believe that I can live on that and still have some wiggle room should there be unexpected expenses.

Or . . . With regard to the expansion, I've drawn up a full project-management plan with conservative timelines. Would you like to take a look, as I've brought it along with me?

We see that you have quite a lot of savings and we have a range of products available.

Translation. I want to sell you something . . .

Answer. That would be great. If you could give me all the information, I can talk it over with my partner [or whoever else you decide upon]. Given that I'm at the research stage of my decision, I'll take away the leaflets and evaluate them against other products. [If they persist, simply repeat this line until they get the message.]

How much 'stress' could you take in that scenario?

Translation. If things went wrong, how 'wrong' could they go before you were in over your head?

Answer. I have actually considered this in depth. Let's look at the 'pressure points' on my situation:

[Increasing mortgage payments] Could you tell me how much of an impact a 1% interest-rate rise would have on my situation? I could/couldn't handle that. How about 2%? [Keep going until you find your number.]

Or . . . [Saving €250 per month] I have wiggle room of €x in my budget. As a result, if my salary was cut or I suffered an adverse fall in my level of income, I could sustain €x. As a result, I feel that €250 per month is comfortable for the short term.

Or . . . [Business-expansion plan] If market conditions weaken, I have a Plan B in mind. Let me go through that with you . . .

It seems that you are right on top of things. Was there anything else?

Translation. You know more than I do about your situation. What exactly did you come in for?

Answer. I'm just wondering if I have all of the angles covered. Do you know if there are any changes to requirements, special offers, charges, etc.? As I said earlier, you're dealing with individuals, households and businesses all the time. Have you some nuggets of advice for me, as I really do want to clear my mortgage/increase my savings/expand my business? If you felt you had anything to add, it will have been a very worthwhile hour for me.

So, how was that? How do you feel now about meeting your bank manager? Still a bit afraid, but excited and open to all the opportunities that such a meeting might offer? Good. This is just one example of how beneficial it can be to talk about money.

Here is a checklist of who to communicate with; alongside are financial issues to discuss or monitor, in order to make sure there is no 'financial bomb' ticking away without your being aware of it. All these people have the potential to help you gain traction on your road to financial well-being, so don't be shy – make sure to communicate with them on a regular basis.

Who to communicate with	Issue to discuss or monitor
Your income providers	
Employer(s)	Is your job still safe? Are there any opportunities to earn more money?
Clients	Is your account still safe? Are there any opportunities to expand the business you have with them?
Revenue office	Budgetary expectations on the part of the government: Are they planning to change child benefit, policies on business grants, tax rebates (for better or for worse)?
Distributors (i.e., any person or business who links you with customers, e.g., websites where you sell things, people who refer business to you, advertising outlets)	Are they still happy to work with you/refer you? Are there any other opportunities to increase their level of business with you?

Your suppliers

Your mortgage provider	Are interest rates going to change (if relevant)? Are there any changes they can suggest in order to help you pay it off faster?
Your utility providers and their competitors (electricity, fuel, TV, phone, internet)	Are they planning to maintain their pricing structure? Have they got any special offers?
Your financial service providers (accountant, bank manager, financial adviser, stockbroker)	Are they planning to maintain their pricing structure? Could they review your current situation and suggest ways to increase your revenue, decrease your costs and ameliorate your effectiveness?
Your remaining service providers (grocer, butcher, decorator and all others that are recipients of your money in the budget that you wrote earlier)	Are they planning to maintain their pricing structure? Have they got any special offers?
Your discretionary-income recipients (hairdresser, beautician, travel agent, websites with special offers on holidays, etc.)	Are they planning to maintain their pricing structure? Have they got any special offers?

**The people who can help you move forward
(I call them 'goal realizers', a.k.a. your dream team)**

Mentors	Are they planning to maintain their pricing structure (if relevant)? Have you made much progress towards your goal (in terms of where you thought you might be by now)?
Accountability partners	Check out Chapter 11.
People who can put you in contact with those people with whom you want to communicate	With whom do you want to be put in contact? Why? How can you assure the person that they should feel confident about helping you make these connections?
Your children	What dreams do they have that will require your finances (from the doll they want from Santa to their university of choice)?
Your child's school/college	If they are planning to do Transition Year, what trips (and expense) are involved? Is there a rental scheme to get books or will you be buying them? How are the registration fees going to change next year?

Your partner	Check out the board-meeting section in Chapter 11.
Your siblings	Are they planning any parties or holidays that involve you?
	Are you all going to give each other gifts at Christmas or do a 'Chris Kindle'?
	Are you going to club together and buy a gift for your mutual cousin?
	Are they thinking of getting married abroad?
	Are they thinking of having a surprise party for your parents' anniversary and expecting all of you to share the cost?
Your friends	Are they thinking of going to Galway for the Races this year?
	Are they thinking of having a spa weekend as a hen party?
	Are they planning to buy a big present for your friend's thirtieth?
	Would they be interested in sharing a house this year for two weeks in the summer in Donegal, to which you could take all the kids?

STEP SIX

Share your financial journey

'I will, if you will!' Having someone to talk to about your financial goals

In the previous chapter I hope I convinced you that communication about your goals, especially about your financial ones, is vital, and can get you where you'd like to go much faster. Now I'd like to talk about a particular kind of communication. I've told you about asking for help, asking for information, exchanging information and building rapport, especially with the stakeholders in your financial situation. Here I'm going to take it up a notch and show you how to turbo-charge your communication by establishing accountability systems.

The concept of accountability systems may sound a bit formal and daunting, but all it means is having people you can talk to in a focused way about your plans and goals. You already have accountability systems and accountability partners without realizing it. It's the person that you rope into walking three kilometres with you every night when you start a diet; the study buddy who has their head in the books with you over Christmas; the friend who makes sure you don't text 'that person' when you're feeling blue after a night out and you really shouldn't be texting them. An accountability partner is a person with whom you register a goal and then ask them to hold you accountable for achieving it.

One of my accountability systems that has led to extraordinary results is my weekly board meeting with my boyfriend. Every Friday night we go to the same Thai restaurant close to where we live. The owner always throws her eyes to heaven when she sees me coming with my thick black folder and laptop. She doesn't even try to hide her sentiments any more. 'Crazy woman,' she says while seating us. You might be thinking, 'Have you got nothing better to do on a Friday night than talk about the business?' Indeed, we tried at ridiculously early hours in the morning (but that didn't work for too long); we tried various different afternoons during the week (but there were too many distractions); we tried on a Monday morning, but that's the time of the week when you want to kick-start the week, not talk about it. One week, we tried a Friday evening. We didn't have any other meetings, there weren't any pressing calls or emails, and we were in a reflective mood. It was perfect, and now it's become my favourite time of the week. I love sitting down with my boyfriend, over good food and wine and without any time constraints, and talking through our common passion, our business.

We order our food and then chat over what's gone on in our day thus far. Afterwards, I take out a sheet of paper and look at the key themes of the meeting. What are the main things that we're going to talk about? We have only ever had a maximum of four. For example:

- A new project (e.g., moving from live training to eLearning).
- An ongoing project and the next instalment (e.g., writing the next chapter of this book).
- A new customer.
- A theme (e.g., our internationalization strategy).

This is where the bulk of the time and of our concentration goes. We discuss each of these in turn, which might take two hours. Where are we at now? What are we hoping to achieve? What resources do we need, do we have, do we need to source? What is the timeline for this project? How is this shaping our vision? If we were to look beyond this project, how could we move further in this direction?

We always go through each of our customers. What have we done with them this week? Have we delivered what we said we would? Have we thanked them? Is there anything else of benefit that we could do for them? We have a conversation about them and make sure that they're feeling appreciated. After all, without them, we wouldn't have a business.

Contrary to how most meetings are run, it's only at this point that we look at the minutes from the last meeting. If we were to start with the minutes, we would spend the night looking back at what we did or didn't do and delving into the details. We prefer to discuss the previous week's meeting after discussing our big vision, because often, as the week unfolded, our approach needed to change. It's not that we shy away from assessing whether we did what we said we would; it's just that we look at that after we've focused on what's driving us forward. We don't waste time doing a post-mortem on things that we discussed the previous week, things that are no longer that important given the more developed, bigger picture that we've just discussed.

The next thing we do is to look at the diary for the past week. We look at what each of our staff has done and how we will work with them, in line with the goals for the next week. From a Friday-evening perspective, the week is coming to a close; we're tired and yet relaxed, and so we can look calmly at what everybody is doing and when in the week ahead. We take the time to plan, which will enable us to get off to a good start on Monday morning (or often Saturday morning in my case). We can also see if we are overstretched and make arrangements to remedy that. Alternatively, if it's a quiet week, we can get ahead on something that needs to be done later anyway.

Along the way, we discuss finance, but only if necessary. It might come up during a discussion about a new project. It might have come up the week before and we address it again when we tackle the minutes. It might come up when we talk about our staff or a certain thing we're doing that week. However, we don't make a point of talking about it at every meeting. The reason is that it is a detail in the grand scheme of what we want to do, and if we don't need to worry about it, we don't; we have lots of systems set up to ensure that everything is running smoothly and that if an issue is beginning to form, it appears on our radar early.

Letting money rule the way we run our business is the tail wagging the dog. It's supposed to fit in around us and not the other way around. The business needs to make more money all the time but that fits in neatly with our own business objectives; and, since the money side and the business side are aligned, we can get on with what we actually want to do, rather than focusing on an individual figure each week. I love to spend time with Excel, and I do look at all of our systems in between meetings anyway. If they're okay, there's no need to go back over finance for the sake of it. Our board meetings are about the big picture and achieving our dreams.

We finish the meeting by going through the non-staff members of our dream team. We look at all the people who help us with our business, from our accountant, to our Development Adviser in Enterprise Ireland, to our Enterprise Europe Network contact, and so forth.

By the end of the meeting, we have:

- rigorously gone through each and every element of the business;
- discussed the key areas that we want to focus on and developed an action plan to drive those forward;
- looked at our relationship with our clients and discussed each of them in turn;
- held each other accountable on what we were supposed to do the previous week;
- drafted the company's diary for the coming week;
- checked in with our 'dream team'.

All of this, along with the non-business benefits of relaxation, quality time, and lovely food and wine, makes for a feeling of achievement and a wonderful night.

So what are the real motivations behind my board meetings? Why do I have them? First, I think board meetings are so enjoyable. I love to sit with my boyfriend over dinner talking about something that we both love. Who wouldn't? In fact, my birthday last year was on a Friday night, and when my boyfriend asked what I'd like to do, I had no hesitation in saying that I just wanted to have our usual board meeting. (The restaurant owner might have a point about me being a bit crazy!)

Over the years, our board meetings have allowed us to achieve the following:

Clarifying the vision. They've given us the chance to really talk about what we want to do and why we want to do it – in effect, to shape our future. Along the way, we've found things out about each other that were interesting, contrasting and sometimes the cause of arguments. I'm glad this happened because we had the time and space in which to debate them between us, and when we knew where we stood, we could move on. Had we not done this, we might have set off in directions that weren't in unison. By discussing issues in the abstract, before they created problems, we were able to reconcile our points of view and avoid misunderstandings and a lot of resistance further down the line. Imagine discovering that we really didn't see eye to eye on a very big project, at deadline time. That would have been a catastrophe.

Avoiding procrastination. Procrastination squirms under a spotlight. Write down something that you would like to achieve, along with a list of actions to take with a timeline for each; and then have somebody ask you whether you did them or not – that's quite a good motivation. If you don't do it week after week, it gets embarrassing. If you aren't doing what you promised to do out of laziness, you will eventually be found out. If you've lost interest, you can review why and plan to do something else instead. But you *won't* find yourself in the position of life having passed you by and you *won't* find yourself saying, 'Oh, I can't believe that we're in September already and I never got around to doing such and such.' Procrastination is not allowed. Yes, some things don't get done, but that's because other priorities replaced them. Notice I said 'priorities' – if you choose not to do something (e.g., start a small online business) in preference to something else (watching the soaps in the evenings), your actions illustrate that you placed more importance on the latter. Most people would think that setting up a new revenue stream would be more important than watching TV, but, as we all know, after a day of hard work, the sofa can be very inviting. However, if you have a list of things to do and you have somebody holding you accountable at the end of the week, you'll want to be able to say 'I did that' – so you may look twice at that sofa before sinking into it.

Tracking progress. We have a documented diary of our business's progression. It's a wonderful feeling to go back three months, six months, a year, two years, to see how far we've come. We look back at what we thought were ambitious goals, at stumbling blocks, and at how different our vision was back then. We haven't let life pass us by, but we have taken snapshots of it. I get a real boost as I look at what seemed impossible a year ago, at the way we worked around it and at how normal it all seems now.

Looking at the bigger picture. It gives us the space and time to think. Life has become so full of incessant demands, communications and exchanges of information. I often practically set up an office for three hours while on the train home to Cork. I have my laptop, pen-drive, phone, headphones and charger; and I can send emails all round the world while I'm whizzing through Portarlington or Charleville. These days, we're always connected to everyone: anybody can reach us and make a demand on our time. So it's wonderful for you to be able to stop for a while, actually look around you and see where you want your life to be, without constant distraction. I've been in situations where my heart hardly had time to beat, I was so busy. Is that any sort of a state to be in when making strategic judgements about my life and career? I've been in meetings where I could hear the phone vibrating in my bag and see emails zooming into the bottom corner of my screen, while I was mentally reminding myself to get back to somebody who'd left a voicemail. Should you be making very important decisions while a multitude of people are vying for your attention? At our board meetings, my boyfriend and I invest this time in ourselves, in each other and in our business. As a result, I'm not flapping around on a Wednesday thinking, 'What exactly am I doing?' and then getting to Sunday night and saying, 'Now *next* week will definitely count.' How do I know how this feels? Because I've been there and where I am now is not only much nicer, but also more effective and exciting.

Celebrating achievements. I think the best thing about our board meetings is that they have often marked the turning points in our business and subsequently in our lives. I will never forget sitting beside the window in Mi Thai, a red curry with duck in front of me, and saying to my boyfriend, 'Will I go? Will I just go to Malta and see what happens?' I realized later that going to Malta was the first step in really opening up my business to the whole world of international trade. On one Friday recently, we made a breakthrough on something that we'd been working on for months, and I waited until our board meeting to tell my boyfriend what had happened; we spent the entire meeting going through exactly how we were going to take it to the next level. I remember savouring the moment just as I saw him walking through the door and thinking, 'Thank you, God, for making the world a beautiful place. I'm going to enjoy every single second of telling him this!' Imagine if I'd just caught him in between meetings, or exhausted after eighteen holes of golf, or as he was rushing out the door. Instead, I waited until Friday night because I knew we would have time to savour the news.

At this point you might say, 'But it sounds like all you do with your boyfriend is talk about business and finances. Isn't it very bad for a relationship to be talking constantly about money? Doesn't it lead to rows? Are you such a material girl that all you can do is talk about money all the time?'

That's a good question – and a complete misconception. Indeed, my boyfriend and I talk about business and finance a good deal, as we are both business owners. But what we talk about the most is how to create the life we've dreamed of for ourselves. Money and business get discussed, as they are means to this end. And I would like you to take that message to heart – whatever your situation, money is a crucial part of creating the life you want to have, and talking about money with your significant other is therefore a crucial part of your relationship.

A lot of rows about money need never start if two people in a relationship make an effort to be aware of, and understanding about, each other's financial situation and attitudes towards money. Inevitably, there will be differences, but if you can bring those out into the open and discuss them in a calm, relaxing atmosphere on a regular basis, you'll find that this really beats addressing money matters only when you're under financial strain, tense and probably unable to think clearly.

So, if you feel ambivalent about being so upfront about money – afraid it will make you seem money-obsessed – you need to see the bigger picture. It's my view that money can be used to create an enormous amount of good in the world, assuming that it's directed in the right way and with genuine intentions. I want our company to be a multinational one and to employ many people in exchange for their high skills and tremendous contribution; I want to pay them salaries that will in turn fund their children's education, enable them to go on holidays and create memories of a lifetime. I want our company to pay huge sums of money in tax, which can be used for the capital development of countries, making the vulnerable in society better off, and creating conditions of economic growth so that other businesses will flourish. I want to invite thousands of people to be part of our company's story as staff, mentors, innovators, suppliers, clients, leaders, joint-venture partners, etc. I want wonderful people to develop our business and our business to develop wonderful people. I want to bring financial literacy to each corner of the world. I want our company to be held up as an example of technological innovation in business. I want to encourage the entire industry to be better. I want to make our clients feel appreciated. I want to be the very best person that I can be and to develop an organization that lives longer than I do. I want to inspire those who feel stuck, just as I was inspired by others when I felt stuck. I want to be the person that gives people the confidence to say, 'It's okay to think like that, feel like that and be like that.' I want to be the light that pierces the darkness of fear. This may sound a bit over the top, but this is truly the way I feel. Indeed, I might fail, but I will learn and gain experience by trying.

I love my board meetings and cannot recommend them enough. So, if you think you could benefit from establishing your own, here are some steps to help you:

- Find a time in the week (or every two weeks if once a week is going to be too difficult) when you are least likely to be distracted. A nice atmosphere is absolutely key.
- You can have these meetings with yourself, but I would strongly recommend sharing them with someone whom you highly trust, or, ideally, with your other half and/or any member of your household interested in changing some area of their life for the better. If you are a business owner, have the board meeting with your partner, associate, a member of staff or an adviser.
- Agree at the beginning what you want to achieve (hint: What are the most important things for you in your life/ business at the moment?).
- Write out an agenda based on the themes you choose.
- Focus on what you can do. This is not supposed to be the time when the conversation descends into a full-scale argument about how you can't change things (although sometimes those frank discussions need to be had). Instead, this is a wonderful time for talking about your hopes and dreams, and for figuring out how to move towards them. If there are obstacles in the way, think about what steps, however small, you can take to go forward in some way.
- Write down what you intend to do between one board meeting and the next, and then hold yourself accountable.

Board meetings are only one example of an accountability system. Even if you're not in a position to have a weekly board meeting, I would recommend that you find accountability partners, as they are a tremendous help when it comes to reaching your goals. However, it's important that they do the same with you: the best accountability systems are based on reciprocity. If you're trying to achieve something that takes willpower, perseverance and strength, it's much more fun when you're doing it with somebody else, so you can keep each other going if one of you flags.

I have struck up two new accountability alliances. I met Sarah, who's married to a friend of my boyfriend, during a weekend break in Galway. Over a glass of wine after lunch, I started to talk about how nice it was to have the whole weekend off, meander through Market Lane on a Saturday morning, take the time to cook and reminisce about the wonderful four years I spent there while at college. She told me that I should take more time off and I said, 'Yeah, yeah, I know. Everybody tells me that and I know they're right, but I never seem to do it.'

Then she asked me a question that completely changed my view of things. She said, 'What things will you regret when you're eighty?' Indeed, I had never thought about it this way. So I started to think. I certainly wanted to make my mark in the world. But would I regret not spending more time in the office? Very unlikely. I came up with a list of ten things I was sure I didn't want to miss out on, and she said, 'You have the time to change that now, so why don't you?'

I turned the tables then and asked her the same question. Throughout the afternoon, we explored what we'd like to see if we were looking back on our lives sitting over a glass of wine decades hence. Our partners periodically stuck their heads in the door and asked, 'What are you two doing, you've been in here for hours.' After that, we agreed on a list of things to do, so that we didn't get to the autumn of our lives with regrets about what might have passed us by. The things on my list were personal, and the things on Sarah's were professional.

As for my other recent accountability partner, I met Mary-Anne at a business-development programme that we attended a couple of years ago. We were both in the start-up phase of our businesses, a very exciting stage. However, we were facing the same issues: getting bogged down in emails, having high aspirations and trying to do everything at once, as well as attempting to be innovative and successful. The programme was great for touching base and questioning how far we had come since the last time the group had met. When the programme came to an end, the two of us decided that we would have a monthly meeting to keep up the benefits of the course. We share business tips and techniques. We question each other's high-level objectives – for example, she'll ask me, 'Have you written that proposal that will actually drive the business forward or did you spend an hour reading other people's social-media updates?' Since we are at similar stages in our businesses, she can shine a light on my situation and show me things that I'm too close to see. Similarly, I can look at her enterprise efforts from an objective perspective and say what I see.

Having an accountability partner is one of the most precious things you can have because:

- It's much more fun than doing something on your own. If you spend a lot of time managing situations on your own, it's sometimes great to share them with somebody. You can tell them about your successes and difficulties while helping them with theirs. It's lovely to give and to receive help.
- Somebody else is holding you accountable, which provides extra motivation. For example, Mary-Anne recommends not opening your emails until after lunch, as you can get sucked into replying to non-urgent emails at the expense of real development. As a result, if I'm meeting her next Tuesday and she asks me about that, I'd like to be able to tell her that I stuck to it all week, rather than having to sheepishly say that I'll be better next week. Knowing that I have to answer to Mary-Anne makes me much less likely to click on that icon.
- If you start to flag, a good accountability partner will pick you right back up again. They will remind you of the reason why you started the initiative in the first place, what benefits you will derive from sticking with it, show you your success

to date and help you to put your foot forward just that little bit more. We all have an impulse to help others and to enjoy the warm and fuzzy feeling that results. It's wonderful to be able to help another bridge a gap that looks like an impassable abyss to them, and bring them closer to their goal.

I'm not saying that I would have failed to achieve anything without my accountability partners, but I don't think I would have done as much so quickly, so effectively or so enjoyably. In addition, I don't think that I would have sufficiently acknowledged my success along the way or been boosted by it to the same extent.

It's lovely sitting down with my boyfriend on a Friday night, looking back on a successful week, dreaming about what's going to happen next and then pencilling it into my diary, hopeful of its manifestation. It's fantastic sitting down with Mary-Anne and telling her excitedly about our latest opportunity, one that we went for and got. I've often found myself spontaneously sending my thoughts to Sarah, telling her about things I've learned about myself from taking time out, or the experiences that I would have missed out on by not making the effort that she reminds me to make. Similarly, it's awful to admit to any of the three that I didn't do what I said I would do. Imagine hearing yourself say out loud, 'Yes . . . I know I promised myself and you I would do that . . . I know I'm holding myself back . . .'

I have been lucky, perhaps, in that I've never had to go out looking for an accountability partner; they've just crossed my path. I think the best way to find one is to let it happen naturally. However, it's not quite just up to fate. I've often been the person to say to someone, 'Why don't we write a list of things that we both aspire to do and catch up again in a month's time and see where we are?' Also, remember things that are on your mind will spontaneously come up in conversation. You might find that you have very similar ideas or diametrically opposed views (either works when you're looking for an accountability partner). Simply by talking about certain issues, you may find your accountability partner in the strangest of places.

Picture this. You're at a friend's hen night. You both met at work over the past year and just clicked. As a result, she asked you to go out for dinner with her friends and family, but you don't know anybody. You're a little nervous, but you do get talking to a couple of them. You mention to her friend from college that you would love to get that New Year's Resolution feeling back into your life, as you've been meaning to sign up for that Monday Salsa Slim class. She says, 'I would love to try that – it sounds like a great bit of craic. I would be too nervous to go on my own, though.' Suddenly, you make firm plans and, motivated by each other, resolve to go to the class. You swap numbers and it becomes a running joke for the night. Since everybody on the hen night knows about it and you now have somebody who is both relying on you and supporting you in your decision to go – and you know it will be a conversation at the wedding reception – when Monday evening rolls around, you get straight into the car and off you go. That's the wonderful power of accountability partners.

In my experience, a good accountability relationship has several characteristics:

- *It's with somebody you can trust.* This is absolutely key. Most important of all is the fact that they will keep the relationship confidential. You don't want to be hearing about your successes or blips from somebody else. Also, you don't want to have to watch what you're saying in order to make it 'rumour-proof'; on the contrary, you want to be able to throw yourself into it and go all out. If someone pops into your head as a potential accountability partner, but on reflection you're afraid they might repeat stuff, hold something against you in the future, judge you or take your ideas and use them for their own gain, pass on the choice of this person – otherwise, you'll always be watching what you say and not getting the true benefit out of accountability. One other thing: if you're going to talk to this person about, let's say, money, that doesn't mean you also need to talk to them about your relationship, work–life balance, career, kids, etc. You don't need to give them the low-down on your whole life; this is not a confessional. Have a mutual, deep understanding about just one aspect of your life where you don't hold back and you might be surprised by the impact it will have.

↬ *It works both ways.* They have the same issue as you, or they want to work on an issue of their own. If you fear that somebody will look down on you if you fall off the wagon, it won't make for a productive relationship. They can't support you if you're too inhibited to tell them you had a lapse in the first place. And if you fear that somebody will make you feel bad about a failure, you'll end up discouraged. However, if two people are striving for the same thing, they can resonate with each other and keep each other going. If, like Mary-Anne and me, you're both at the same stage, it's great. You can understand where the other is at and really identify with how she's feeling. You can help to illuminate their issues and feel genuinely delighted for them when they achieve something they've been striving for. On the other hand, Sarah and I are at completely different stages in our lives and careers. We have different priorities, professions, hobbies, etc. Our only connection before we became accountability partners was the fact that our partners were childhood friends. As a result, she can take a look at something that I do from a perspective that I simply don't have. The conversation we had about regretting things at eighty was completely alien to me – a goal-focused, 'here-and-now' person with a tendency to concentrate on the short term, like me, would never reflect on that. She brings a slant to things that would otherwise be missing from my life.

↬ *It's with somebody who takes you seriously and is empathetic.* Have you ever related a dream (e.g., climbing Kilimanjaro) and somebody said, 'Sure, you will never do that' or 'Why would you want to do that?' Sitting at Weight Watchers, I used to hear story after story in which a woman asked her co-workers in the office not to tempt her with fattening stuff; and they would roll their eyes and say 'Here she goes again' and 'How long will this one last?' These are exactly the kind of people you *don't* want as an accountability partner. You want someone who believes that, if you haven't already achieved something, it's because you haven't found the right way of doing so, or because the time wasn't right, or because you weren't able to muster enough effort until now. You need an accountability partner to whom you can outsource your self-confidence. If you don't believe that you can do it, but somebody else does, that's okay for now. It's crucial that they understand why you want to go somewhere and how you're going to go about it. They believe that you will lose a certain amount of weight, reach a certain level of turnover, hold a dinner party for twelve people, pay off the mortgage, start up your own business, win that promotion, do that course, landscape your own garden, do your MBA, etc. At this point you may not see how it will happen, but they believe that it can. And then you can use their belief in you as fuel to keep you going while you're actually working at the thing you want to achieve. An accountability partner who doesn't think it can happen will serve only as a constant source of resistance and annoyance, so steer clear.

- *It's with somebody you get on with and can have fun with.* This may sound obvious, but if you want to make a part of your life better and you haven't already done it, it probably takes a good deal of perseverance. It may be enjoyable, but it's not like eating a cream cake. As a result, it's important to keep your spirits up. I genuinely look forward to meeting my accountability partners because they are great people who are wonderful company. I thoroughly enjoy talking to them about my successes and listening to theirs. I love discussing where I'm getting stuck and soaking up their perspective on things and their encouragement. I love the little conversations that we meander into and I love just having a laugh with them.

~ *It's with somebody who isn't going to be affected by the changes you're trying to make in your life.* Obviously an accountability relationship with your other half falls outside this guideline. But, apart from that, what's important is to find accountability partners who are detached from your own situation, that is, if you get what you want, it's not going to make a blind bit of difference to them. Remember that, by definition, you're going to talk about an issue you want to change. Maybe your closest friends and family are too close and just the thought of discussing that particular matter with them strikes fear into your heart. This is why you might be better off talking to somebody who is at a distance from those who know you best. If you're confiding in somebody who will be affected, they are naturally going to think about how it relates to them and give you an opinion based on that. For example, if you set up your own business and you talk about it to a co-worker who works in tandem with you, they might start to think about what it could mean for them and their job. Or let's say that you and your family go away every year with your friend and her family somewhere in Ireland. However, this year you would like to save up to take the kids abroad. Your friend may be comfortable with the current arrangement and your goal will affect her holiday plans. Do you think she can objectively help you in this? Finally, let's say that you go out with a friend every weekend. You decide that you want to take three months off work and travel around Australia. This will directly affect her social life, so will she be a good accountability partner? In each of these three cases, my point is not that you should secretly go out and achieve what you want and to hell with the consequences for those around you. Quite the contrary, in fact – I think you should discuss your goals with people, but only when you're ready to defend them against attack. This is a different business from asking others to help you get up on your feet.

~ *And, on a practical note, it's with someone who's actually in a position to help.* Do they have the time to spend with you? Can they grasp the key issues? Do they understand the journey that you want to take? Do they have experience with some element of the situation? Can they listen to your difficulties and offer relevant advice?

I'd like to expand on the penultimate point on the list: discussing your goals more widely only 'when you're ready to defend them against attack'. You should be aware that, at some point, somebody is bound to question your goals and ask, 'Why do you bother at all?' Sometimes this can come from a malicious source: the person could be envious or begrudging. Other times, people cannot grasp possibilities beyond their own situation, or yours, and genuinely don't see the point in trying to change things. Or it could be that people are worried about how your changing will affect them and they will try to encourage you to stay where you are. People might even say that you are getting 'too high and mighty', if you want to strive towards an ambitious goal – a sour grapes feeling rooted in their own disappointment in themselves. Sometimes, and this is the most poignant one, people have seen you try and not succeed before. They have seen your disappointment and have been there to pick up the pieces. It's difficult for them to watch you start again, because they don't want to see you hurt again. And yet these people will be your greatest cheerleaders and feel genuinely overjoyed for you upon your success. So they might not be ideal accountability partners, but they are definitely on your side.

How do you feel now about taking an accountability partner on board? After having read all of the above 'dos' and 'don'ts', you now have a feel for who would make a good accountability partner. Are you enthusiastic, thinking, 'Oh, I know just the right person for this. It will be so exciting'? Even if no one springs immediately to mind for your particular goal, now that you're primed your instincts will kick in and as soon as you meet the right person you'll know.

Or, on the contrary are you thinking: 'But having an accountability partner is terrible. It means that if I fail to reach my goals somebody other than me will know about it. How humiliating. I never reach my goals – what am I going to tell them?'

If you find yourself thinking this, the accountability partner isn't the problem. It's your own lack of belief in your ability to achieve that goal in the first place. Already, you're picturing the conversation in which you're admitting failure. You're already overwhelmed by your goal and thinking that you won't achieve it anyway.

There are two things that I would say to put you back on track. First, you may need to revisit your goal-setting techniques and make your goals even SMARTER. If you genuinely feel that you might fail before you've even started, is it because the goal is too big? If so, break it down further and make a list of every little thing that you could do right now to move it forward a millimetre. This worked for me when I wanted to internationalize – remember? All it took to get me going was replying to an email about meeting a delegation to the Dublin Chamber of Commerce. Just replying to an email – a tiny step in the right direction. Read back over Chapter 4 if your goal seems too daunting and get yourself going again with some techniques from there.

Second, discussing a big scary goal with an accountability partner can be a great experience. If you can find the right one, they can share in the excitement of your dreams. I met my best friend one day for a coffee in Java's in Galway. We were both first-year students at college at the time. I told her that I was thinking of going to Edinburgh for the summer on my own. I didn't have a job, I didn't have accommodation, and I didn't know anybody there. She said, 'I think that's crazy, but wouldn't it be soooo exciting?' I met her for a coffee in Merrion Street a few years later (yes, we have consumed a lot of coffee over the years!) and I told her that I was thinking about going to Malta. I said, 'I don't know what I'm going to do when I get there, I don't know how it's going to go, I don't know what's going to come out of it. I'm just going to go.' She said, 'I'm so looking forward to hearing about what you're going to tell me when you come home.' She believed in me at times when I didn't believe in myself, or at least I wasn't quite sure. And in turn over the years I've been the one to cheer her on and be excited for her. Sharing my wildest dreams with her made them seem real and therefore achievable.

You're going to laugh at this, but I told Sarah that I was going to enrol in a set-dancing class in Dublin. I danced throughout my childhood, and if any of you are familiar with set dancing, you know it's one hell of a cardio workout. These classes take place all over Ireland and the closest one to me was on a Thursday night. I'm always full of resolve and energy on a Monday, but, week after week, I never got to that class. I told her this and her immediate reaction was, 'It's hard to start a new hobby when it's getting dark and cold; perhaps consider it again in the spring when it will be easier to find the time.'

This motivated me to go out and do it. I can imagine that some of you might think, 'Didn't she just let you get away with it?' The thing is, would it have made any difference to the lost Thursday nights of the previous month? No. There is something in business called a 'sunk cost'. This means that the money is spent, it can't be retrieved, and so you may as well not take it into consideration in the future. For example, let's say that I'm going to start selling plants and I'm thinking about pricing them. It costs me €0.10 for the seeds, €0.60 for the pot, €1 for the person who sells the plant and €0.30 for the compost. The total cost of the plant is €2, so I might sell it at €3.50. I don't add in the price of the new glasshouse that I bought a few months ago when I came up with this idea to the calculation. I bought it, I can't return it and there aren't any ongoing costs. It might turn out that I don't need the glasshouse after all, so the expense is 'lost money'. However, I will sell my plants now and try to make as much profit as possible. I won't price a 'bit' of the glasshouse into each plant to try to recoup my costs, as the glasshouse is there whether I sell the plants or not. If I do make a profit, I can offset the cost of the glasshouse against it for tax purposes; but if the plan doesn't work out, I can't pack up the glasshouse and sell it on. One way or the other, it is a 'sunk cost', because I can't retrieve the money I spent on it. Similarly, the previous Thursday nights were 'sunk' – they had come and gone. There wasn't any point in going back over them. Instead, Sarah encouraged me to look forward and to get going again.

This may seem like a pretty simple goal. A set-dancing class isn't exactly life or death now, is it? The thing to remember is that how your goal looks to other people is irrelevant. I had a problem with my work–life balance and this is what Sarah was helping me with. I wasn't taking enough time out, wasn't exercising enough, etc., and I needed somebody to push me in the right direction. So it wasn't so much about the dancing class in itself, but about whether I was taking the right steps towards my bigger goal of achieving a better work–life balance. Sarah knew that, could see I was disheartened and gently put me back on track by suggesting I forget the past and focus on renewing my resolve instead.

12

Why having to account for your actions (and inactions) is good for you

In this chapter I'm going to walk you through an example of a working accountability relationship, showing you just what a fantastic contribution it can make to realizing your goals.

Say you have settled on a SMARTER goal: you want to save €10,000 by putting aside 10% of your wages each month. I imagine the thoughts of a person ready to embark upon achieving an ambitious financial goal would be along the lines of: 'So here I am. I'm going to give it a try. I think it's crazy to imagine that I could save €10,000, given the fact that I only earn €30,000 a year and that's before the taxman gets near it. It's impossible to think I would ever have that much. I love my nights out too much. I love going for coffee with the girls and people-watching. I don't really think there is any money for me to save. If there were, I would have saved it by now, wouldn't I? All I need to do is to get on top of my bills. If stuff would just stop coming up for a while, I would be grand. Anyway, Susan Hayes seems to think that I can do things differently. Let's see how it goes. I'm going to do like she says – dress up, head for a coffee shop and settle into a budget on a Saturday morning. Oh, look at that dress in Karen Millen . . .'

Ummm, see how easily you can get sidetracked or discouraged. This is where sharing your goal with an accountability partner comes in. You meet for the first time with your accountability partner to decide on a goal and to work out the details of getting there. The first round or cycle ends when you meet again and you look at how you did – what went well, what didn't go so well, what you learned, what you'll try next time. And each time you meet to look at how things went you finish another cycle. Let's eavesdrop on one side of the conversation (as accountability can be symbiotic), say, a week or a month later, at the end of Cycle 1 . . .

Your situation at the beginning of the meeting. 'It didn't work. At all. I hate this. I made a mess of the budget.'

What you tell your accountability partner. 'I thought that I actually knew every single cent that I spent; I thought that I would write it all down against my revenue and expect to have €200 at the end of the month. Instead I was €30 in the red and I was giving out to myself for "not sticking to my budget". I looked back and noticed I had forgotten to factor in x, y or z.

'I had either (a) forgotten about some small (or not so small) expense or (b) believed that life was going to press "pause" while I got my finances under control. For example, I thought I had done a really great job looking back over my receipts from the week before and my direct debits and everything. I got to the other end and the bottom line was not at all what I expected. I was *way* down – what had I forgotten? One of the things was that I had got my hair cut. I hadn't thought to include that as an expense, because typically I wouldn't be getting my hair done every week – it was a periodic thing that caught me off guard. Same as the kids' uniforms in September, a wedding, Christmas presents, birthdays, impromptu this, that or the other. I didn't remember to include them in the weekly budget because they don't happen every week.

'Also, I was writing the budget by working out how much I would spend on shopping, petrol, rent, etc. I gave myself €20 to eat out, in case a friend invited me to lunch or something. However, given that much of my life is spent on the move, I didn't account at all for the "I haven't a hope of waiting until I get home to cook something" expenses, or the "The bus didn't come on time, so I'd better get a taxi instead" money, or the "I think I would actually be better off driving so I'll need money to park" costs. What do you think at this stage? Am I poor at budgeting? Should I throw in the towel?'

The issue. It looks like you've been focusing on the wrong thing.

★

At this point, the right type of accountability partner will encourage you to reflect on what you got out of the experience. Indeed, you should think about all that you learned in that time. You gleaned an awful lot. After discussing things with your accountability partner, you might have a different perspective on the week's experience, which would go something like this:

'Ahhh, so that's where the money goes. If I hadn't actually looked, I would never have thought about integrating these things into a budget. First, if I were to take into account the number of cut-and-blow-drys I get in a year, and divide the total over my budget timeframe (i.e., 52 weeks or 12 months), I could actually get this right the next time. I get so stressed about miscellaneous items popping up that I haven't factored in. There is one answer to that – factor them in. Yes, I will become aware of them as they come up, though I might forget about them before they do. That means there will be some unexpected expenses, but now I know to look out for them and include them in my budget. It can only get better from now.

'Second, if I planned my day better, both my health and purse might thank me for it. Instead of spending €15 on a chicken curry at 9 p.m., I could get soup and a sandwich before going to that evening event, which would minimize the "I haven't a hope of waiting until I get home to cook something" expenses. If I gave myself an extra twenty minutes to get the bus, my stress levels and my pocket would be delighted, and I would be able to save the "The bus didn't come on time, so I'd better get a taxi instead" money. If I could motivate myself to get on my bike, my lungs would be happier, my frustration with red lights would vanish and my time and cost issues with parking would be non-existent. In fact, look how much money was lost and how many calories were gained through lack of planning. I could improve my budget AND my figure at the same time.'

You're certainly getting a lot of information from teasing out things with your accountability partner. Fair enough, the budget didn't quite work out. However, you're now much more aware of what's going on in your finances and can locate the cracks through which your money was slipping.

Now consider the following:

- What did you learn from the exercise?
- Did it work out like you thought it would?
- What happened to drive it off course?
- How could these issues be remedied?

By the end of the conversation, you should:

- be aware of what you've learned.
- have specific strategies to deal with these issues in the next cycle.
- have gained a more objective perspective.
- have soaked up the motivation to continue.

Let me tell you, you're doing great. The first time I tried sticking to a budget, I didn't do as well and didn't learn nearly as much. The reason for this was because I did it in fits and starts. I started with great intentions, kept with it for a few days and then got bored or dispirited. Here is where an accountability partner can really help. If you know that you have to meet and 'report back' to somebody at the end of the week or month, and you're looking forward to a chinwag over a coffee, your motivation will be much greater. Also, you might find that you've taught them a thing or two. They might say, 'Oh. That's clever. I would never think of putting a haircut into a budget.' Better yet, they could do it along with you, and you would both have a laugh about what went wrong and how you could remedy it.

Now it's a week later, and you have your second meeting.

Your situation at the beginning of the meeting. 'I just wasn't motivated . . . I'm fed up with it all, really.'

What you tell your accountability partner. 'It's like this. I had a bad week. I was under pressure at work. The kids got sick and I was up all night with them. I was cranky with my partner. I didn't have time to feed myself, never mind cook for the entire household. I had to go out for a drink with a friend because she needed a shoulder to cry on. Everybody was pulling out of me and I got nowhere near eight hours of sleep a night. Where was I supposed to get time to look after money and stick to a stupid flipping budget?'

The issue you need a strategy to deal with. How to weather rough patches and still stick to your objectives.

The right type of accountability partner will sit you down, talk to you like a friend and give you the space to relate all the things that happened in the week. You really need an accountability partner at times like these. I don't say that because I want to add to your woes, but because you need to outsource the responsibility for keeping your ultimate goal at the top of your agenda, as you certainly don't have the time or the energy to do that yourself. At the end of such a horrible week or month, wouldn't it be great for somebody to ask how you are and to be genuinely interested in the answer? You want to be able to manage your money better for a reason; you have chosen a goal for a reason; otherwise you wouldn't be reading this book. You must want to achieve something for a certain reason. Now what is that reason? What is the bigger 'why'? Is it big enough, inspiring enough? What is the thought that you'll be using to sustain you through difficult times? Things happen all the time, throughout our lives. They can wreak havoc with our plans. So how will you get 'back in the saddle' when life happens? Just because it didn't work this week, doesn't mean it will never work. Regroup, take some time to vent and rant, remind yourself of your bigger 'why', and let your accountability partner help you to get back on track.

Now, take a deep breath, start afresh, wipe the slate clean and let a new week and a new opportunity begin. Consider the following:

- You didn't manage to work towards your objectives as you had a hectic week.
- Can you think of ways to avoid things getting this hectic again?

~ Or can you think of ways to adapt your strategy so that you can stick with it even when things get tough?

~ How can you get back in the saddle?

By the end of the conversation, you should have:

~ let off some steam and vented everything that you needed to.

~ revisited why you undertook this journey in the first place.

~ gained a more objective perspective.

~ soaked up the motivation to continue – again.

Before you know it, your third meeting is around the corner.

Your situation at the beginning of the meeting. 'I hate it. It's so unpleasant. I have to deny myself everything I like. This is no way to live.'

What you tell your accountability partner. 'I did it. I actually was much better this time. I took everything into account and was a lot more on the ball. However, I didn't enjoy it. I kept thinking of all the things that I could buy, instead of putting away the money "for a rainy day". It was even sunny this week and the world around me rubbed it in my face that I wasn't "allowed" to spend. My towards motivation was invisible. I cut 10% of my spending power, and it was terrible. I was miserable as I made tea for myself at home watching TV, when I could have had a nice frothy coffee in a lovely coffee shop with atmosphere, people, music, where I could have indulged in a little people-watching. I almost had to shut my eyes walking past my favourite clothes shop, and couldn't stop dreaming of the new dress that I wasn't allowed to buy.

'Having said that, it was interesting to find that I had a good bit left over and some of the saving actually was pretty painless. I just planned in advance. On Sunday evening I went through my favourite cookery books and picked out some new recipes. I planned my meals for the week over a cup of tea with MTV Classic in the background. I wrote a list and spent a pleasurable hour wandering around the supermarket doing my grocery shopping. I spent the equivalent of five "I'm too hungry to cook and I'm ignoring the calories in this" type of meals on a basket of shopping for the entire week. I did actually have some money left over (just as I had budgeted) and I was sooo tempted to go book a cheap Ryanair flight somewhere nice, or get a massage, or buy stuff that was on special offer, thinking I might need it sometime – or just to relax things a little during the week. However, I kept telling myself, "Don't. You're resetting your financial thermostat. Don't go back to zero." '

The issue. You were focusing on the wrong thing again.

Well done. Your accountability partner should be patting you on the back. It sounds like you were suffering from withdrawal symptoms. In a way, you were. You were changing habits that it will be difficult for you to shed. As for the temperature on your financial thermostat, it was trying to pull your purse back down with it. You correctly identified that it was trying to 'do its thing' – but your awareness of it has really diminished its power over you. It's interesting that you say that your 'towards motivation' is invisible; this means you're focusing on the wrong thing. It sounds like you believe that saving 10% of your wages is doing without rather than with. I suggest that you pick a figure to work towards: maybe you can start lower and work your way up to 10%?

Alternatively, you could give a concrete form to what you're going to do with the savings. What is worth more to you than all the things you're giving up? Is it the education your kids will have if you transfer the money into a fixed-interest account? Is it being 'lean enough' to set up, with confidence, a standing order for a fixed amount that's paid into a hands-off account, with a view to funding a wedding, travelling next year or the time out needed to do something you love? Is it the feeling that you have a solid financial cushion under you so that you can take a leap of faith and try an activity you've been holding back from? Is it the knowledge that, with a larger sum of money, you can sustain 'adverse economic shocks' (this is a term that we use in economics to describe a spike in the price of oil or a currency crisis)? If saving 10% of your salary isn't doing it for you, what would?

Consider the following:

- Did the first hint of achieving your goal work out as you'd anticipated?
- What did you like and dislike about the experience?
- What have you learned from the week?
- Does the satnav need to be recalculated?

By the end of the conversation, you should have:

- reflected on all you've learned.
- become aware of the financial thermostat trying to dwindle your balance.
- really thought about where you're going.
- really thought about how you're going to get there.
- really thought about how to continue.

Now you're at a very powerful stage. You have learned that your dreams and thoughts can be turned into very real possibilities. But, having tried it on for size, do you want to adjust it? It's as if you knew the castle in the forest existed and someone has cleared a way for you. Is the castle as wonderful as it is in the fairytales or is it actually less interesting than the other castle that caught your eye on the journey? It looks like it's time for a major strategy meeting.

Your situation at the beginning of the meeting. 'I now know that I could, if I wanted to, achieve my original goal, but I'm not sure whether I actually want to work as hard as this to get there.'

What you tell your accountability partner. 'You know what, if I have to say no to a fun night out with my friends, wait for another week to get the kids' hair cut and don't have the budget to put credit on my phone (which I'm uncomfortable about), it's not worth it. Seriously. This carry-on of saving 10% of my salary just drains lots of things out of my life. I might have to wait an extra couple of months to build up that nest egg, but I have firmly decided that I'm okay with that. I don't want my life to be a bread-and-water diet for forty years and then a "cruise-till-I-croak" retirement paid for with the money I've saved. Life is for living throughout. Indeed, I've learned a lot over the past couple of months and I'm far more vigilant than I was before. I want to work towards that €10k being in my account, instead of simply saving 10% of my salary. Maybe that's what I wanted all along. I certainly don't want this boot-camp feeling to go on forever.'

The issue. You have fully experienced what's involved in going for your goal: the journey where you discard everything holding you back. The vision that you have for your desired destination is now a little fuzzy, as experience has changed the way that you look at your goal, and you need to decide fully what you really want.

Here your accountability partner should be taking your feelings on board. If you had said this back at the beginning, you shouldn't have been allowed to get away with it. But by now you've given it a proper go over a decent span of time and you've really seen the impact on your life. However, there comes a point when you need to re-evaluate. You absolutely need to make up your mind about what you want to do.

Make sure you really think about your goal before you discard it entirely. Are you at the Red Cow roundabout and trying to find your way into Inchicore after setting out from Cork? Perhaps you're late; maybe you thought you'd be there by now. That's okay. But it wouldn't be a great idea to drive back to Cork just because you can't find your way around the roundabout. Let's rethink the time that it's going to take you to get there. You can find 10% of your salary to save, but you want to bring that down a little. Right. How much longer are you willing to wait to get your goal in exchange for saving slightly less? That might prove to be a valuable trade-off.

Consider the following:

- Now that you know what it feels like, is this really the goal you want?
- Should you lower your expectations?
- What have you learned from the week?
- Are you toning down the goal because the goal itself is not exactly what you want, or because the speed at which you want to reach it wasn't right?

By the end of the conversation, you should:

- have reflected on all you've learned.
- be crystal clear on where you want to go now.
- be motivated to keep your spirits up.

At this point, you might be thinking, 'But lowering my expectations by saving less feels like I'm giving up and being lazy. How can I know the difference between dropping a goal that isn't right for me and letting myself off the hook altogether?'

There are such things called 'destructive goals'. These are things you strive for that don't serve you well. It doesn't just mean that bad things can happen, but that things can happen that aren't in your best interests. Imagine that someone wants to lose weight because they don't like their body. Along the way, they realize that dieting hard is actually not helping at all, as they dislike their body even more for having cravings and not submitting to the strict regimen. Maybe losing weight is not the goal they really need to achieve – what they need is to be at peace with their body, and dieting is not the way to get there. By dropping the strict diet altogether, they're not being lazy; they're being very wise. You must have heard of people who strive to become rich, only to find in the end that it's an empty victory. Again, if someone drops the goal of earning more in order to focus on enjoying life – after having lost their previous belief that money was the precursor to happiness – they are not being lazy, they are being wise.

I remember setting goals that didn't work out for me from time to time, which I didn't pursue for the following reasons.

a. They were things that I thought I wanted but, on realizing what they looked like, I didn't want them any more.
b. I didn't think that I could aim higher when I first set the goal, and it wasn't until I was further down the road that I realized I could bypass that particular step.
c. I didn't know how to move forward. But as soon as I started to progress, things became clearer and led me in a different direction.
d. Sometimes the opportunity was there, but I didn't go for it because I let the urgent take precedence over the important.

The way to tell the difference between getting lazy and dropping a destructive goal is very simple. You need to answer the question: 'Which will make me a happier person now and in the long run?' In my case, for (a), (b) and (c) above, the answer was quite clear. I saw a better way and I went for it. In (d) I got lazy. My actions illustrated that I didn't treat that goal with the importance I felt it deserved. Sometimes we need an 'external stimulus' – this is a fancy term for saying we need something outside of ourselves to give things a boost. As I have said many times already, an accountability partner can add a real timeliness to your goals.

Now let's have a look at one last accountability meeting.

Your situation at the beginning of the meeting. 'It's working! This is great. It's not the goal I originally set myself, but I'm proud to have done this much. I never thought it would work at all.'

What you tell your accountability partner. 'Magical. I'm saving 5% of my salary each month and it will take me about six years to get to €10,000. I'm happy with that. It's interesting what's after happening, though. I seem to always have about 2% left in the account at the end of the month. I never have credit-card interest to pay any more. I'm saving a fortune because I'm able to take care of my yearly bills all at once and I'm not paying any "pay-monthly" sur-charges. My planning is second nature by now and I look forward to my Sunday-night shopping trip. It kinda draws a line under the week. I don't need to worry as I have it under control. If a friend calls me to go out at the weekend, I have that "budgeted in". Even if I don't hear from anybody, I can either pamper myself or get the wheels in motion for a meet-up. I've actually come to really enjoy tea at home with a movie. I find it easy to resist relatively low-value-added uses of my money now, after that financial diet left me starving. In fact, I have €500 left in the account this month that I might just transfer across to the "goal account", as I know I'll have 2% spare again in a few weeks. I don't know how I could ever have been happy with nothing in the account by the time the next wage slip came through. You never know . . . I might just hit my initial target in time after all.'

The opportunity. Success is breeding belief, which, in turn, is becoming reality.

Your accountability partner should be hugely excited for you. You see, sometimes when we aim for the moon, we reach the stars instead. Imagine that you had never started this journey. You would have yourself convinced by now that you couldn't do it, when all you really had to do was to make some adjustments. In fact, you're in a much more comfortable place. I wouldn't be surprised if you did reach your goal and even within your initial time-frame . . . just like with a satnav.

Consider the following:

- The journey that you have undertaken so far.
- The changes in your thinking.
- The rise in your financial thermostat.
- How your satnav is redirecting you back towards your initial 'impossible' goal.

By the end of the conversation, you should:

- have reflected on all you've learned.
- have fully savoured the result of your journey.
- have thought about how your old ways no longer interest you.
- be interested in maintaining your good habits.
- be open to improving even more.

All this might strike you as an awfully time-consuming process. Having an awareness of things always seems to be more time-consuming – because it consumes mental energy. But the choice is this. Don't devote any mental energy to it, and the problem will remain a problem. Or, devote mental energy to it, accept that you'll feel drained at the beginning because it's new and unfamiliar, but the problem will be solved – and you'll avoid wasting the time that the problem would have eaten up and the worry that would have ensued when it became a much bigger issue – as ignored problems always do.

Indeed, the process that I went through above is time-consuming. However, how many years have you been spending, managing, worrying about, saving or investing money? This process is a snapshot from a lifelong journey. If you want to make it faster, go for it. Zap straight through to knowing exactly what you want and put every inch of effort that you can into it. You don't have to take months and months; it can happen as quickly as you want it to. But do you know exactly what you want, without a doubt, and do you feel up to giving it your all?

From experience, I can tell you that there are times when you'll learn lots, and I do believe that you need to give yourself the time to go through that learning process. Your motivation will flag and it will need to be buoyed. You might come across parts of the journey that you don't find comfortable or enjoyable at all. You might gain a new understanding of your goal and be surprised or disappointed to find that it doesn't look like what you had thought. You might decide that the path is just too rocky and that there is an easier road to your destination. You might just find that you arrive there by default anyway. One thing is for certain, though: you'll grow, mature and benefit from the lessons that you learn. And, paradoxically, there is no faster way to achieve this than by taking the time to put a support system into place, that is, by choosing an accountability partner and talking things over with them at regular intervals.

Is there an alternative to what may appear to some as a painstaking process? Yes. In fact, there are two. One is to do nothing, say nothing and just remain where you are. This won't take any time at all. The other is to know exactly where you want to go and stick with it, applying laser-like focus and not flagging once. Not so easy. Also, remember it's important to share this exacting journey with somebody whose company you enjoy!

And one last thing. An accountability partner will help you to make sure that you achieve your actual goal. Tunnel vision is not the same thing as focus. If you close your mind to everything but the fairytale castle you're aiming for, with nobody to give you another perspective and valuable feedback, you might just walk right past the real object of your goal: the kingdom that would have been yours for the taking.

Identify the costs and benefits of your choices

13

Revenue is vanity, profit is sanity

In the last chapter, you got a taste of how you might go about weighing the pros and cons of your goal, through working with an accountability partner. In our example, you decided to save 5% instead of 10%, because you realized you had to take your feelings into account – saving 10% was too much of a struggle, and you felt it wasn't worth it.

And this is something we'll come across again: when it comes to improving your finances, feelings weigh as much as, and sometimes more than, hard numbers. You have to take them into consideration. But you still need hard figures, so that you can base your decision on something tangible, instead of being led solely by your feelings. That way, you'll have a much better grasp of the trade-offs you're prepared to make to reach your goal.

Trade-offs are, in fact, costs. How much does it 'cost' to renounce your daily cup of coffee versus how much does it cost to have it? You might save €3.50, so you're making €3.50 in revenue, but there is a loss involved: changing a habit, getting less coffee into your system, forgoing the five-minute respite that goes with actually drinking that cup of coffee. Only you can know whether it's worth it.

Examining whether to have the cup of coffee is a profit-and-loss exercise. Most of you will know, intuitively, what a P&L exercise is: it's when you calculate how much money comes in and how much money goes out for a certain activity. You get a monthly salary, and that is money coming in. What you might not know intuitively is what it costs you to have that money come in. So it costs money to make money, in a way. And just like the cup of coffee example above, you have to factor in how much it costs to make a certain decision.

To a certain extent much of the rest of this chapter, as well as the next, is focused on people who are in business (and the examples I use are based on the business world), but even if you're not a business person I believe you can learn lessons from thinking about some of these issues – in particular about how business people identify when they're actually making money, or when they're fooling themselves and they're very busy getting nowhere.

I gave a presentation one night for a group of entrepreneurs that was held in a café attached to a small, beautifully decorated shop selling some very delicious, mouth-watering delicacies. Afterwards, as everybody was mingling, I took the opportunity to look around the shop and got chatting to the owner. I asked her if she had considered talking to the multiples and supplying them with such high-quality foods. She rolled her eyes and said, 'I've been there and done that. I used to toil endlessly supplying great amounts of what you see all over the country, and I made a lot of money. However, I lost just as much by not having any quality of life. Now, I just have my own shop, supply some local businesses, have a high mark-up, lock up and go home at 5 p.m. I have a couple of staff and a comfortable standard of living. I don't have the turnover (or the prestige) of the big business that I used to have, but revenue is vanity, profit is sanity.'

I think that phrase deserves discussion – revenue is vanity, profit is sanity. Think back to the story I told you in Chapter 7: how I discovered that I was actually making a loss on someone I considered to be a key client and how I was working flat out, raking in the money, but earning no more than my salary had been before I set up in business. So let's get into the shoes of a small-business owner – you – who has deservedly built up a good reputation. You've been offered two contracts and are deciding which one to choose. Let's take a look at the details and walk through the decision-making process.

Contract A	Contract B
Revenue €10,000	Revenue €5,000

At this point in time, many people would sign up Contract A straight off the bat. However, this would be premature. Indeed, you may receive more money into your bank account, but how much money needs to leave that account in order to service this contract? You don't know that yet. The next thing you should do is examine the costs related to this activity.

Contract A	Contract B
Revenue: €10,000	Revenue: €5,000
Materials: €1,000	
Consultants and subcontractors: €4,000	
Miscellaneous: €500	Miscellaneous: €500
Profit: €4,500	Profit: €4,500

Now it looks like the first contract involves the manufacture of a product, while the second involves a consultative service. What do you do?

Some of you will say, 'It doesn't matter, take your pick!'

More of you will say, 'Take Contract B, it looks easier, as there seems to be a lot more work involved in Contract A.'

Others will say, 'Find a way to make both happen. If the business is on the table, go for it!'

What you should really say is: 'I have incomplete information. What about the cost of my own time in here?'

As you delve into the briefs of the contracts, you discover that in the case of Contract A, the number of hours spent would be three times that of Contract B. In addition, you would need to hire a temporary worker to manage your other clients while you threw yourself into Contract A. Let's now take that into consideration.

Contract A	Contract B
Revenue: €10,000	Revenue: €5,000
Materials: €1,000	
Consultants and subcontractors: €4,000	
Miscellaneous: €500	Miscellaneous: €500
Cost of own labour: €4,500	Cost of own labour: €1,500
Cost of temporary labour: €1,000	
Profit: –€1,000	**Profit: €3,000**

Now, despite the fact that you were turning over €10,000, you find that you would actually be running this contract at a loss. On the other hand, the profit from Contract B is positive, and hands-down beats what's on offer from Contract A.

Is this now a done deal? You take the second contract and off you go? Well, there are two more things that you need to think about.

The first is to look beyond today and into the future. Given that Contract A involves some sort of product manufacture and that you retain the intellectual property rights (i.e., you have the right to sell the same product to customers other than your client), are there other sales channels that you could make use of for this product afterwards? If there is a demand for the product – and there must be if somebody offered you Contract A to make it – could this opportunity force you to spend time and money developing something that could be scaled upwards? In other words, something that, once developed, is easy to sell widely without any further major spending. For example, I spend €10,000 developing a product, and I'm then able to sell €20,000 or €100,000 of that product without needing to invest a lot more time or money. On the other hand, if I'm providing an accounting service, for example, it would take me a lot more time to generate €100,000 than €20,000.

In the past, you may have said that you would love to take on something like Contract A, but that you didn't have the time, or you didn't want to spend €10,000 and then find yourself without any buyers. Here, you're actually getting a product funded by a contract. The alternative is to supply a highly profitable service to fulfil Contract B, send the invoice and get paid. This is perfectly fine, but afterwards you'll need to go in search of new business again and, though you may have gained in reputation, experience and contacts, you'll need to 'start from scratch'. In the case of Contract A, you could take the product and generate another €10,000 contract, but this time, because the product already exists, you'd be able to keep your costs to around €2,000. And you could repeat the experience again and again. Therefore, you could judge this situation completely differently.

If a company or individual is in start-up or expansion mode, Contract A would be the one to opt for. However, if it is set up, established and happy with its current offerings, the decision is much more clear-cut: simply take the one that is profitable.

Finally, as I will discuss in more detail later, there are non-quantifiable costs and benefits with all opportunities, and they can often outweigh the accounting in any decision. Here, the company might also be taking several other things into consideration that you can't measure with a ruler, calculator or an Excel spreadsheet:

- Is there a possibility of future business with this organization?
- Could I generate more business because of the prestige of working with this organization?
- Will taking on this contract affect the level of service that I can offer to my existing customers?

∼ How much customer service will be involved in this contract – follow-up calls and emails, managing communication between stakeholders, 'touch-base meetings', client entertainment?

∼ Am I going to be under pressure with this contract and how will these elevated stress levels affect my life outside of work?

In essence, the point of this exercise is to illustrate that higher revenue does not automatically mean higher profits. It is absolutely key to delve into an opportunity and identify whether:

∼ it is profitable, now and in the future;

∼ it can be scaled upwards or whether 'capital' is being developed (i.e., is something being created which can outlive the contract);

∼ the non-quantifiable benefits or costs stack up with the numbers.

Equipped with this analysis, you can really make some very effective decisions, the positive impacts of which you should be able to feel right into the future.

In this example the company knew the difference between revenue and profit. But what happens when the people running the company are less clear about the difference? Many years before I started my own company I read an interview with two friends who were in business during the boom years. They didn't talk about the pressures of business in terms of finding customers, getting paid or issues of scale. Instead they spoke about how hard it was to find reasonably priced (and conscientious) labour and to keep up with demand, and about how often the bank called them to offer credit in various guises. They were turning over five figures a week and working themselves into the ground.

One of them recalled one year when their accounts showed €500,000 turnover and their bank balance was €50,000 in the red. This isn't uncommon for a business at certain stages of its life, but the thing that stuck out for me in this interview was that they had absolutely no idea this was going to be the result of that year's output. As far as they were concerned, the money was rolling in the door. They didn't worry about the costs involved in servicing the business. They borrowed to buy premises and materials, instead of renting, because they believed credit was cheap and it would save them money in the long run.

They carried on with that mindset until their accountant sat them down one day, wrote down a large five-figure sum on a single sheet of paper and asked them to tell her how long it took them to earn this amount of money. They replied proudly that it would take only about six weeks. She then asked them how long it would take them to earn that amount of profit. That stumped them. They hadn't a clue. She then said, 'You'd better think about that long and hard, because the only thing you two would be doing during the six weeks is working to pay the bank – that is in fact the amount of interest that you'd be paying on your borrowings.'

That story really struck me and I made a note to learn from their experience. I truly have and I hope that you will too.

Here's another story showing how there's more to profit and loss than meets the eye. One day I was at a talk delivered by an entrepreneur. She spoke very passionately about her product and her business story. Her primary brief that day was to speak about financing a business, and she took us on a journey that included County Enterprise Board grants, Enterprise Ireland investment, Venture Capital funding and Angel investor money, as well as the owners' own capital and countless hours of unpaid wages. The business had been started about eight years before, and there were five people involved. They'd won several local, regional, national and international awards. Their marketing efforts were innovative, eye-catching and, most of all, highly effective. The story was one of perseverance, tenacity and hard, risky slog, and we were all inspired by it. Then one person asked how much her product was retailing for. She replied that, depending on the spec, around €25,000.

It was her answer to the next question that made my jaw drop. 'How many have you sold?' She didn't need to think. 'Twenty-two.'

You won't need a calculator to work out that eight years of work by five owners and tens of staff, millions of air miles, three premises, energy costs, sundries, consultants, prototypes, etc., comes to a hell of a lot more than their turnover. They were suffering hundreds of thousands in losses every year. Despite an amazing product, incredible drive, memorable marketing and highly talented people, they were losing money hand over fist.

Were they worried about it?

Actually, this was part of the plan. They knew they were far too small to scale the business, so their aim had been to set it up and then sell it to a large multinational, which would be in a position to make it profitable.

I hope these stories show you that revenue and profit are far from synonymous. And I hope you realize that, to a certain extent, it costs money to make money. Now I don't mean that 'you have to have money to make money'. Don't get discouraged, thinking you can never get out of the vicious circle. What I mean is this: is it possible to make money cost-free? Yes. Can you continue to make money cost-free? No.

In Chapter 18, I suggest a number of ways to start making money from scratch, and many don't involve any outlay. For example, you can start an online business, a training endeavour or act as a distributor without any costs at the beginning at all. However, after a while, you will have to spend money in some way. At the very least you'll need to pay tax on this revenue stream. You may also have to pay for phone, stationery, electricity, petrol and internet access. You will be able to offset the costs attributable to the business against your revenue for tax purposes, but you will still need money to pay for them in the first place, even if you don't turnover anything at all. If you want to move to the next stage and set up a company, you will need an accountant, business cards and letter-headed paper, staff, subcontractors and a marketing budget. If you make a product, you'll need a manufacturing plant, inputs, distribution and transport.

In other words, there is no business that doesn't cost something to run. In basic economics, the costs are called the 'four factors of production' and categorized as land, labour, capital and enterprise.

For example, let's say that I'm going to set up a fashion boutique:

- *Land.* I would need a premises in order to hold and sell my stock (premises which I would need to buy or rent).
- *Labour.* I would need people to work in the business (including myself).
- *Capital.* I would need rails, hangers, shelves, lighting, doors, windows, a till, etc.
- *Enterprise.* I would need to act in an enterprising way, selling goods at a higher price than what I paid for them.

The same rationale would apply to a very low-cost business. Say, for example, a teacher decides to give grinds in her own house:

- *Land.* She still has to pay for her own house via rent or a mortgage (either now or in the past).
- *Labour.* She has to pay herself a salary out of the money that she makes from the grinds.
- *Capital.* She has to buy textbooks, notebooks and stationery.
- *Enterprise.* She needs to act in an enterprising way, selling the grinds at a price above that of all the other inputs

Remember that she has to buy each of these things before she can actually deliver the grinds. Afterwards, she can offset her costs against the revenue that she makes, to minimize her tax liability, but the Revenue won't compensate her for these costs.

As you can see, in every case it does cost money to make money. I've used the cheapest ways of making money to show you as examples. I won't expend any effort in trying to illustrate that a pharmaceutical company with millions of euros' worth of buildings and machinery and a thousand staff costs money because, well, you don't need me to figure that out.

It's important to acknowledge and consider your costs when

thinking about creating any type of additional revenue stream. It's even more important to minimize costs without compromising on impact.

By now you might be thinking: 'This is money coming in versus money going out – I thought we sorted that out a few chapters ago when we established a budget? Take the teacher giving grinds – wouldn't her rent or her mortgage payment be factored into her budget? Same thing for the textbooks that she needs to buy – she might as well factor them into her budget, since she needs to buy them even before she can make money giving grinds. How is a budget different from a P&L exercise?'

A profit-and-loss account is one where you examine your revenue, take away your costs and then arrive at your profit. A budget is where you take a certain amount of money and apportion it according to your spending needs. Using the example of €100, if I'm thinking in profit-and-loss terms, I ask myself, 'How much of that will be left over for me after all costs?' If I'm thinking in budgetary terms, I ask myself, 'What things can I buy with €100?'

Let's take the example of a bakery:

Day 1. Brenda the baker gets a phonecall from client 'Cookies & Cream', which would like 100 croissants. She knows that she can sell each of them for €3. So the value of the order is €300.

Day 2. Brenda needs to pay for the ingredients, three hours of a staff member's time, the electricity for the oven and the delivery of the croissants. Her costs are:

Costs	Unit cost	Total order
Ingredients (per croissant)	50c	€50
Labour (per hour)	€15	€45
Electricity (per hour)	€5	€10
Delivery	€10	€10
Total		€115

Day 3. Brenda delivers the croissants and gets cash-on-delivery. She lodges €300 in her bank account. Next she sits at her P&L Excel spreadsheet to offset her revenue against her costs. €300 minus €115 leaves her with a profit figure of €185.

Day 4. Brenda pays each of her four bills. Obviously we're keeping the figures and logistics simple for the sake of this exercise, so let's say her bank account had a balance of zero when she lodged the €300 cheque from her client on Day 3. Now that she's paid her bills she has a bank balance of €185.

Day 5. Brenda sits down at her budgeting spreadsheet again and works out how to budget her profit. She has an insurance bill of €100 due and must get some new supplies so that she can bake some muffins for her next client. These will cost €35. She decides she wants to save what's left over to help her business through the quieter season in August. That accounts for the remaining €50.

Day 6. Brenda is now very clear about the difference between a P&L account and a budget.

A profit-and-loss exercise is an extremely important tool, even if you don't have a business. It can help you weigh the pros and cons every time you're faced with a big life decision, such as going for a promotion, leaving your job to raise your children, or leaving your job to create your own business. And, just as in the example of the two contracts at the beginning of this chapter, you'll need to take things into consideration that aren't necessarily quantifiable in a neat way. But you'll also find out about the real financial cost of each decision. And this will help you see much, much more clearly.

Let's consider a complete list (or as complete as I could make it) of the costs and the benefits of going to work. Yes, going to work has a cost: as you now know, it takes money to make money. First, let's start with the financial side of things and then progress to the non-financial perspective.

Financial costs of going to work

Cost	Explanation
Transport (and the time spent in transit)	The hours and money spent on buses, taxis, trains, planes, automobiles, etc.
Lunches	Going out for lunch or buying a meal at a cafeteria.
Childcare	Crèche, au pair, etc.
Coffee	11 a.m., 3 p.m., 'I'll just buy a coffee and then settle into my day.'
Clothes	Your 'work' clothes and shoes, uniforms, 'something to wear to the Christmas party', dry-cleaning, etc.
Appearance	Make-up, perfume, jewellery, etc.
Travelling expenses	Travel and subsistence expenses if you're outside of a physical workplace, as well as spending money 'just because you're travelling', e.g. tourism activities, drinks, a taxi to the airport, gifts.
Going out	'It's Anne's birthday this week, so a couple of us are going for dinner if you would like to come too?'
Presents	'Anne is leaving this week, so we're all going to put €10 into a kitty and get her something.'

Social welfare	If you didn't work, you could claim social welfare, so by working you are 'losing' that money . . .
Working more hours than those stipulated in your contract	If you stay after work or take work home without getting paid for it, this is essentially time that you could be spending earning money elsewhere – these are billable hours, after all.
'I'm running late'	'I slept in, missed the bus and now I have to take a taxi. I thought I was going to have the time to get breakfast/lunch ready, but I'll have to buy it when I get into work.'

Financial benefits of going to work

Revenue	Explanation
Salary	The money you get periodically from your employer/business.
Bonus/overtime	The added revenue that you receive throughout the year from seasonal bonuses or the opportunity to work more hours in exchange for more money.
Experience	The more experienced you are, the higher the rate that you can charge as time goes on.
Networking	Should you ever decide to move on, you'll have contacts who can put you in the way of employment opportunities that aren't advertised, which, should they materialize, would turn into money.
Pension	Your job/company may be contributing towards a payment plan for your retirement.
Benefits	Your job/company may be providing you with extra benefits, e.g. health insurance, gym membership.

Expenses	If you incur travel, subsistence or out-of-pocket expenses, the company should refund you accordingly.
Training	Your company may be paying for you to sit exams as well as paying your salary while you take study leave.
Social welfare	At the time of writing, if you are an employee of a company and your PRSI payments are up to date, you can claim social welfare in the event of unemployment, maternity leave, etc. – so, although you're not getting that money now, by working you are earning the right to it, should you ever need it.
Facilities	You may have access to a parking space, internet, stationery, etc.
Discounts	You may be able to acquire goods and services at discounted rates because you work at a company or because you own your own company.
Tax efficiencies	If you have your own company, you can offset your losses against your gains, which can increase your disposable income.

Non-financial costs of going to work

Cost	Explanation
Stress	Work-related issues dominating your thoughts – a particular client or situation; constantly planning for the next day; office politics.
Worry	'What if I don't reach that target?' 'What if we don't close that deal?'
'Not enough of you left'	You turn down engagements with your family or friends because you're too physically tired or mentally exhausted after work.
Fear	'If I lose this job, I won't be able to get another.' 'I'm afraid of taking a month off because it might jeopardize my job.'
Opportunity cost	'If I didn't have to work today, I could study to pass exams that would further my career.' 'I could start to build a company that would bring me much greater rewards.'
Family and social life	'I can't go to [insert event] because I have to work.'

Arguments with those around you	'Why are you working this weekend when you know it's my birthday?'
Outside influences on your time	If you work at premises that are out of the way, you'll have to spend time getting to and from work, time that you might have used to run errands conveniently. This may force you to waste time in queues during peak periods, sit in traffic during rush hour and pay premium prices when consumption is at a high volume (electricity, etc.).
Change your circumstances	If you have to relocate or work shifts, it can bring about huge changes in your household and social circle.
Guilt	A feeling of regret for having to endure the above costs.

Non-financial benefits of going to work

Benefit	Explanation
Socializing	If you're at work, in most cases, there is an additional social outlet in your life, either at your place of work, through regular contact with clients and service providers, or through contact with the retail public. You can benefit from this mutual communication and develop lifelong friendships (or more).
Use of skills	If you train and study, by putting those skills into practice, you can sharpen, hone and develop them for your betterment and enjoyment.
Feeling of contribution	If you're working on a project, or providing customer service, or helping with the production of a product or service, it can give you a rewarding sense of contribution.
Achievement	If you set out to reach a certain level or progress up through the ranks, you can get a sense of achievement and encouragement.
Enjoyment	If you can find or create a position that enables you to spend all (or most of) your time working on something that you love, you can enjoy every moment that you work.
Flexibility	Over time, your needs, desires, interests and circumstances change. You can weave these changes into your career through actions, opportunities, research and courage.

Peace of mind	If you're in a position that provides you with financial security, you can budget and plan with as much reliability as your contract allows.
Pride and inspiration	As other people look to you for advice and inspiration, you can guide them wisely and encourage them with stories, taken from experience, of how things can be done.
Prestige	If you have achieved a significant amount in your life, you may be thought highly of and invited to share your story in different media, formal or informal.
Constant learning curve	As technology evolves, new concepts become normal protocols, and you're constantly kept in the loop about current market conditions.
Personal development	You can decide that your career is a journey of personal, emotional, psychological and intellectual development through courses, experience, assignments, situations, scenarios, negotiations and discussions.
Personal goals	You might find that your career spills into other areas of your life – perhaps you get to travel a lot, which could become a hobby of yours. You might meet people who become great friends. You might get involved in a charity project at work, which might have always been your ambition.

Now you can look at your job or your business and decide which costs and which benefits are relevant to your situation – you can mix and match the different entries in the tables above to suit your own case.

Assessing your life in these terms can throw up some surprising conclusions. I was speaking at an event and a woman called Tracy, whom I had met years before at a networking meeting, came up to me afterwards. Like many others, her business had been hurt by the recession and she wasn't doing as well as before. In a former life, she had worked in financial services in Dublin. Just when she was worried that her business might not bear the stress of the recession, the company she used to work for offered her a job in her old department. She lived about ninety minutes away and said the money they were offering was fantastic.

At first, this seemed like a dream come true. No more worrying about whether the phone would ring. She would have financial security, a defined role and much more structure in her life. Admittedly, it would involve a lot of time during the week, but she would have quality time at the weekends, and, without the pressure of a slowing business and less money coming in, life would be better for everybody all round.

She decided to sit down with the figures before she went back to her old job. In addition, she took out a sheet of paper and lined up the pros and cons. She was utterly shocked at what materialized on the sheet of paper in front of her.

First, when she counted the cost of childcare, petrol and tax, the shine came off her initial feelings about her high salary. Next, she thought about the length of her working day and realized she would either have to become an 'alarm-clock hero' or move to Dublin four nights a week. The latter was out of the question, so she would have to be on the road by 6.30 a.m. and wouldn't be home until 7 p.m.

She put down her paper to think for a couple of days. At the moment, it was easy, for example, to make a split-second decision to go to the park with her kids: yes, it would involve driving there and back, but the sun was shining, the kids wanted to play ball, and she didn't need to ask anybody for permission. She could catch up on work later, when they were in bed. She began to think about how she would manage if she took the job and one of them needed to go to the doctor. She thought long and hard about how she felt about the business she had built up by then: her brand, her customers, her efforts. Would she be able to keep the business running on the side when she had the new job? Not a chance. She had to get some sleep, after all.

In the end, although it tore her apart to do it, she turned down the job. Yes, she would have earned more money with the role in Dublin, but the non-monetary costs were immense at that stage of her life. However, the realizations didn't stop there. The role she had chosen at that point in her life was really in the home, bringing up her kids, and, by her own admission, the reason she had started a business was to contribute to the family budget. Would this always remain the case? Who knew? As the children got older, she might or might not dedicate more time to her enterprise. However, for now, she would stop worrying and focus on what was important to her, her home and family – and then do what she could with her business in the time that was left.

I'm sure you won't be surprised to hear that her business actually picked up a little when she started to think about it as an addition to her life rather than as a source of stress. She automatically thought about all of the small and big things she could achieve within it, rather than looking back at Celtic Tiger accounts and wondering how she was going to return to that sort of profitability. This experience forced her to really think about her objectives. She realized she was focusing on the goalposts of the past rather than on the playing pitch of today.

14

Profit – it's not just about the money . . .

In the last chapter we looked at how you could evaluate the costs and benefits of going to work, using a woman's decision whether or not to close her business and go back to paid employment as an example. I really want to drive home how crucial it is to look at your life choices in this way, so I'm going to continue with some further cases.

Let's take the example of a woman who earns €50,000 in her job and has two children: one is in a crèche, the other in primary school. She lives just outside Dublin but works in Dublin. She sits down one day to work out her P&L and finds the following results. These are, respectively, her benefits (on the left) and her costs on a weekly basis.

Benefits			Costs		
		Revenue per week			Expenditure per week
Salary and bonus	48 working weeks	€1,041.67	Petrol	€60 per week	€60
Overtime	€100 per week	€100	Lunches	€50 per week	€50
Health insurance	€100 per week	€100	Childcare	€1,000 per month	€250
			Coffee	€20 per week	€20
			Work clothes	€400 per month	€100
			Appearance	€200 per month	€50
			Work nights out	€200 per month	€50
			Presents	€80 per month	€20
			Running late	Three breakfasts	€24
			Tax	50% of salary and overtime	€570.83
Total of weekly benefits		€1,241.67	*Total of weekly expenses*		€1,194.83
Total profit					€46.84

So her weekly earnings are €1,241.67, and her weekly expenses are €1,194.83. This means that her actual profit, the balance of her earnings minus her expenses, is €46.84 per week. However, she also needs to take into account the non-monetary effects that her work has on her life as well as the opportunity costs.

Scenario A

She absolutely loves her job and has always been a career woman. She adores her kids and wants to be an inspiring mum for them along the way by boosting her job prospects, income and opportunities. She wants to keep up with technology, continue to sharpen her skills and to expand her network. She treasures the time that she has with the children three evenings a week and always makes sure that weekend time is family time. However, she knows that her stress levels would rocket and her happiness collapse if she were to stay home with them all day – she's afraid her brain would turn to mush. On the other hand, guilt pierces her heart every day as she drops her kids off and she is appalled that she hasn't even €50 per week to show for it. As a result, she tries to look objectively at her job and writes a list of pros and cons to her working week.

Pros

- She loves working with the people at her company, eight hours a day. They are a very focused, forward-looking group but well able to have a bit of craic throughout the day.
- She worked diligently to get her professional exams and those hard-earned letters after her name. She doesn't want to let those skills get rusty now.
- She thoroughly enjoys her role at the company, feels that she contributes immensely to the team and is constantly striving forward and achieving. She has her eye keenly on her manager's position, as she has heard rumours that he is considering leaving to work for a competitor, and she would absolutely love to go for that promotion.
- She loves the title on her business card . . . and she loves telling others about it too. Even if she doesn't say so herself . . . although she should.

Cons

- Her job is fast-paced and high-powered. While she loves that, it also means that she brings home a lot of mental baggage that can permeate the weekend and even affect her sleep. She can be irritable and cranky when her youngest makes a mess of the floor or things just don't happen right, though her kids and husband are blameless in this. This isn't the type of mother she intended to be.
- She feels that she is always watching her back. She's afraid to talk about school plays, being kept awake by colic or the excitement that a child can bring, in case her boss might overlook her for the promotion because he thinks she's getting broody. She feels that she can't always be herself, that she's often trying to emulate the corporate man.
- She knows her husband would be happier all round if she stayed at home with the kids, and this feeling edges its way into many arguments.
- She has her day, month and year planned to within an inch of its life without any real time for her personally.

Outcome

She isn't going to give up work – she loves it too much and it's part of her identity. As a result, she's going to stick with the job. However, she needs to address the fact that so little of her top-line salary figure is actually reaching the household purse. In addition, there was a series of pretty serious negatives that she listed above and we need to take a look at those also.

Benefits			Costs		
		Revenue per week			Expenditure per week
Salary and bonus	48 working weeks	€1,041.67	Petrol	€60 per week	€60
			Public transport		−€30
Overtime	€100 per week	€100	Lunches	€50 per week	€50
Health insurance	€100 per week	€100	Childcare	€1,000 per month	€250
Additional revenue from promotion		€500	*Childcare savings*		−€150
			Coffee	€20 per week	€20
			Break the habit and drink tea at work		−€16
			Work clothes	€400 per month	€100
			Appearance	€200 per month	€50
			Work nights out	€200 per month	€50
			Presents	€80 per month	€20
			Running late	Three breakfasts	€24
			Cut this out – it's a silly waste of money		−€24
			Tax	50% of salary and overtime	€820.83
			Claim all tax refunds and benefits		−€100
Total of weekly benefits		€1,741.67	*Total of weekly expenses*		€1,124.83
Total profit					€616.84

By implementing a small number of changes, she increases her profit *thirteen*-fold. As we spoke about in an earlier chapter, she repairs the holes in her expenditure column before filling up on the revenue column. She cuts her financial costs in the following ways:

- By simply taking public transport from just outside the city, she can cut her petrol bill in half, because she wastes a lot of petrol doing short journeys and sitting in traffic.
- Her sister-in-law mentioned to her that she was interested in minding some children while her own two kids were still toddlers. Since she wouldn't be charged the premium rate of a crèche and her husband could pick up the children early on a Friday, they could cut their childcare bill by €150 per week.
- She realizes that her coffee spend is just a comfort thing. She actually doesn't need to drink it and the process of getting a cup of tea at work every day for free would actually bring about the same feelings. However, she leaves room for that one treat on a Friday! This isn't being tight, it's just changing something tiny which has zero impact on her life and a positive impact on her pocket.
- The running-late budget is silly and there is no need for such waste. Better planning would sort that out and fast.
- Because she was earning so much, she really didn't think she needed to be poring over her tax documents trying to save a couple of euros. However, when she actually adds up all the tax benefits that she could be earning, it turns out to be quite significant.

Dealing with the negatives in her situation

- The stress of her job, and its impact on her home and family life, isn't a financial issue but a time-management one. She needs to find ways to become more efficient at work, so that she can develop boundaries that prevent her working life from oozing into every other area of her existence. She also needs to practise mindfulness techniques, which will make her focus only on the here and now; these will ensure that when she's participating in family life, she is there in both her body and mind. She needs to be more balanced between the high-powered career woman and the home-making wife and mother. They don't have to be separate but they do have to co-exist in harmony.

~ She needs to have a frank conversation with management regarding her own career path and to learn to be more confident in herself. If the company wanted another corporate man in the boardroom, they would have hired one. She is there by virtue of her own personal skills, abilities, insights and perspectives. If she can't be herself for eight, ten, twelve hours of the day, then who is she deceiving? She needs to call a meeting with the decision-makers in the company and spell out exactly what she wants to do and the realities of the situation. She absolutely wants and feels she deserves this upcoming promotion. She needs to put forward the rationale that she has a specific and very valuable skillset, a strong record and an immense amount of creativity, innovation, perseverance and vision to offer. She is well able to rise to the new challenge. She needs to be proactive about the situation, rather than reactive.

~ She needs to sit down with her husband and speak to him about how they are going to raise their children as a family. They are both parents and partners. As in any relationship, they need to compromise. If this feeling edges its way into arguments, she needs to draw it out and deal with it out in the open. If he's feeling that she doesn't spend enough time at home with the kids or that she's just cranky when she is there, she needs to think about this. As already mentioned in the first point in this list, she should try to become more efficient at work so that she can impose boundaries, and she should try to develop mindfulness techniques, to ensure focus when she's at home. On the other hand, she must talk to her husband about how he is participating in family life. Is there a way that he could contribute more time or more of himself, so that everybody is happier all round? (Now you can see why there was a whole chapter devoted to communication!)

~ If she is a career woman, a mother, a wife, a sister, a daughter and a friend who doesn't devote any time to herself, she won't have sufficient personal nourishment to be able to play all of her roles successfully. She may not think that she has the time, but, if she was called into an emergency meeting at lunchtime to deal with a crisis situation, unimportant things would fall by the wayside. If she forgot her phone before flying to another country for a weekend, highly important things would find a way to get to her and all the rest would wait. If she stayed in a hotel for a week without Wi-Fi, all her emails would still be there for her when she got back. She must schedule some time out for herself, as if she were attending an important meeting, a doctor's appointment or a big family party – something that you would consider important enough not to miss. Because that's exactly what 'me-time' is.

Scenario B

In this case, the woman really doesn't enjoy her job and would love to be at home with her children. However, she doesn't think this is possible, as without the money coming into the household purse, the family's finances will come under pressure. She examines what life would be like without her full-time job.

Benefits			Costs		
		Revenue per week			Expenditure per week
Salary and bonus	48 working weeks	€1,041.67	Petrol	€60 per week	€60
			No more petrol for work		*−€60*
			Petrol during leisure time		*€30*
Overtime	€100 per week	€100	Lunches	€50 per week	€50
			No more lunches for work		*−€50*
Health insurance	€100 per week	€100	Childcare	€1,000 per month	€250
			No more childcare		*−€250*
Leave job		*−€1,241.67*			
Social welfare		*€200*	Coffee	€20 per week	€20
			No more work coffee		*−€20*
			Additional coffee morning		*€20*
			Work garments	€400 per month	€100
			No more work clothes – personal clothes spend only		*−€50*
			Appearance	€200 per month	€50
			Work nights out	€200 per month	€50
			No more work nights out		*−€50*

Benefits		Revenue per week	Costs		Expenditure per week
			Presents	€80 per month	€20
			No more presents		*−€20*
			Running late	Three breakfasts	€24
			No more running late		*−€24*
			Tax	50% of salary and overtime	€570.83
			No more tax		*−€570.83*
Total of weekly benefits		€200	*Total of weekly expenses*		€150
Total profit					€50

Although now set against a context of just €200 in revenue, not only can she generate a profit from leaving her job, but she gains €3.16 per week. Therefore, her monetary fears didn't have any basis *whatsoever*. However, there are a number of positives and negatives that she also needs to consider.

Pros

∽ More family time.
∽ No more time spent at a job that she doesn't enjoy.
∽ Less stress from commuting, spending time at work and a more satisfied sense of self.
∽ Much more control over time.
∽ More time to spend on homework with the eldest.

- More social time with family and friends and hence her baby will still have lots of interactions with people.
- She has been feeling a lack of achievement and contribution of late. Instead of staying at work to address that, she intends to find it in her own home, where it will come about naturally. She feels that her personal development will still evolve, only on another path, as she immerses herself in motherhood. If anything, it was becoming stilted in her old job and she is excited by this new challenge.
- She'll no longer feel guilty about dropping the children off at the childminder's on her way to work.

Cons

- Should they pay for private health insurance out of their own pocket now? If so, this should be added to the explicit financial cost of giving up her job.
- She is a professional woman and if she leaves the workforce for a number of years, it may be difficult for her to find a job and then reintegrate at the level to which she's become accustomed.
- The household is losing an entire pillar of income, and if there were a threat to her husband's job, they might find it difficult to meet mortgage payments and other financial commitments.
- She would now be contributing only a tiny amount to the household, and she doesn't want to be entirely dependent on her husband.

Outcome

She decides that, given that there are more positives than negatives associated with giving up work, and that the positives have a good deal of weight attached to them, she would be better off handing in her notice. She addresses each negative in the following way.

- They can always get private health insurance and call competing companies to see if there is a better deal on offer.

- She can deal with getting back to work when the time comes. However, she can also keep an eye out for some CPD (Continuous Professional Development) events going on in her industry that she can attend periodically or sign up for an evening course specializing in one area of her sector. She can read newspapers and magazines and join LinkedIn Groups related to her field. She can skim through job advertisements to see how the requirements of positions evolve. As soon as the time comes for her to go back to work, there will be many resources available to her.

- Her husband is in a relatively secure job, and they can cross the bridge of any threat to his job when they come to it. She could encourage her husband to speak with the decision-makers and influencers in his own company to ascertain if there is any uncertainty regarding his job security. In addition, perhaps there might be some opportunities on the horizon for him, which could improve their financial situation.

- Finally, regarding the dependence issue, after doing the exercise above, she has come to realize she has been relying on him all along, and this is simply an issue that has to be discussed and ironed out between them. First, she needs to be comfortable in the knowledge that she is a very worthy, valuable 'worker' in the home. If they had to pay for a crèche, a chef, a psychologist, a driver, cleaning services, etc., – that is, everything that she does in the course of a day – her husband would be working round the clock. Next, she needs to discuss this with her husband, and they both must acknowledge the fact that they are reliant on each other. He needs her work as much as she needs his.

Scenario C

In this case, there is vague dread and a feeling of boredom; for a long time this woman has been thinking about changing jobs or starting her own business. She performs this exercise with a view to making a decision about starting her own business or looking for a more prestigious job. The numbers are easy to work out for this woman. She just needs to figure out if she can set up a business that would cover her expenses and give her more than the profit she is getting currently from her job. In order to answer this question, she needs to break it down into steps.

Step 1. What are her new expenses? If she is working from home, there are a lot of things that she won't need to spend on, and as a result we can cut these out. Also, because she is starting in business and will probably have a number of expenses to begin with, as well as a relatively low turnover in her first year, she won't have to pay any income tax. She won't need childcare any more, etc.

Costs

		Expenditure per week
Petrol	€60 per week	€60
Working from home – no more petrol		− €60
Lunches	€10 per day	€50
Working from home – sandwiches at lunch		− €30
Childcare	€1,000 per month	€250

No childcare payments		− €250
Coffee	€4 per day	€20
Coffee at home		− €15
Work clothes	€400 per month	€100
Personal clothes spend only		− €50
Appearance	€200 per month	€50
Reduced appearance spend		− €25
Work nights out	€200 per month	€50
No more work nights out		− €50
Presents	€80 per month	€20
No more presents		− €20
Running late	Three breakfasts	€24
No more running late		− €24
Tax	50% of salary and overtime	€570.83
Zero tax payment for first year		− €570.83
Higher phone bill		€50
Own stationery		€4
Interest payment	€1,000 *over 52 weeks* x 1.04%	€20
Total of weekly expenses		€174

Each of these line items is self-explanatory, apart from the 'interest payment'. We will return to that in Step 4.

Step 2. Add up her new expenses total as well as the profit from the base case in Scenario A (i.e., €46.84). You get €220.84.

Revenue hurdle	Amount
Total expenses	€174
Profit at base case	€46.84
Weekly hurdle	€220.84
Annual hurdle (weekly × 52)	€11,483.68

If her total weekly expenses are €174 and she can cover those and earn €46.84, it will make absolutely zero difference to the household budget on a day-to-day basis if she leaves her job and sets up her own business. As a result, she has to be confident that she can make €11,483.68 per year before taking this leap.

Step 3. Does she envisage that she could turnover this amount of money? She is a professional and she knows five people whom she could call right now and possibly get business worth €1,500 from three of them, which she could complete within two months. This would give her a start and some breathing room to find her next clients.

Step 4. In order to set up the business, what things would she need and how much would they cost in total? Does the family have this amount of money in savings and can they be spared? The very basic things that you need to do when starting a business are: register the company, get a website and print some business cards. She would be well advised to do a 'Start your own business' course, which would include learning how to design a basic website. Also, she will need some miscellaneous bits and pieces to get started. She would need approximately €1,000 and some good competitive service providers to do this.

Initial Investment	Amount
Register the business	€100
Host and secure a web domain	€150
Website development	€250
'Start your own business' course	€100
Business cards	€300
Miscellaneous	€100
Total	**€1,000**

The family does have this money, but this was previously earmarked as part of a budget to take the kids to Disneyworld next year. She doesn't want to compromise on that, so the newborn company borrows this money from the household at a rate of 1.04% – the same rate that they would have got if they had put it into the bank. This is the interest payment referred to earlier.

Pros

- This would be so exciting. It's something that she has always wanted and now she really thinks that she can do it. It would be a lifelong ambition that she could achieve within days.
- She has used a range of skills in her life, but now she would need to build new or call on existing skills in sales, marketing, management, accounts, communication, etc. This would be a fresh challenge for her.
- She could stay at home with the kids and be a lifestyle entrepreneur, combining this dream of hers with being at home every evening to hear their stories as they come in from school.
- She could build up the business so that eventually she would have others working for her or use technology to expand. She would be setting herself and her family up for the future.

∽ This would be a major achievement for her and she would love to be able to tell her children in years to come that she always followed her dream . . . and made it work.

∽ If the kids are sick, she can be there. If they want to take a holiday, she can work around it. If her sister offers to baby-sit, she can catch up on things. The lack of fixed times and dates gives her freedom to take and to create all the opportunities around her.

Cons

∽ If she gives up work and stays at home with the kids, it's unlikely that she'll be able to get any work done during the day – which means she can work only when they've gone to bed in the evening or when they're with her husband or a friend. As a result, her time with her husband will be cut down and also the quality of that time may be reduced.

∽ The safety net of the reliable figure that tops up her bank account on the 28th of every month will be gone. While she does feel that she can surmount her revenue hurdle, she still doesn't have any guarantees.

∽ If she sets up her company, at the time of writing, she signs away any access to social welfare in the form of Jobseeker's Benefit or Allowance.

∽ Her day-to-day social life will now become just her immediate family; she'll spend a significant part of the day with a pre-school toddler. If she really liked the people that she worked with and enjoyed the camaraderie at work, this will have an impact.

∽ At the office, she has a routine. She gets up at a certain time, is at work for a certain time and then leaves at a certain time, without needing to worry as soon as she sits in the car to drive home. This way of life will dissolve into one day flowing into the next without boundaries or deadlines, unless she has the discipline to enforce them.

Outcome

She decides to go for it because the numbers stack up and the positives far outweigh the negatives. Also, it's important to note that only €46.84 per week is holding her back from her dream: when you strip away all that she spends from what she earns, €46.84 is all that's left.

However, each of the negatives is important and needs to be treated accordingly.

- She needs to sit down and speak with her husband, in order to come to some sort of arrangement about how they are going to take time out for each other in their new regime. They decide that, each Friday night, they are going to have a board meeting at home with a bottle of wine and a take-away. Also, they make it an iron rule that Sundays are to be a family day and nobody's work is going to get in the way of that. They are also going to go away every six weeks for a weekend on their own. They can do this by saving the €50 each week that she used to spend on work nights out. Their relationship is the bedrock of their family, and they are not going to let it be compromised.
- She doesn't have any guarantees that she can surmount the aforementioned revenue hurdle; however, it is guaranteed that she won't succeed if she doesn't try. She has got perseverance, will and tenacity, and she is going to put all her efforts into making this work.
- Willingly signing up for zero welfare benefits if this endeavour goes wrong is worrying. However, she can't let fear hold her back. Instead, she needs to move forward and think about how much better off they'll all be if this business works.
- While her day-to-day social life will now become just her immediate family, by the very nature of business she is going to be communicating with a whole new set of people. Also, because she'll be at home with the kids and working during the evenings, she can meet her friends for coffee, join

a mother-and-toddler group and visit more people than when she was restricted to a nine-to-five schedule at work. She is going to put a series of things in place so that she can keep to her schedule. Her husband is going to help with the housework and cooking. They are going to split the tasks between them, and she is setting a personal goal of having all her jobs done before he gets home, so that family time is exactly that. She's going to ask her sister to act as an accountability partner; each week she'll be sending her an email containing her aims and objectives for the new week as well as her performance from last week. She knows that she has only four hours every night to do everything, but, since her two kids came along, she has learned very quickly how to pack it all in. There is nothing stopping her here; she just needs to focus.

Maybe you find yourself nodding at this last scenario; maybe you've always wanted to start your own business, but until now you've brushed aside the idea, thinking that you couldn't afford to lose your stable income. And now this whole P&L thing sounds just like what you needed to find out whether you could make a go of it or whether you'd be better off staying in your job. As you know I have a strong bias in favour of business, being a business owner myself, so of course I would encourage you to go for it.

A couple of years ago, I couldn't have imagined international contracts. I couldn't have imagined writing sales proposals. I didn't even think that I would ever have a business, never mind that I would one day be making a distinction between my 'domestic' and my 'international operations'. Sometimes my days are stressful – I think of one when a delayed flight out of Dublin meant that I missed a connection between Amsterdam and Helsinki, and when I eventually turned up in Helsinki, the hotel told me they had no room reserved for me – but I'm the sort to get a kick out of overcoming those problems, and, in the end, with the aid of technology, I still got plenty of work done. In my opinion, an actual 'bad' day would be one where I looked at the clock every five minutes waiting for the day to pass. I've been there and found it an awful waste.

If you're unhappy in your job or even just holding back from taking the leap, your salary is the cost of your dreams. I walked away from a job that was paying me a salary, in which I had been happy for many years. However, it was a job and not my own business. The brand that I was building up wasn't mine. I had contributed towards it, but it wasn't authentically me. I remember sitting at the traffic lights outside King's Inn and getting the feeling that I couldn't ignore what was in my head. I had to do it, even though it scared the hell out of me. That feeling was 'Could I actually make enough money to scrape by?' and then 'Could I make more than that?' The answers were two very nervous yeses. I knew from that moment onwards, every day or every hour that I didn't jump meant I was holding back. That was the exact moment when my fantasy became a possibility.

After I made the leap, I didn't hurl myself out of bed the next morning to the sound of a cash register going 'ka-ching'. I did get going, but there was no sign of all the money I thought that I was going to make. As for the non-monetary benefits, they stuck their heads in the door here and there, but that's all. In fact, I have to admit that, on more than one occasion, I really did compare the life I had chosen against the security of the one past. Also, hard as I thought I'd worked in my salaried job, I found myself working even harder in my own business, and it edged its way into all my waking and sleeping hours. I again stood back and calculated that, on a per hour basis, I was working a lot more and making a lot less than I had been in my old job. What the hell was I doing? At that stage, I had two choices:

- Find another job.
- Do things differently.

However, this was like asking myself:

- Should I take a step backwards?
- Or take a step forwards?

Of course, I chose the second. Again and again and again and again. There have been many times since I started the company when I questioned where I was going, and wondered whether I was moving forward at all. But I learned that these moments were either passing weaknesses or signals indicating that some sort of change was needed in my business. So I learned to weather them or to harness them.

Have I ever been tempted to throw in the towel? Yes, many times, but it never lasts very long, and, thus far, I have always chosen just to move forward instead. Quite simply, every day, I enjoy those monetary and non-monetary benefits that I talked about previously. Happily, they're always getting bigger and better. The learning curve that comes from stepping outside your comfort zone is a big benefit in itself.

Now, it's time for you to take a look at your sources of revenue and to identify if you are making a profit or a loss. Go to the P&L Excel spreadsheet blueprint, which you can download from www.savvy-womenonline.com, and fill it in for the financial side of the decision. If the final figure in red is on the right, you are making a profit (since the revenue is greater than the expenditure). If the final figure in red is on the left, you are making a loss.

You also need to take a look at the non-monetary costs and benefits, as it's crucial to be aware of them. You can't measure them with a ruler, calculator or an Excel spreadsheet; however, if you are honest with yourself, your instincts will tell you how important they are. Use the grids below to think about the impact of choosing one option over another. If you want to take stock of your life as it is, compare what you are doing now (i.e., being employed, staying at home with the kids, running your own business, studying full time, travelling, etc.) to doing the complete opposite.

(Note. Some of this may not have any relevance at all, so please feel free to strike things out, but only after you know for certain that they genuinely won't form part of your decision-making process, rather than because you're hiding from them.)

Cost	*Within each set of parentheses, cross out the words that don't intuitively feel right for you . . .*
Stress	This option will (reduce/increase) my (and my family's) stress levels (a little/significantly/a lot) to the point where things will change dramatically.
Worry	This option will (reduce/increase) my (and my family's) worry levels (a little/significantly/a lot) to the point where things will change dramatically.
Not enough of me left	This option will (reduce/increase) the quality of the time I spend with the important people in my life (a little/significantly/a lot) to the point where things will change dramatically.
Fear	This option will (reduce/increase) the amount of fear that I feel (a little/significantly/a lot) to the point where things will change dramatically.
Opportunity cost	The impact of not taking this option is (a little/significant/a lot) to the point where things will change dramatically (better/worse).

Family and social life	This option will enable me to go to (a few/significantly/a lot) (more/fewer) family functions and social events – from doing homework with the kids, to the periodic coffee with my cousins, to family celebrations, to a friend's wedding in a foreign country – to the point where things will change dramatically.
Arguments with those around you	This option will lead to (a few/significantly/a lot) (more/fewer) arguments with those that I love to the point where things will change dramatically.
Outside influences on your time	This option will lead to (a few/significantly/a lot) (more/fewer) outside influences making the decisions for me and my family – from being on call, to needing a flexible babysitter, to choosing holiday time off, to somebody else choosing when I can spend time in my own home with the family – to the point where things will change dramatically.
Change your circumstances	This option will lead to (a few/significantly/a lot) (more/fewer) lifestyle changes for me and my family to the point where things will change dramatically.
Guilt	This option will lead to (a little/significantly/a lot) (more/less) guilt to the point where things will change dramatically.

I list below the non-monetary benefits:

Benefit	Within each set of parentheses, cross out the words that don't intuitively feel right for you . . .
Socializing	This option will lead to (a little/significantly/a lot) (more/less) social interaction with people to the point where things will change dramatically.
Use of skills	This option will lead to (a little/significantly/a lot) (more/less) use of my skills on a periodic basis to the point where things will change dramatically.
Feeling of contribution	This option will lead to my feeling (a little/significantly/a lot) (more/less) that I'm contributing to something that is important to me to the point where things will change dramatically.
Achievement	This option will lead to (a little/significantly/a lot) (more/less) of a feeling of meaningful achievement in my life to the point where things will change dramatically.
Enjoyment	This option will lead to my feeling (a little/significantly/a lot) (more/less) enjoyment in the time I'll spend taking this decision rather than what I'm doing now to the point where things will change dramatically.

Flexibility	With reference to my values, I can be (a little/significantly/a lot) (more/less) flexible with this option to the point where things will change dramatically.
Peace of mind	I will feel (a little/significantly/a lot) (more/less) secure, financially and otherwise, with this option to the point where things will change dramatically.
Pride and inspiration	I will have (a little/significantly/a lot) (more/less) pride in myself and inspiration if I choose this option to the point where things will change dramatically.
Prestige	I will have (a little/significantly/a lot) (more/less) prestige and social standing if I choose this option to the point where things will change dramatically.
Constant learning curve	I will learn (a little/significantly/a lot) (more/less) if I choose this option to the point where things will change dramatically.
Personal development	I will grow (a little/significantly/a lot) (more/less) intellectually, personally and emotionally if I choose this option to the point where things will change dramatically.
Personal goals	This option is something that I (want/don't want) to do (a little/significantly/a lot) to the point where things will change dramatically for myself and my family.

Now you need to rank each of the things in this grid in order of importance. For example, having the social life of work may override the stress of traffic in the morning. Prestige might mean nothing at all to you in comparison with being able to attend more family events. You might simply want to do an MBA for yourself and your kids are old enough now to have 'less of you'. There is no right or wrong – a piece of paper won't judge you. Let your own inner thoughts dictate and listen to the messages of your answers.

Finally, compare the non-monetary costs against the hard numbers of the spreadsheet, and, if you have done this exercise seriously and sincerely, you should be much clearer about any financial decision that you are faced with.

Challenge your beliefs about making money

15

Can you handle more money?

We have now been through a lot of exercises together. You've established solid foundations for your new financial life: you've created a budget, cut costs and learned to communicate about money. In the last two chapters you learned how to do a profit-and-loss exercise, without forgetting to factor non-monetary costs into your financial decisions.

Now comes the litmus test. At the beginning of the book I asked you to take your financial temperature, and I explained how everyone has a kind of financial thermostat, a certain set-point they always come back to. But if your personal set-point is low, how can you handle more money? If you experience an unexpected windfall, you might feel a kind of low dread or even outright panic, because your bank account is showing a financial temperature that is 'too hot' for you. So what do you do? You might go on a shopping spree to get back to your set-point, to get back to a place where things are comfortable.

You don't believe me? I'm certain you think, 'Oh, but sure isn't it normal to enjoy money? Money is not there to be hoarded, it's not a good unto itself, it comes into my life to be used. And, in the case of money, used means spent.' Therein lies the rub: when it comes to money, 'used well' does not necessarily mean 'spent' (or 'invested', or 'saved', for that matter; what you can best do with money depends on what plans you have). But be aware that, by spending excess money, you are, in fact, making sure you get back to comfortable territory. In fact, the simple phrase 'excess money' gives it away: it's only an excess compared to a lower figure that you take as a yardstick, as a norm. And this subconscious norm prevents you from being able to handle more money comfortably.

However, the whole point of this journey and becoming

financially literate is about being able to make more money. I'm sure as you went through the exercises in the previous chapters, the thought must have struck you more than once: 'Wouldn't it be so much easier to fit everything into my budget if only I had more money?' And that is the problem. If you had more money, it wouldn't necessarily be easier, since your financial thermostat might prevent you from increasing your financial temperature. More money will help you only if you can handle it – if the amount of money you have matches your financial thermostat.

But just how do you reset your financial thermostat? Let me share a personal story that was a game-changer for me. I was at a workshop in Limerick several years ago. The guest was an entrepreneur who took the stage by storm. He was very energetic and excited to share his insights. He picked a random person out of the audience and asked him a very personal, sensitive question 'How much do you want to turnover next year?'

The reason that I say it's personal and sensitive is because business people don't like to speak publicly about how much they've made in a year after they've done it, let alone announce to an audience beforehand how much they want to make. Now that you know how to communicate about money and how to build accountability in your goal-setting, you're in a position to recognize what's holding us back: the fear we mightn't actually do it and somebody might take us to task for it.

However, this person was asked directly in front of an audience of a hundred people, and he gave his number. The speaker was inspiring and motivating, so everybody was feeling good about life, their business and the world at this point. 'Right,' the speaker said. 'I'm going to ask the rest of you to answer the same question silently. What is your number?'

I thought, if I could bring in €60,000, that would really stretch me and I would be delighted with myself.[1] The speaker then invited us

---

1. As I write this, my figure has increased several times, as I have repeated this exercise over the years.

to think of ways to do it. We had five minutes to come up with a set of financial strategies – it was simply a mathematical exercise, so there wasn't any time for emotion or hemming and hawing here, as the clock was ticking. I took a blank sheet of paper and started making some calculations:

€60,000 ÷ 52 weeks = €1,154 per week

How am I ever going to make €1,154 per week?

I told the doubting voice in my head to keep quiet as I needed to work this out in time for the deadline.

€1,154 ÷ 6 days = €193 per day.

At the time, I was charging €60 for an appointment (which could take several hours) and could do about two per day, because I often had to travel significant distances between them. At this rate, even if I worked seven days per week, every week of the year, I couldn't make my target. I had only three minutes left to figure it out. Over the next two minutes, I played around with all the variables in this equation:

Revenue per working week =

price per appointment ×

number of appointments per day ×

number of days in the working week

I asked myself what I could add to my offering to increase the price. I projected what would happen if I raised the price to €100 per appointment, became more efficient with my time during the appointments and cut my travel time between meetings to the point where I could do three per day. I came up with the following:

€100 × 3 meetings per day × 6 days = €1,800

I couldn't believe it. I had come up with a way of making €1,800 per week. However, at that rate, I would soon have run myself ragged. During my last minute, I worked out how many days I would need to work, at €100 a meeting, if I wanted to make my €60,000 per year.

Daily revenue target: €300

Weekly target: €1,154

1,154 ÷ 300 = 3.84 days

So, imagine – if I worked four days and spent another day taking care of my administration, I could even take weekends off.

The speaker darted around the room asking people about the findings of the exercise. As soon as the pressure of the clock eased off, the self-doubting voice let rip. 'Oh, so your customers are just going to say yes to a 66% price rise, are they?' 'Where are you going to get three clients per day?' 'In your grand plan, you forgot Christmas week, St Patrick's week, the first week in January, etc., so you probably would need to work the fifth day of the week as well. On top of that, who on earth is going to want to have a mentoring meeting on a Friday evening?'

However, I started to think about it. If I spent an hour a day on the phone, I would actually be able to get three clients a day from time to time. Also, if I ran a search through my database to focus on people within one area, and if I organized several meetings with them on a single day, I could probably keep my distances close together. My voice started to strengthen against the self-doubt. Finally, given that I had rounded up my number of work days per week from 3.84 to 4, I quickly calculated how many actual weeks I would need to work:

€300 per day × 4 days per week = €1,200 per week

Yearly revenue target: €60,000

60,000 ÷ 1,200 = 50 weeks

It looked like I could plausibly make the €60,000 a year, if all these best-case scenarios went to plan. I was delighted with myself. I could visualize myself slotting an hour into my diary for all those sales calls I would make and ensuring Google Maps was open on my computer so that I could factor distance into the equation when setting up the meetings. I imagined myself squeezing my eyes shut as I told people that an appointment cost €100 and hoping they wouldn't hang up the phone.

The return to reality was somewhat brutal, I must say. Suddenly the speaker went back to the person in the audience whom he had originally asked. He looked him straight in the eye and said, 'If you wanted to make quadruple that dream amount next year, what would you do differently?' He then invited the rest of us to take fifteen minutes to answer that question.

What? Quadruple that amount? €60,000, times four?

My first reaction was, 'Oh for God's sake. I just used up all the ideas I had and was impressed with where I'd got to. If I worked around the clock, I couldn't hit almost a quarter of a million in revenue. This is ridiculous.' Clearly, the speaker knew what our reaction would be.

He pointed out the difference between what he had said and what we had all heard. 'I'm not asking you to come up with a way to make quadruple the amount; I asked you what things you would do differently, assuming that you were going to turn over quadruple that amount.' There were twelve minutes left. Before it could even open its mouth, I told my self-doubting voice to shut up while I tried to make some headway with this exercise.

I started to come up with some interesting ideas. It was like shining a flash lamp around areas of my brain that had previously been dark. I considered how many people I could see in a day if I booked a small meeting room in a hotel and invited them to come to me, instead of me going to them, thereby cutting out the time and expense of travelling in between meetings while preserving the individual tuition I was offering. I could ask the hotel what rate they would give me for the day and bargain them down by explaining that I would be bringing a number of new people to the hotel who might be buying coffee and food. In fact, I would be acting as a distributor for them. (My dad is from West Cork and I learned a lot about bargaining from him!) What if I offered to train people who didn't mind being trained with other people at the same time? I would offer them a discount – €80 per appointment, given that my fee had increased to €100. What if I were to print off some vouchers that I could give to each person who attended a mentoring session with me? They could pass the voucher on to a friend or family member. Let's say I offered €20 off a meeting, that would still net me €80, which would be higher than what I was currently charging and would result in new business.

Suddenly the speaker said, 'Time's up.' I was almost annoyed at him, as I was really getting into my stride.

He then said to us, 'Now, think about your previously "ambitious" goal . . .'

I was shocked to realize that my first goal of €60,000 felt almost tiny by comparison, and easy to reach.

Admittedly, I didn't get as far as €240,000 (i.e., quadrupling my ambitious €60,000). But I started thinking to myself, 'If I were to put some of those techniques into action, I could get to €60,000 much faster. And maybe, dare I think it, I could actually do better.'

The speaker completed the process by saying, 'Now, compare the techniques you just wrote down with the way you were doing things up to now.' Can you imagine how I felt? Two meetings a day? €60 per appointment? I was killing myself for nothing, driving hundreds of miles between meetings. This exercise shone a harsh light on my work process and exposed it for what it was: a terribly labour-intensive, highly inefficient, marginally profitable business that was all entirely of my own doing.

I would love to tell you that I hopped into the car and revolutionized my business from that moment onwards. I didn't. Life resumed. A voicemail needed to be answered, emails needed replies, meetings had to be held. That's what often happens, doesn't it? However, over the following weeks, months and years, I implemented each and every step I had dreamt up doing the exercise in that Limerick hotel room. I didn't do them all at once, but I took one step forward, then another and another and another. I'm proud to say that, after two years, I hit that target, and comfortably too.

Have you ever attended a spinning class? They're gruelling. I remember taking one such class while on holiday. The instructor was putting us through our paces and my lungs were slowly closing. He told us to increase our effort to 60%, 80%, then back down to 50%. He continued with this 'volatility' (as we would call it in stock-market terms), and then asked us to hit 120%, 130%. I was almost in too much pain to think, but I remember saying to myself, 'How can I give 120%? That guy should go back to school and learn some maths.' However, I did actually cycle faster than when he asked for 100% effort. Have you ever, ever said to yourself, 'I never knew that I could do that?' Hold that thought, because you're about to do it again.

This technique works not only for your financial thermostat, but for any comfort zone in your life that you would like to expand. I have used it over and over again. However, sometimes it can absolutely stump you. I remember sitting down a while ago with my boyfriend and, again, we started at a very high figure (corresponding to the first €60,000 step in the above example), but no matter what way we did the figures, they simply wouldn't add up; irrespective of the different processes or marketing ideas we came up with, we simply could not hit our target number, never mind stretch it. Also, we couldn't raise the price unless we offered a totally different product. That simple exercise coldly said to us, 'No. No way. You can't do it that way – you have to completely change what you're doing.'

Now, there is 'impossible' (i.e., increasing the number of hours in a day) and there is 'impossible' (running two marathons consecutively). The latter is one that seems utterly 'undoable', but I have heard of it being done, unlike the former. The two of us were sitting opposite each other at the Helix in DCU, near where our business is based, with defeated looks on our faces. I said, 'There is nothing for it, we'll have to completely revolutionize what we do.'

That's what I love about numbers – they are so informative. They never lie. I walked out of the Helix and didn't know how I felt. I had always been proud that, by working for myself, my income was never capped and I could always increase it. The numbers I had just looked at certainly felt like a cap and that hurt my ego. On the other hand, I felt excited. I had this feeling that we were moving on to the next stage of the business. After that exercise, I knew we neither could nor would continue as we were. I couldn't ignore the information on that sheet of paper. We were going to have to change completely.

Now I would like you to do this exercise for yourself. As you are reading a book and I assume you are alone, you don't have the energy of a live workshop to keep you going. So it might be more difficult to quiet the voice of self-doubt on your own. To help you, in this chapter and in the two that follow, I've listed some common misconceptions about making more money – the ones that are most likely to crop up in your mind as you think of ways to generate more revenue. And I have tried my best to craft a pep talk to go with each. So go ahead, and blast these doubts away.

Let's begin with two misconceptions that come up very often when people talk about making more money. First, if you are ambivalent about making more money, if you are somehow suspicious and find it vaguely distasteful or even morally questionable, you might find yourself thinking the following: ***Being in business is very tough – you have to be a heartless shark to succeed nowadays, or you'll be eaten alive by unscrupulous people.***

Would you buy from a 'heartless shark'? Of course not. You'd be put off by them. There is a phrase in marketing – 'people buy from people'. This doesn't refer to the actual transaction, but to the fact that people base their buying decisions on the relationship that develops with the seller.

Maybe you've had this experience: you're in a shop looking at some clothes that you don't really have any intention of buying. A very friendly sales assistant helps you find the right size, suggests some accessories or gives you undivided attention as you're trying on something. You leave with a bag of purchases, just because you had such a nice experience.

In fact, as you leave the shop, you wish that every clothes-buying experience could be like this: a competent, knowledgeable, really helpful person assists you to choose clothes that truly flatter you, clothes that you know you'll be wearing for years to come. It's like having a stylist or a personal shopper, without having to pay for the service. What good value for your money, and what a good investment.

Does that sales assistant sound like a heartless shark? She might be a skilled seller, but, more than that, she might have been sincerely trying to help you and to want you to be happy with what you bought. I had an investment club meeting in Mayo one day and

I was staying in a B&B in Claremorris. I decided to take a walk through the town and I walked into this lovely clothes shop. The prices were all quite high, but the woman behind the counter showed me some things on sale and seemed genuinely proud of her stock. She knew every piece of clothing in the shop, what it would go with, the type of person who typically bought it, absolutely everything. She really made me feel that during that half-hour in the shop she was my personal stylist. At the time, I had only recently graduated and I bought a skirt for €120 – which was more than I had spent on complete outfits before that – but it felt right, because of the experience. If she had pushed me into a changing room while throwing clothes at me, saying, 'That would be wonderful on you, dahling,' I would have been out the door in no time.

In fact, I like this analogy of the shop assistant, because I once read a true story that illustrates the exact opposite. It was about a shop assistant who wrote of her experience when a domineering, high-powered exec came to work in her shop. The new exec was selling stock like there was no tomorrow. No matter who walked in the door, they walked out with bags full of stuff. The shop assistant began genuinely to worry about her job. After all, the sales in the shop had rocketed because of this new person and she was completely overshadowed. This continued for a few weeks, until the manager arrived to witness this great transformation in action.

As the three of them were going through some administration, unbeknownst to them a long-standing customer appeared at the counter with more than a handful of clothes. The new woman turned around to her and said loudly and within perfect earshot of the manager, 'Oh, hello. Are you taking all these? That's great – green is SO in this spring.' The customer interrupted her, 'I'm not here to buy, but to return. My daughter was in here this week and said she felt pressured into buying these horrific things that don't suit her, or her pocket for that matter.' The manager recognized the customer and said, 'I'm terribly sorry about that. I'm sure it was a misunderstanding. Of course we'll give your daughter her money back.' As it happened, three more people brought back their unwanted purchases. The shop assistant regained her position and the shop regained its reputation.

Being a 'heartless shark' serves nothing and nobody, and is the surest way to see your dream of making more money evaporate. Somebody who cuts corners and swindles their clients is not building a sustainable business. You might be afraid that you'll have to fight for every inch of progress in a very competitive marketplace, and that in order to do so you'll have to adopt an 'eat or be eaten' mentality. This is not the case.

In a later chapter, I'm going to show you how to create a few more revenue streams, or increase existing revenue streams, to the tune of a few hundred euros to begin with, rising to a few thousand euros later on. We're not talking multibillion mergers and board members going at each other's throats.

Also, there's a misconception that it's somehow 'purer', more virtuous, not to be in business, not to have to go after money. Hum, no. Once again, you define this in your own terms. It is perfectly possible to be successful in business and to remain a kind, caring person. A successful business is one that provides real value to its customers: in other words, a business that fulfils a genuine need, and fulfils it excellently. You won't have to cut corners and swindle your partners and your customers unless you so decide.

Yes, you might have to stand your ground and defend your own interests, sometimes. You might have to learn to become more assertive and better at negotiating good outcomes for you and your business. I think this is a positive thing. But it doesn't have to be at the expense of the values you hold dear. I have never sold something I didn't wholeheartedly believe in. And I never will. I'm absolutely sure that, in order to be successful in business, you need to be likeable, trustworthy, honest and honourable. These are quite nice qualities to have.

Another misconception has to do with change in general:

But if I try and I succeed, I'll become a selfish, greedy bitch/bastard, just like all rich and successful people, and I could lose my family and friends.

How do you know your successes will turn you into a greedy bitch or bastard? How do you know your family will disown you if you pursue your dream of making more money? It might only be in your head.

First, let's examine why you are afraid of becoming 'greedy'. It might be your preconceptions speaking. Maybe you grew up with the idea that the only way to become rich and successful is by treading on other people to reach your aims, by using people as a means to an end, by lying to take advantage of others. Who put these ideas into your head? Most probably the people with whom you spent a lot of time. Maybe your family. Don't blame them. They might have passed on to you only what they themselves had grown up with. From a positive point of view, this belief system might have emphasized how important it is to take care of others around you, not to be selfish, to help out, to be honest and generous. All good things, but things that were perhaps expressed in a negative and unhelpful manner – in suspicion of people who were ambitious for themselves and their families. Maybe they even saw ambitious people behaving in ways that were selfish and inconsiderate.

When you feel held back by this belief system, it's because you know that the people around you still adhere to it. So you're afraid that, when you become more successful, these people will turn their backs on you. Again, you can't blame them. They might not be aware that they are sabotaging your efforts. Their belief system cannot make sense of your new behaviour, of your new successes, so your behaviour and your successes are identified as negative things. You have done something that they're not equipped to understand, because it's outside their comfort zone. So their reaction is negative, or even downright hostile. Maybe they're afraid. It's not that they want to put you down; it's just that you're doing things that they don't know how to handle.

Having said that, the chances are that those close to you will recognize that you are still you and won't tar you with a negative brush. Most likely, indeed, these thoughts are just your own doubts talking and trying to hold you back by threatening you with terrible, terrible things – that you'll end up like Scrooge, alone and the object of general revulsion and hatred. In fact, the people around you will quite probably be very happy with your progress, especially if they see that you are happier and more relaxed. Most likely, those around you really want the best for you and will cheer you on.

So, what do you do? First, let's deal with the people who really love you. Most likely they'll be very happy to help you however they can. And if you feel they're uncomfortable with your newfound resolve, you need to communicate with them about this issue. If you explain that you want the best – for both of you (or for all of you), they will be that much more receptive to your plans. Maybe they're afraid that you'll see them as 'not good enough for you' any more. Have you heard of the husband/wife encouraging their spouse to have second helpings simply because their other half was starting to look a little 'too good' on a diet and they felt threatened? Have you heard of the friend who encouraged their going-out-with buddy to put off travelling for another year simply because they would be left on their own? Have you heard of the parent encouraging their child to stay where they were, instead of looking for a better job elsewhere, because they were afraid that their child would move on and move up and they would be left alone? Maybe they just need to be reassured that you'll still love them, that this change is not the prelude to your walking into the kitchen one day and saying you're leaving them behind. They probably just need reassurance that you will still be you, and won't turn into Cruella de Vil. You need to think about how you can help them through it, bringing you both forward.

Having said that you need to communicate and share your vision, I know there are few things more off-putting than somebody who, just because they have embarked on a self-improvement plan, wants to impose it on everyone around them. Don't force things on your partner or your family. They'll come round in their own time, on their own terms. There are lots of ways you can share your new life with the people you care about, so that they see the benefits, rather than just an unwelcome change from how it used to be. In the case of the fitter spouse, they could encourage their partner to look at an alternative way of living so they can be healthier and happier together (but if the not-so-fit spouse doesn't want to take up spinning just yet, the fitter spouse should not force them). The prospective traveller needs to encourage the home-bird to look up flights and book a holiday to see them – or emphasize how the two of them will have that much more to talk about when the traveller is back from their adventures. The ambitious child needs to involve the parent in the planning of their move, while reassuring them that they will always have a place in their heart.

Second, let's deal with the people who will try to sabotage your efforts because they don't want you to succeed – most likely some of your friends, perhaps co-workers or distant relatives. Do you spot a pattern here? These people who you're afraid won't like you any more or who will be hurt by your success are putting their own desires first. They have certain ideas about the way you should live your life, and ideally – according to them, at least – you should live your life on their terms.

Why would someone 'disown' you because you became success-ful? Because it doesn't suit them. Now the choice is yours: will you stick to your goal and risk falling out with them? Or will you give in to their relentless teasing and sabotaging efforts? I can't answer that one for you. I know that my reaction would be the first one: I wouldn't be deterred. I can't stand the mentality of giving the cold shoulder to people who want to do better for themselves. Holding back those who are ambitious enough to want to improve their lot isn't helping anyone. And I really think that other people's reaction to your success is the best test of their real feelings for you: if they don't want you to succeed, they don't love you as much as they and you may have thought, do they?

Money is the root of all evil.

When you think of it, what could be so bad about having more money? Maybe you were constantly told as a child that 'Money is the root of all evil.' Or you think that, if you have more money, this means others will have less – that you are depriving other people either locally or in other parts of the world.

What evil? The evil that makes people sacrifice anything for money – time, love, family, respect? However, it doesn't seem that money is the problem here, but rather the lack of it. If people actually had a healthy attitude towards money, the pursuit of it wouldn't result in such negative consequences. The popular saying is incomplete. In the Bible it is part of a longer comment on greed that starts, 'For the love of money is the root of all kinds of evil . . .' In other words, the real problem is an unhealthy attraction to pieces of gold and silver, or numbers on a bank statement.

The attitude towards money that drives extreme greed is often born of a deep-seated fear that someone won't have enough. However, if you can learn to be self-sufficient, your vision won't be clouded in that way. You won't need to clutch so tightly at what you have, if you feel there is so much more to be made. The only things that dictate how much of it you get are your attitude and your efforts.

Look at all the wonderful things you can do with money. You can donate to people in need, buy things for people that need them, send your kids to the schools that you want, so that they can take care of themselves later on, take time to spend on the things you love rather than on the things you need to do to bring in money, visit the places you want to visit, eradicate the stress that comes from worrying about not having enough. You can take your family and friends on holiday and be in a position to help them in an emergency. You can pay higher taxes so that wealth is redistributed. You can buy things in shops, which keeps people in jobs. You can invest in innovative projects that wouldn't have seen the light of day had it not been for your financial contribution. The good uses of money are endless.

If I have money, somebody else doesn't.

Let me give you a brief economics lesson, in which I will refer to the 'Multiplier Effect', the 'Marginal Propensity to Consume' and the 'Velocity of Money'.

Say I earn €100 and I deposit €90 in the bank. The bank lends out €81 to Brian, who spends €72.90 on a new fridge. The hardware shop where the fridge was bought puts €65.61 into the bank. The bank lends out €59.04 to Catherine. She spends €53.14 on a car repayment and on and on and on we go. To see why I picked these particular figures, multiply each number by 0.9 to find the next one. This is because each person's 'Marginal Propensity to Consume' is 0.9. This is another way of saying that out of each €100 that comes somebody's way, that person will spend €90. Now, how much of an impact does this initial €100 that I earn have on the economy? This is such an established economic principle that there's a formula for it:

$$\text{Multiplier Effect} = 1/(1-\text{MPC}) = 1/(1-0.9) = 10$$

Therefore, for every €100 that I earn, €1,000 of extra money is created in the economy. As a result, the more you can earn and spend, the more people will actually benefit. Think of it: the bigger slice you take out of the pie, the bigger the pie actually becomes. This explains why, during the difficult times we are in, there is so much talk about 'consumer confidence' and getting people to spend money again. Imagine if I earned €100 and stuck it under the mattress (which can happen when people are very worried about losing their job or the economy at large) or didn't earn €100 at all – look at the number of people who wouldn't benefit.

Now, one last bit of theory. Because the above scenario has a great impact on any economy, there are serious differences between an economy in which this process takes a day and another in which it takes six months. The faster this process (called the 'Velocity of Money'), the better it is for the economy. The more you can earn, and the faster you do it, the greater the effect you can have. If people and companies notice an upswing in business, they start to spend more. This intensifies the effect, which is how economic growth is created. So don't for one minute think that if you have money somebody else doesn't. In fact, it's the opposite – if you don't have money to spend, many other people will be missing out further down the chain.

Your desire to succeed stems from your desire to give your family a better, more comfortable, worry-free and opportunity-rich life. What could be more generous? Your family will actually be grateful that, thanks to you, they're able to enjoy holidays in the sun, meals at nice restaurants, wonderful Christmas gifts, music lessons, you name it. And you'll be a role model for your loved ones. You will have shown them that, with a little bit of effort and planning, one can change one's condition for the better. What more precious lesson can you teach your children than to show by example? 'Go ahead, give yourself a goal and a plan to get there, work at it, and you will get there, just like I did.' How would it feel to know you didn't have to worry about your children's future, because they have it within them to take care of themselves? Because they know how to set goals and how to work at reaching them? Sounds like a mother's dream come true, to me.

16

Are you afraid of change?

Now that we have dealt with any ambivalent feelings you might have about whether it's a good thing to want to make more money, let's examine other unhelpful thoughts that might be holding you back. You might be familiar with these thoughts, because they usually appear every time you dream about making a big change in your life, or taking on something new.

I'm already overwhelmed by everything I have to do – errands to run, appointments and stuff to remember – how can I possibly find the time and the energy to improve my situation?

Well, for one, the systems in this book will make you feel in control and help you organize your finances, so that you'll stop worrying about them and spinning your wheels. It doesn't take long to put these systems into place.

Nevertheless, this is the conundrum that many are faced with. We all think that we don't have any spare time until something comes along and we have to deal with it. Yet, when the emergency happens, we do somehow find the time. Isn't improving your finances an emergency? In a way, it definitely is.

Schedule an appointment with yourself each week. Maybe it's a Tuesday night after the kids have gone to bed or maybe it's an hour over coffee on a Saturday. Maybe it can't be fixed to a certain point in the week, but make absolutely sure that it happens. Treat it as you would a very important appointment – after all, you're making the time to meet your financial freedom. You don't need a huge amount of energy, as each week you'll be making small steps that will have a powerful incremental effect.

The other thing to remember here is that if you don't take time out to stop running and actually see where you're going, things will always remain the way they are now. Not a very nice thought, is it? I set up my business in September 2010 and it did well quite quickly. I was bringing in a fair bit of business and getting paid on time. I was working really hard all day, every day, but enjoyed running my own company. I was paying myself a salary, paying the phone bill, paying the accountant, paying my taxes.

But by the end of the month, I was back to square one, as I had to start all over again. It looked like my 'capital' wasn't increasing. It looked like I could never take time to work on making the business more effective because I was so busy just keeping it afloat. Effectively, I had moved from one job to another. It was just that by then I not only had to do the job, but find the people to pay me each and every month too. At least when I was employed, I only had to do the former. And, as I explained already, though I increased the revenue I generated, after paying for everything, I was financially no better off than I had been when earning a salary.

I was running to stand still. Is that what you're doing now? If so, you need to take a step back. If you feel that you can't afford to, that you have to keep everything going or something will give, my question to you is, 'If that's the case, can you afford to keep going like this for years?' That is what will happen if you don't, even for a short amount of time every week, stop the treadmill, step off and take a look around. The choice you're faced with is this: always, always putting out fires, running from one emergency to the next and never finding a minute to catch your breath – or taking a step back and tackling the source of the fires, so that they don't start so often, or at all, in the future. Which one would you choose?

I remember ringing my boyfriend the day I realized that though I was running and running, I was really just jogging on the spot. It was an awful discovery – here I was thinking I was doing great, but if I continued to work at that rate on the same things all the time, my development and bank account were set to plateau. I felt absolutely miserable.

This was the genesis of our board meetings. As we talked, I said,

'Why don't we have a strategy meeting? Let's talk about where we're really going with this business.' I wanted to create an organization that would outlive me and could function without me micro-managing every aspect of it. I didn't want to be in a position whereby if I got sick, the business suffered a terminal illness. But that was, in effect, what would have happened. In order to change directions, I had to stop, look and listen. I had to work *on* the business, not *in* the business.

Please, if you think that you haven't the time or energy to change your life and achieve your goals, take this into consideration: you're missing out on much bigger and better things. The life you dream of is just one strategy session away.

So, start strategizing. Where can you find a spare hour? How much time do you spend in front of the TV? How much time surfing the net? How much time doing things because other people do them and you somehow feel you're supposed to be like other people, whereas you don't really enjoy those things? If you feel you 'have to' do something or it won't get done, how about delegating it? Teach your husband or partner and children to do household chores. Motivate them by telling them that, in the time that they'll free up for you, you'll be working on how to take them on holiday.

But maybe your most pressing concern is that change is overwhelming?

This is the way it is, I can't change it. I'm lucky to have a job at all.

This is absolutely not the way it has to be. The United Nations Universal Declaration of Human Rights states that we are all born 'free and equal'. Some people do amazing things with that freedom – whether they're technology geniuses like Bill Gates or Steve Jobs, great creative minds like Moya Doherty or Steven Spielberg, or inspiring leaders like Aung San Suu Kyi or Nelson Mandela. Each of these people has just twenty-four hours in their days, just like you.

Ah, you say, 'But they're super-humans. I'm not nearly as talented as them.'

Well, you don't have to be a Gates or a Doherty or a San Suu Kyi, but you can certainly take steps, tiny and not so tiny, to bring about change in your life. Let's take a look a lot closer to home. I think parents are incredible people. Look at the change in lifestyle that a baby brings to a house. One or two people go from having to look after only themselves to suddenly spending their waking and sleeping moments caring for this small, demanding person. They now need to become far more efficient with the twenty-four hours they have, as usually they need to do a whole lot more on top of what they were already doing.

So you can of course make changes to better your own life. You just need to discover which changes need to be made (that's the easy part) and then make them (admittedly a little less easy, but doable all the same).

Remember what you articulated in Chapter 1 as your ideal life? What did that picture look like? Was it to go for a promotion, increase your salary and revolutionize your working day? Was it to reduce your working week and be able to sustain your current lifestyle? Was it to set up a business? Indeed, you may be lucky to have your job, but your job is also lucky to have you. Therefore, decide what your ideal scenario looks like, think about how you could propose this idea, or at least elements of it to begin with, to your employer, so that you can improve your situation. It can be scary, but it can also be exhilarating.

As you know at this stage, my dream was to set up my own business and I will never forget when I willingly signed up for that P45 in order to start the company. I remember having thoughts like 'If I don't have my salary, what will I live on?', 'It's too scary', 'Where will I get a job if it doesn't work?' and the whole blizzard of doubts that competed with my desire to become an entrepreneur.

Did I feel lucky that I had a job? Of course I did, but I could be even luckier by pursuing my real dream. However, when the temporary high from this light-bulb moment had faded, the question remained: what was I going to do next?

I did what every business person does: I looked at what it was that I could offer to the world from which people could benefit. I searched for those people and asked them if what I could offer was of more value than the amount of money that I wanted to charge. And it worked.

So don't be fooled into being resigned to your fate (whatever that means – I believe we create our own fate). 'That's the way it is' is an empty statement. It's the way that it currently is, but you absolutely have the power to change it. This book shows you how, but you have to decide whether your desire for success is greater than your resistance to change. You don't have to change the world, give up your job tomorrow or start a multinational – you just need to figure out a set of steps that will bring you closer to the financial place where you want to go. And that is the entire purpose of this book.

Or perhaps you are afraid that it's your character that's standing in the way?

If I want to make more money, I'll have to ask for it, to go after it; I'll have to ask for a raise, or find clients if I create my own business – I'll have to get myself noticed and I'm simply not the kind to attract attention to myself. I hate attention.

You don't have to draw any attention to yourself from the outside. Perhaps you think that in order to take control of your finances, you need to become a hot-shot exec and then the local paper will want to interview you and people will talk about you, and none of it will be good. Or you think that you'll have to become a braggart, always tooting your own horn.

This is not the way that it has to be at all. If you want to take control of your finances, by the very nature of taking control you set the rules and the parameters. If this is a personal mission that you don't want to share with anybody, express your thoughts, fears and ambitions on paper. If you don't want to go out into the world and 'sell' face to face, the internet allows you to shield yourself behind a computer screen. If you don't want to pick up the phone to your boss and start making your dreams a reality, you can always start by sending an email asking to have a discussion.

You're not alone either. I once knew of a very confident and successful businessman. Or at least he was confident on the outside.

He loved to provide his coaching services and knew they were of benefit to his customers, but, at the beginning, he struggled when asking them to pay. This was holding him back from actually making a difference to the lives of hundreds of people who would gladly part with their money in exchange for the life-changing techniques he could show them.

Then he came up with a great idea. He employed somebody to process the transactions and gave them a small commission on all of the sales they put through. As a result, he could sell his service and then say, 'You might ring my PA and she'll go through all the logistics with you.' The customer then contacted the PA, and at the end of the conversation she would ask 'May I take your credit-card details to confirm your place please?' Did she feel worried about asking for payment? Not at all: it was her job. She treated this task much as she did turning off the lights in the building before she went home. And he didn't have to talk money with his customers. That's what is called a 'win-win'.

Also, remember, if there is anything that you do to bring in money outside of a fixed salary and benefits, i.e., exchanging goods or services for money, this is entrepreneurship at work. If you prepare the accounts for a family member, if you mind kids for a neighbour, or teach somebody to play music, you are in business. You don't have to have a business card and a Company Registration number to use these exercises.

If you're worried that by achieving financial freedom, people will begin to talk about you or treat you differently, you need to go back to basics and figure out what financial freedom means. If it means taking the kids on holiday and you're worried that the people next door might begin to ask where you got the money, well – it's their problem, isn't it? Are you going to deny your family an experience, just because of what the neighbours might think?

If financial freedom means paying the bills without worrying, how are people on the outside going to know? In fact, the people who truly matter in your life might very well be the ones who would help you out of a financially difficult spot if you asked them to. And don't you think these same people will be sincerely happy for you if your pocket is treating you better?

Of course you might be avoiding change because you can never be 100% sure that you'll be successful . . .

If I try and I fail, it will be horrible. I'll never get over the humiliation.

I feel your pain. I really do. On one shoulder, there is this little voice saying, 'Imagine, you could do this, you could do that. Life would be great.' On your other shoulder, there is the voice that brings you back to earth, saying, 'Of course, it would be great. That's like saying the land across the river is plentiful – when you ain't got no boat to get there.'

You have always wanted to ask for that raise. However, things are tough at the moment. The boss is busy this week. You're not feeling confident enough to send that email, but you save it in 'Drafts'. That's okay, you tell yourself – you're not denying yourself your dream; you're just putting it off until it's the right time. Someday.

You have always dreamed of setting up your own business, but what about the mortgage? What about the kids? What about everything that depends on you? You see famous entrepreneurs on TV and even friends of yours who run their own businesses successfully, but you have no idea how to get there or how they do it without starving. You should have started years ago, when you were young, carefree and had far fewer claims on your money than now. No, you might as well leave it at this stage. Maybe when the kids are bigger, when the mortgage is paid off, when things settle down. That's okay, you tell yourself – you're not denying yourself your dream; you're just putting it off until it's the right time. Someday.

Only there's a problem: as the cheesy saying goes, there are seven days in the week, and last time I checked 'Someday' wasn't one of them. I ask you now, where does that 'Someday' lead you? Well, there are two roads that you can travel. One leads you right up to the old-age pension and thinking back to all the things you could have done. You remember the ten years of your life when you could have slotted in a business but you watched *Emmerdale* instead.

You think of the hours and hours you spent polishing mirrors that wouldn't have got any worse, if your duster had visited them only half as often. You think of the better lifestyle you could be living now if you'd learned to take control of your finances years ago. You run into old acquaintances and ask them how they are finding retirement. They say it's great, but they miss the buzz of working in a job where they thrived. They have a glint in their eye as they talk about their company, the people, the huge sums of tax they paid to invest in a country that would take care of their grandchildren, the lives they changed by creating a few jobs, the full life they lived, the lessons they learned, the fun they had. They aren't worried about money, but rather about where to go next, what do to, who to see.

Do you know where the other path leads? To a scary place. One where you ask, willingly, for that P45, that pay rise, that new path. One where you don't know what will happen next. One where the diary isn't planned, where the road ahead can't be mapped. One where you will sometimes think to yourself, 'Am I *stone mad?*' One where others will say to you, 'Would you just be normal like everybody else?' But you know what – that is one exhilarating ride. There is nothing like the feeling of getting to a place on that journey and thinking, 'How the hell did I manage to get here?' People ask how you are and instead of giving them the perfunctory 'Fine, and how are you?', you reply with vigour, pouring enthusiasm and all the passion you have into your answer. You spend every day getting paid for indulging your hobby, because now you're in that dream job or in that situation where you spend your day doing something that you enjoy. You sometimes want the hours that you sleep to speed up so that you can get up and just live more. You have the same sense of excitement that you had before a weekend or a fortnight's holiday, but now you experience it all the time. You feel enlivened by the breadth of things that you can do – the world is your oyster and you're not afraid to claim it. You feel sorry for people who complain about their surroundings and yet are apathetic about doing anything about it. You feel great. People tell you that you're inspiring, although you're not trying to be. People tell you that you're courageous, but you don't feel as if you're getting up each morning to face the dark unknown; you feel as if you are shaping your own destiny. People who are further down that path than you look at you with a wistful smile as they remember what it was like to be at this stage – the energy, the vitality, the sense of achievement. They wish you all the best and say, 'Enjoy it all.' You promise them that you will. And then you do.

I remember often asking my mother the same question in various guises: 'What if x doesn't happen?' She would retort, 'What if it does – how will you deal with that?' By the time I had figured out how to deal with the positive outcome, it had already become a reality in my mind. I had inadvertently set the satnav and was already on my way there, before I even realized it.

I once attended a conference where one of the sessions was led by a life coach. She asked the audience, 'What would you do if you couldn't fail? Take a minute to think of this.' As I was driving from Galway to Dublin one day, I suddenly remembered this particular question. I had been contemplating something I was sure was impossible and I said to myself, 'Just between Athlone and Kinnegad, think about how you would go about this if you knew you couldn't fail.' By the time I got to Dublin, I had it sorted.

Failing is only definitive if you give up once you've failed. If you pick yourself up, dust yourself off, learn from your mistakes and try again, that failure wasn't a failure; it was only a stumbling block on your way to success. Do you think my life as a business owner is always smooth and worry-free? Of course it isn't, but I'm continually learning how to deal with the obstacles that I encounter. I'm sure that in the past you came up against things that presented themselves as problems, but which now, because of your experience in dealing with them, present themselves as simple issues instead. However, if you hadn't tried to learn because of fear of failure, those problems would still be that – problems . . . minus the benefits. After all, our business was started right in the middle of a recession, when it would have been very tempting to recoil in fear, thinking, 'What if I fail?'

You might say, 'Well, this is all very nice, but I'm talking about *real* failure – the one where you have to file for bankruptcy, or you lose your house, or your spouse leaves you. What do you say to that?' To which I would reply, you don't have to gamble it all. Take only as much risk as you're comfortable with. You never 'have to' remortgage the house. In the following chapters I'll give you lots of ideas about how you can try out a business idea without much – or, indeed, any – risk.

If you fail, think of the lessons you'll learn, the adventures you'll have and the wisdom you'll gain. And what if you succeed? How will you deal with that? The reality of success is probably even better than in your wildest imaginings.

And remember – nobody will have to die a horrible death just because you gave your dream a try. So what's holding you back?

17

The secret about making money . . .
is that there is no secret

So you've accepted that making money is a good thing and that changing your life is not as daunting as you might have believed. What remains to be tackled is the set of misconceptions many people have about how to go about actually making money. It's not some unfathomable dark art, nor is it as complicated as rocket science. Instead, it's a practical matter of finding a natural fit between your life and your interests and the wonderful opportunities that are out there. But, first, let's look at the doubts you might have . . .

I have nothing to 'sell'. I have no skill, no talent, no ability, that people would want to pay for. I am so ordinary.
Absolutely everybody has something to sell; all that you need to do is to find out what it is and put a name to it. Let me give you some examples.

Are you somebody who enjoys organizing? You may be the type of person who always likes things to be put in their place, tidy before you go to bed and easy to find. You are the kind of person who writes lists and somebody whom your friends turn to when they want to organize a well-planned party. You look forward to days when you can turn on the radio, close the door and settle down to write Christmas cards or file your bank statements.

Are you somebody who is very discreet and likes to help? You can empathize with people, give objective advice and lessen someone's load. If somebody has a problem, they feel comfortable in coming to talk to you. You genuinely like to listen and really love the feeling when you see a friend's shoulders relax as the tension they had accumulated dissolves.

Are you somebody who loves to bake and cook? You love to sift through recipe books, or while away an afternoon looking for the freshest ingredients at farmers' markets. People love to come to your house for a dinner party and you equally love to plan and execute a menu.

Are you somebody who loves to travel? Airports fill you with excitement and you find it easy to converse with people who have been on even one holiday in their lives. You find yourself 'just checking' if there are any cheap flights available, and before you know it you've spent hours looking up hotels, package holidays and dreaming of your next vacation.

Are you somebody who loves to dance? You look forward to your evening class all week, and on a Saturday night you love to boogie. You don't see the point in counting down minutes on a treadmill, when you can have so much fun at Salsa Slim. You love the movement, the people you meet and just how energized you feel throughout.

Are you somebody who loves to speak a language? You always found it easy to study languages in school and enjoy listening to how the words sound. You always like to speak a couple of words when you meet somebody from the country of your chosen language. You may have visited the country and revelled in getting by, or better, when talking to the native speakers.

You may be wondering at this point if I've forgotten what I was originally talking about. All I've done is listed some hobbies and possibly painted an accurate picture of how you integrate them and things you like to do into your life. The secret to your skills is right there.

I once got a personal trainer to put together a programme for me in a gym. Over the course of the conversation, I asked her how she had found her way into the job. She told me that she had trained to be a teacher and went on to work in a school for ten years. However, the best part of her day was when she could get into her tracksuit and into a sweat. One day, she had a light-bulb moment and thought, 'Why am I spending only an hour a day doing something that I could be spending eight hours doing – and earning money while I'm at it?'

I recently spoke to a group of female entrepreneurs, and at the beginning of the event each gave her name and explained what she did. One woman really impressed me with the ingenuity of what she offered. She sold systems. She said that she'd always loved organizing and she'd made a business out of it. She developed filing systems for people, sorted out people's accumulated balls of receipts into efficient accounts. She could walk into a messy office and put it right. It was almost Christmas when I spoke to that group, so a great many of them were coming to their year-end and tackling all the administration that comes with it. I observed that as she spoke many of the women quietly turned to each other and laughingly said, 'I wish she would come into my house.'

I remember being at another talk and listening to a prominent Irish business woman speak about the challenges of juggling motherhood with entrepreneurship. She told us about how she'd ended up hiring one of the members of her staff. One day she took out a piece of paper and wrote down how much it would cost to employ somebody and pay for their flights and accommodation if they were to do her travelling for her. Someone from the company would therefore be at meetings, but not necessarily her. On the opposite side of the page, she tried, but couldn't, quantify the value of the energy and time, both commercial and personal, that this person, if employed, would save her. The next day she began to look for some body who was happy to travel and not to return home every night.

Now – can you match these concrete, real-life examples with the abstract profiles above? I could go on and on – and I will in the next chapter, where I'll outline many, many ways that you could generate revenue simply by doing the things that you love.

Let me share a quick insight with you from a recent Christmas. I had been giving a training session in Amsterdam and had to make my way to the station to get my train to Brussels. It was dark, and on that short journey I marvelled at the colours, smells and sounds of the Christmas markets. It was such a wonderful sight to see. Afterwards, as I was on my way southwards, cruising past Rotterdam and Antwerp, I wrote some of the passages in this book. I was thoroughly enjoying the writing, and I sat back and thought, 'This is simply wonderful. I'm getting to spend time seeing things and doing things that I really love and money is flowing smoothly into my bank account as I'm doing it.' If you work in a job where all you have to look forward to is watching the clock drag towards the time that spells your release, what would a happier, more productive and fulfilling day look like? Just find something that you like doing, and get paid for it – it doesn't have to be something arcane or rare or especially technical. You don't have to build the next Google or the next Facebook.

I'm not an entrepreneur at heart.

What do you mean by that? Define 'entrepreneur'. We often hear stories of people with incredible drive, passion and enthusiasm who bring a company back from the brink and turn it into a multimillion-euro business. We read articles about inspirational people who invest their life savings and redundancy payment in a product that takes the world by storm; or we hear that somebody was born with a sweeping vision – and with a cashflow statement in their hands.

Indeed, these people are entrepreneurs, but who says you have to be exactly like them? It's much more important to pay attention to their characteristics – what are those? Can you replicate them? The qualities that I would say best describe an entrepreneur are 'hard-working', 'goal-focused', 'creative' and of course 'enterprising'. Do you think any of these words could be used to describe you?

'Hard-working' – does this mean working hard? It could. It may mean toiling day in, day out, or it may mean working smartly and getting results. You could spend eight hours a day working to put money in another person's pocket and what do you get in return? Your salary, the safety of knowing that the money will be there at the end of the week, the ability to switch off at the end of the day, and the knowledge that if you need to take a sick day or statutory holidays, you'll still be paid. There is nothing wrong with that and that indeed may suit your personality or where you are in your life right now. On the other hand, maybe you've never been encouraged to think differently about how to make your living, and in this book I hope I'm giving you plenty of food for thought.

People who work for themselves or set up companies have a different set of goals. They want their pay to be uncapped, their lifestyle to be flexible, and they want to let their creative flair flow. They don't want to ask for days off, or ask for a pay rise, or let their energies be spent majorly benefitting another, or be narrowly instructed on how to spend their day. The point here is that you can be very hard-working, but for different rewards. If you are hard-working by nature, you can put that talent to work for yourself, by focusing your energy on something that will reward you exclusively. The only thing that you need do is find the thing you want to work hard at. The rest of this book will help you to do that.

'Goal focused' – if you have paid any heed to Chapter 1, you'll see how powerful goal-setting can be. It eliminates procrastination, addresses limiting beliefs and sets you on the right path. Did you ever wonder how some people can do well in their careers, make lots of money, be high achievers in a hobby, look well and constantly have a sunny outlook? Do you think that these people have all the luck and, if you are honest, would you admit to being slightly envious of them? Before giving in to the thought that fate has it in for you and has assigned all your luck to them, stop and think. Can you spot a pattern in this person's behaviour? They seem to be able to achieve in all areas of their life. Did you ever consider that they might be using the same technique over and over again – in all areas of their life? The power of goal-setting is immense and can have a very significant impact on all aspects of your life. It's not something that you're born with, but it is something that you can acquire. After a little practice, it becomes second nature and you can apply it to whatever endeavour you set your sights on.

'Creative' – what does creative mean to you? Have you ever added a twist to a recipe? Have you ever added jewellery and accessories to an outfit? Have you ever matched your eyeshadow to your nail varnish? Have you ever thought of an imaginative game with the kids? Have you ever added a lampshade, photo frame or candle to bring colour to a room? Have you ever suggested 'another way of looking at things' to a friend who was upset, angry or afraid? Each and every one of these examples is being creative. There is creativity in each one of us. We all leave our mark on the planet – think of it as a 'creative footprint', the much more positive version of a carbon footprint.

Many people think that only artists are creative, but this narrow view doesn't correspond with reality. According to Gardner's Theory of Multiple Intelligences, there are in fact nine forms of intelligence. They are not mutually exclusive; we have and use all of them, although a few might be our dominant traits.

Visual/linguistic. You have the capacity to learn from pictures, 'see' things in 3D and use visual aids as memory hooks.

Existential. You are spiritual and can contemplate deep thoughts. You can be understanding of people's emotions, and are open and willing to consider ideas that others might consider strange or 'weird'.

Logical/mathematical. You design processes for everything. You like organization and 'strategize' when solving a problem, coming up with a sequence of different steps.

Interpersonal. You are very good with people and they naturally warm to you. You can walk into a party alone and know everybody by the time you leave.

Intrapersonal. You can 'deal with yourself' very well. You are happy with your own company and have a very grounded understanding of who you are and where you want to go.

Musical. You enjoy music at a level that many others can't. You find it easy to learn how to play instruments and learn best by listening.

Natural. You like to spend time gardening and have a natural affinity with animals. You can 'clear your head' with a stroll through a park as you get lost in its infinite beauty and peace.

Bodily/Kinaesthetic. You are a natural sportsperson. You have dexterity, coordination and a love for physical games.

Linguistic. You find it easy to learn languages and love these tools of expression. You like to read, write and listen to well-spoken people.

By the very nature of each of these kinds of intelligence, they are all different, and yours is likely to be a mix of a few that is specific to you. You find some things easy that others don't, while you can't wrap your mind around other things that come quickly to other people. Some people love to put systems in place (logical/mathematical), while others hate the constraint of organization (natural). Some people love to articulate ideas (linguistic) while others get impatient with having to express themselves through words (musical).

Which intelligences describe you best, do you think? Take some time to reflect. Which of the styles above resonated with you? The answer to this question will suggest some ways that you could make money doing the things you love. Your own brand of creativity may be the solution to another person's problem, just as you would be happy to get help in those intelligence domains with which you're not so comfortable. Say, for example, that you are highly interpersonal, but not logical/mathematical at all. A person who is just the opposite of you might appreciate your help as a relationship counsellor. And you could use their help to break down your counselling process into a series of logical steps, in order to work out a preliminary questionnaire to use in your practice, or in figuring out a way to work with clients remotely. Whatever your form of intelligence, it constitutes a perfect competitive advantage.

And going back to the final quality of entrepreneurs – being 'enterprising'. Is that a scary one for you? Being enterprising is simply the act of commercializing a product or service. This is the difference between somebody looking at a bare wall in a coffee shop and thinking, 'I need to get some nice pictures for that wall' and somebody else who thinks, 'I must contact an artist to see if they want to put some paintings on that wall, and I can get a commission on their sales.' It's simply a different way of thinking and then following through with actions. If it seems a little scary at the moment, that's perfectly normal. If it feels alien even to think that way, that's normal too – I'll teach you all about how to adopt these ways of thinking and then the step-by-step actions that will turn your natural talents into a better-looking bank account.

The main thing here is that you don't have to be a superstar to bring in more money; you just need to look at things differently, or think about the things you like to do in another way. You need to incorporate new habits that may seem daunting now, but I hope I've shown you they just require a small shift from how you're already doing things. So let's start from within your comfort zone, and then expand outwards at your own pace.

It's difficult and risky to create a business.

I thought so too. I was an aspiring entrepreneur for years before I realized what was holding me back. I think it was in part that I always felt that in order to set up a business, you needed a building, delivery vans, staff, and so forth. I presumed that you always needed a loan to get started, which you would have to pay with interest, and that you needed a solid business model, as well as lots of courage and savings built up before getting to that point. Oh, and of course, you also needed a good, clever idea.

Rubbish! In order to be in business, you need to have something to sell, a way of finding people who would benefit from it and get-up-and-go. That's about the extent of it. I'm not joking. Indeed I hardly even noticed my first business starting. I was working for a stock-market training company. Its main offering was a training seminar about being successful in the stock market. People often left that course brimming with enthusiasm, but since the course was on a Saturday and the markets weren't open immediately after they left the seminar, they often didn't get around to putting what they had learned into practice for days, weeks or months afterwards. As a result, they forgot how to do this or that. One night, I was at home and someone who had attended the seminar rang me with a couple of queries. They lived in Galway. No matter how much I explained what to do, he couldn't follow me, as I was trying to explain how to use a piece of software and he didn't have his computer in front of him. After some time, I said, 'What about if I meet you? I'll be in Galway on Wednesday evening: let's meet at the Radisson and I'll show you exactly what to do.' Of course, my boss was delighted at my level of customer service.

I said to him, 'Do you think I could charge for this?'

He said, 'Of course you should be charging, that's above and beyond the call of duty.'

The next day, somebody else rang and, as I was answering his queries, a light-bulb went off in my head. I said, 'You know, I do meet people for a charge and go through all their questions while sitting at their computer with them.'

'Oh, that sounds great,' he said. 'How much?'

'€50,' I said.

'Okay, when could you come?'

'Next week at some stage?'

He said, 'That's great, I thought I would have to wait at least a month, that's fantastic.' You should have seen me on the other side of the phone. I was twenty-one, in my third year at college and I could get €50 for two hours' work? I was ecstatic. I went back to my boss and said, 'There were two people looking for this service, maybe there would be more? Maybe I could start an "online-trading education service" where I showed them how to buy and sell online?' He said, 'Why stop there? Why not call it a mentoring service? You could then deal with much more than online trading and train them on all the things that you've learned with us over the years.' I started to call people who had done the seminar with the company and asked them how they were getting on and if they needed any help.

There you have it. My first business. It almost crept up on me. What did I need? A phone, a database of potential clients, a competency. After that, it was simply the impetus to go and do it. The summer I was twenty-one, I spent my time being a real business woman. By student standards I earned a fortune. I travelled the country, and by explaining and teaching I learned more about the markets than any book could ever teach me . . .

You have to know the market place / the stock market / the secrets of business to be able to succeed, and I don't know these secrets.

What secrets? Are a select few born with knowledge of them? Of course not. Indeed, there is information that you don't yet have, lessons that you haven't yet learned about being in business. However, isn't everybody in that category after all? I've been in business for quite a while now, but I'm sure that what I know now will be only a shadow of what I'll know in five years' time. Yet that's part of the journey, and I feel delighted that I have so much more to learn and see and experience.

I'm not saying that running your own company is without uncertainty – you have to make choices and take decisions, even when you're not 100% sure what the outcome will be. You have to go out on a limb. However, those are the very things that business people thrive on. You can put your hand to anything. You can get up in the morning and do accounts, marketing, sales, business development, strategy, outsourcing, client entertainment, emails, administration – the list goes on. Assuming you're not under a pressing deadline for a specific task, there is such variety in that 'job'. The secrets that you are looking for are in the thousand little things that happen each day you're in business. However, you won't learn them until you experience them.

Still, there are a couple of expensive lessons that you don't have to learn the painful way. I can give you the benefit of my own experience. I wouldn't call them secrets, but little tips that may help you along your way.

For example, remember what I said about turnover and profit? In business you should always take in more money than you spend. Hardly a secret, is it? You might think that this is an obvious point – how would a business be run sustainably if it wasn't making a profit? However, remember Chapter 14: many people set out with the incorrect idea about how to run an enterprise, myself included. And the incorrect way of doing things is to focus on turnover, and not on profit. As a result, particularly in the early stages when you're starved for cash, you'll take whatever business you can get. After a while, when you get established, you can get more selective about the work you take on.

You have to have money to make money. We don't have much money in my family. So there's no way I can catch up with famous entrepreneurs.

Really? I think you should know better by now. Do you think that every successful person has had money to start with? J. K. Rowling, the author of the Harry Potter books, began writing the series as a newly divorced unemployed mother living on welfare. When Jim Carrey was in high school in Canada, he lived in a camper van with his family and worked eight-hour shifts at a tyre factory to help make ends meet. Steve Jobs came from a solid blue-collar background, had a tricky time getting through high school, took a course in calligraphy and dropped out of his college course after six months. Moya Doherty nearly turned down the opportunity to develop Riverdance, as she had just organized the 1993 Telethon and felt she needed a break before working on another big project. Imagine if each of these people had held back because they didn't believe they could do it. Look what the world would have missed out on. I could fill the book with examples of very successful people who started with little, nothing or less than nothing and went on to achieve local, national, international and global success.

Perhaps you're thinking there's no way to 'catch up' with famous entrepreneurs. I'm intrigued by this idea of catching up. Who or what are you trying to catch? Who says that life has to be a race, with some people sprinting ahead? Presumably, if someone wants to catch up with famous entrepreneurs, they must want to have a massive company. However, the vast majority of people don't want to do this at all. They wouldn't want to work as hard, risk as much or do what entrepreneurs at that level have to do. Just as in every field – music, literature, sport – in business there is a handful of famous entrepreneurs in every country; they are a rare breed and they have staggering successes. But millions of people make a very good and happy living in business, sometimes simply as sole traders, without ever needing to be the next Richard Branson or Bill Gates. What most people actually want is the freedom not to have to worry about money, or to have enough to take the kids on holiday, or to have a cushion for emergencies, or to have a sustainable business as a source of income, and so on, which leads us right back to Chapter 3. Thinking that, to be in business, you have to emulate famous entrepreneurs is not a very good goal, because it's vague. How will you know when you've made it? If you don't have a specific means of ticking a box and saying to yourself that 'I have definitely achieved this goal', you don't have a huge chance of success – remember the section in Chapter 4 about how not to set goals? Remember the 'M' in SMARTER is 'measurable'.

This idea that you have to have money to make money can be true. If you want to start manufacturing a product, sure, that requires lots of initial investment, and it can be expensive. However, I invite you to rewrite the sentence as 'You have to *do something* to make money.' There are lots and lots of things you can do to make money – I have devoted a whole chapter to it – and all it takes is effort. The first thing is to find out what it is you're going to do and the second thing is to go and do it. It's quite simple, really.

The idea that you have to have money to make money also leads us back to your financial thermostat. Money alone is not a guarantee of financial success; you have to know what to do with it. Take two situations:

A parent leaves €1,000,000 to his son. The son is delighted. He hops on a flight to Vegas to have the time of his life. After two weeks, he has not only spent the money but he is in debt. He had money, but that doesn't mean that he was able to make money. This is the excess money principle that I introduced early on – if you think one million euros is 'excess' money that you can spend as you fancy, you'll be back to square one in no time.

A woman sets up a business with zero capital. She is an accountant and is going to start preparing company accounts for clients. She literally has no money at all to put into this business. She tells her friends and family to keep an eye out for her. Her brother-in-law tells his cousin about her. She compiles the cousin's accounts and gets paid €2,000. With this money, she gets some business cards printed and puts an advertisement in the local paper. The cycle continues and the business grows. This person didn't have any money to start with, but yet she made money from a service-based company.

The only secret about making money is this: to make money, you have to know how to make money.

STEP NINE

Make more money

18

The four principles of revenue generation

We are nearing the end of our journey. Or maybe it is only the beginning. If you've been following the chapters step by step, you've come a long way: you've mined your budget for precious data; you've become familiar with opportunity cost, which has allowed you to cut spending in instances when you didn't derive any enjoyment or profit, in order to be able to afford what you really want; you have an accountability and support system in place, with accountability partners who will cheer you along the way and pick you up when you flag; you have completed the profit-and-loss exercise, so that you know how much your decisions are costing you, and what you're willing to give up or to keep hold of; and you've examined and dismissed all your misconceptions about making more money.

And now comes the last step, the one that will turbo-charge your budget: how can you make more money? Of course, you might feel a bit apprehensive, or excited, or slightly scared, but I hope that, now you've come this far, you see that making more money is absolutely possible.

What I want to do in this chapter is show you that there is always a system involved in increasing your revenue. I know that in recent years a way of thinking called the 'law of attraction' has become popular: according to this idea, focusing on the positive will bring positive things into your life. I'm all for positivity, and I do think that you can 'attract' wealth – but mainly by knowing that you have to take action, and that you can totally do it. However, you can't dream your way to a fat bank account – not if you don't act on your dreams.

You should never disparage or belittle your dreams. In fact, you should value them so much that you should act on them. Otherwise, they will remain just that – dreams. And now you know how to use the information in previous chapters to make a feasibility study for your dream.

You may be thinking, 'But I'm an employee. How can I generate more revenue? I don't get to decide whether I can give myself a raise or not.' This is a very paralysing view and one that doesn't have to be true. Even if you are an employee, all you need to do is apply some business thinking to your situation and you'll find there are many things you can do to increase your capacity to bring in money. As a business person, if I want to increase my income, there are four ways for me to do so:

1. Increase my number of customers.
2. Increase the number of times my customers buy from me.
3. Increase the size of the deal.
4. Increase the number of referrals that I get.

If you're already in business, make sure you do whatever you can with regard to these four points. But if you're in paid employment with a fixed salary, you can still apply these principles. Let's look at each point, from the perspective of an employee as well as from the perspective of a self-employed person.

Increase my number of customers.

~ *Employee: Increase the number of jobs that I have.*
~ *Business person: Increase my number of customers.*

If you find that the amount of money that you earn from your current job is simply not enough, you can look for a second one. If this is not an option for you because of time and other commitments, there are other alternatives. Let's say that you work from nine to five and you need to increase your revenue. You could take a part-time job on the weekends or in the evenings. Alternatively, you could do something that allowed you to work at your own pace from home. You could start a small online business. You could become an agent for a product that you love to use and are already telling your friends and family about. You could start giving grinds in a subject that you studied at college, teach people how to play an instrument or coach them in something in which you are skilled. You could become a mystery shopper and get paid just to give your opinions on experiences that you go through anyway. There are lots and lots of ways to increase revenue if you are an employee.

Finding more customers is the most common way that business people think about increasing revenue. In my own experience, there are more efficient ways, but let's start here. If you're already in business, you can find more customers by casting your net wider. There are many (mainly) cost-free measures that you can take, ones that only cost time, including:

~ Joint ventures
~ Networking
~ PR

The order in which these measures appear reflects how effective each has been for me. Joint ventures occur when two or more people or companies come together to work on an idea. For example, as a financial-markets trainer, I targeted organizations that offered evening courses. I approached them about adding my programmes to those that they were offering. From their perspective, they had an additional product to sell, and from my perspective they and their subsequent customers became new business for me. I find this is very powerful, as the goals of the two companies are aligned and can work harmoniously together.

Networking is great if used in the right way. Networking isn't about meeting as many people as possible, gathering an armful of business cards and giving out your flyers. The people who network most successfully usually meet only a couple of people at an event. They mill around and then get talking to somebody with whom they 'click', and will follow up the next day not just with a LinkedIn invitation (although that's a good start), but with something that genuinely helps their new acquaintance. For example, a networking group is having an event in a fortnight's time and they invite their new acquaintance along. There might be a thread on an online forum to which their new acquaintance could contribute or perhaps get some business from. Or perhaps someone in their networking group and their new acquaintance might be able to work together to their mutual benefit. In each of those cases, the 'networker' didn't give the person any money, but yet provided something of real value to them. You can be very, very sure that if you follow this process in the right networks, networking will be a very strong sales tool.

PR is great too – every person and business has a PR angle, whether you are aware of it or not. All you need to do is to think about it. Is there an answer to 'Why is your company different?' If so, there is your angle. I recently met a local accountant whose 'unique selling point' was that she went to companies' premises so that they wouldn't have to waste any time outside the office. A small, subtle difference, but yet one that a local paper could profile as 'An accountant who shows you how to cut your travel expenses . . . in a very real way.' There is always a human-interest side to a business. I'm sure you've heard variations of the following stories more than once in the news: a mother of one who leaves a well-paid job to start up a business in a recession; a 'necessity entrepreneur' who loses their job and needs to find a revenue stream quickly; or a person who stumbles across a great business idea simply because he spends frustrated hours trying to find a service provider who isn't there. Write a short press release and send it to radio and TV stations. Write a good article and send it with a photograph to your targeted newspaper. You may be pleasantly surprised by the doors that open.

Increase the number of times my customers buy from me.

- ∽ *Employee: Increase the number of jobs that I get paid for.*
- ∽ *Business person: Increase the number of times my customers buy from me.*

If you are in paid, fixed employment, perhaps you could take a look around your circumstances. For example, could you do more tasks and get paid more for them? Could you do more hours and get paid overtime? After I have fulfilled a contract with a client, I sit down with them and we have a chat about how the process went and also other needs the company might have. Often, within that discussion, more business is done, because I take the time to listen, and because I take the initiative and ask relevant questions. In business terminology, this is called a 'needs analysis'. Have you ever taken your boss to lunch and undertaken this sort of 'needs analysis'? Perhaps you prepare the accounts in work, but your boss actually needs to set up some systems on Excel. You might have done the ECDL (European Computer Driving Licence), so you may be well able to help her out. You could suggest that you'll stay late for three evenings the following week and build the spreadsheet for your normal hourly wage.

Perhaps your boss is totally stressed because she has to give a number of presentations this month, but doesn't have the time to format them, input tables and add in animations. You could offer to take them home for a weekend, spend your Saturday on the sofa with music in the background and make money while you're doing it. Perhaps she needs to organize a venue for a client event, or the Christmas party, or travel arrangements for a conference in Sweden. She simply does not have the time at any stage to do this and it's nagging at her – the deadline is approaching fast. You could suggest that you'll do all the research for these, run them by her next Monday morning and liaise with all the relevant people Monday afternoon. You'll make sure all of your other duties are also fulfilled – and you'll do this in exchange for €x. In essence, you are selling 'one-offs' to your boss that may just put you in a whole other light. Just by having this discussion, you could earn more money, make your boss's life easier and make your own job easier, because things will run more smoothly. This could change your job description forever, and, as you become more indispensable, it may lead to an increase in your salary and job security. Why don't you take your boss to lunch with the genuine intention of relieving her of some stress, in ways that she may not have thought about? This would serve to better the company, at a cost below the value of the output (we will work out how to price this later when we turn to 'dollar-izing the sale').

If you're in business, you can also increase the number of times that your clients buy from you with two very simple techniques.

First, suggest ways that you could further help them out. This has a different ring to it than 'Will you buy more stuff?' If all you're doing is selling stuff that people don't need, you probably won't last very long. On the other hand, if you're making people's lives better and easier, and if they value what you do for them more than the fee you charge, your positive impact on people's lives increases in line with your revenue. This is truly a 'win-win' situation. 'Win-win' is not empty corporate speak; it is the only way you can do business sustainably.

Last year a company asked me to do some consultancy work on the delivery style of their training personnel. I very happily under-took the task: but it struck me that there were many things about the content of the training that could have been more relevant, more interesting and, ultimately, more effective. As a result, at the end of my stated contract, I had a 'needs-analysis' meeting and put this to them. I said, 'If I wrote a short proposal on this, would you be interested?' They read it, were happy with it and signed off on it. I remember walking out of their office that day and thinking, 'It's not their responsibility to come up with ways of buying more from me after I give them the service they've asked for. It's mine.' This is a very profitable business lesson to learn and also highlights that, in identifying ways to go above and beyond, you really care for the contract you're fulfilling. As another example, I was in a network-ing group with a photographer. She actually did the photographs for one of my own family events. Afterwards, I bought one family portrait from her and it made a lovely Christmas present. However, she had lots and lots of shots in there that would have made lovely birthday, anniversary and 'thinking of you' presents. All she needed to do was to call me again six months later and ask if I might need to get a present for a family member . . .

Have you ever been sitting in a coffee shop, sharing stories with a friend, and time just flies? You realize that you have actually been sitting there for two hours and your coffee has long gone cold. What would have happened if the barista had walked by your table an hour earlier and said, 'Excuse me, could I get you both another cup of coffee?' You probably would have said, 'Yes, please, that would be lovely.' It never ceases to amaze me how much more business could be harvested, if we only just asked for it. In many cases, if we just remind our customers that we are there and open for business, sales will come. Have you ever called up a customer after, say, three months? Maybe they greeted you by saying, 'Oh, hello. I've been meaning to call for the last month, so you've saved me the effort.' They had their credit cards at the ready; they just needed a small nudge from you.

Why is it that with all the forms of modern, fast, cheap technology, we still send Christmas cards? Isn't it a lovely feeling when somebody that you haven't heard from in months sends you that colourful card, which basically says, 'I'm thinking of you and wishing you well'? If you're in business, do you give cards and corporate gifts at Christmas? Why just at Christmas? I give all my clients a gift after every single time they pay me. I don't do it just because I would like to get more business; I do it because I'm genuinely appreciative of their business. Without my customers, I wouldn't have a business. They are very important people, and I want to express my gratitude to them. Also, it keeps me, our company and our services right there in front of them.

If you want to increase the number of times that your customers buy from you, remind them of your presence. Put a note in your diary to call them, or visit, or take them out to lunch, or something that will remind them of you periodically. You could try the following exercise to limber up and prepare: imagine they have an unspoken desire to give you more business, but they need your help in articulating this. What would be in their email? What would they say they need from you? When you meet them, you'll be in a better position to explain how you can help them further.

Increase the size of the deal.

~ *Employee: Increase the amount that you get paid.*
~ *Business person: Increase the size of the deal.*

In the first chapter of this book, we talked about a comfort zone. You might be feeling that this chapter, with all this talk of taking your boss to lunch and asking for money, is really stretching your comfort zone. Well, now is the time to cower in fear – or maybe not. Because we're going to talk about asking for a raise. It may be a time of plenty in your place of work: business has been flowing in the door and there has been overtime galore on offer. On the other hand, it could be a time of layoffs, cuts and pay freezes. Obviously, it is much easier to ask for a pay rise in the first situation, but you can't choose the economic times or the business environment in which you find yourself; all you can do is simply to react to the current conditions. If your place of work has been under immense stress and now is not the best time to pursue this path, that doesn't mean that you should necessarily disregard this chapter. You can absolutely prepare for when things improve; and you may find that the principles below have a great deal of merit when applied to other, more lateral ways of improving your situation.

Perhaps you feel that, as of now, you are paid fairly for the amount of work that you do. Perhaps you're thinking, 'Who am I kidding? I'm only doing what's expected of me and not exactly going the extra mile . . .' If you don't want to ask for a pay rise for what you're currently doing, that's fine. But why not take some time to think about how you could get paid more for doing something else? For example, meet with your boss and ask how you could add more value to the company in exchange for more money. Alternatively, you could do your own research into how you could make a differ-ence to sales, efficiency, cost, convenience. Could you look into a new sales channel and get a commission on the business you take in? Could you take control of inducting new staff or up-skilling existing personnel? Could you take control of a monthly finance review and present your findings to management?

As long as you can prove that your added value is worth more than the money you're asking for, you may well be able to argue your case. This is called 'dollarizing the sale' in business terms: if I can bring $50 worth of value to your company/life and I charge only $30 for it, it makes absolute sense for you to buy from me. Are there any promotions on offer where you are employed? If not, ask your boss if there are any in the pipeline. Could you design a higher-paid post for yourself? Try this exercise: you're walking into the canteen one day and you see this notice up on the door about a new promotion. It makes your heart leap; you feel that it could be almost written for you and you are absolutely the best person for the job. What does it say? Write it. Dollarize its benefits and go to your employer.

Before the conversation, make sure to research some negotiation techniques – because this will be a negotiation, make no bones about it. You might want to go on to Google to research negotiation techniques. You'll need to come up with what's known as your Best Alternative to a Negotiated Agreement, or BATNA. If your boss refuses to give you a raise, what do they stand to lose? In a real negotiation, you have to retain the ability to walk away at any time. Of course this is not so easy when you're an employee, but 'walking away' comes in many forms. Maybe you've had a call from a head hunter? Maybe you've decided to change jobs or even careers? Maybe you know of a position similar to yours that is open in a different department of your company, or in a different company altogether? You shouldn't of course threaten to resign, as this might backfire, but make sure that you have some weighty arguments on your side. After all, why should your boss give you the raise, if they know you'll continue to work for them, even if they don't give you what you want?

If this sounds absolutely out of bounds at your current place of work, maybe it's time for a change. Research other jobs in your sector. If you see a position that is more highly paid, but your heart sinks as you read down through the requirements and you don't have a certain qualification or experience, don't disregard it. Would it interest you to get that qualification? How long would it take you? Take a look online and see where it's on offer. If you'd never seen the job offer in the paper, would you have wanted to do the qualification anyway? If so, why not go for it? If it doesn't lead you to this job, it may lead you to others. Anyway, other employers might contact the organizer of the course for potential staff. Conversely, the course organizers and trainers might know of companies looking for people with that qualification.

The company offering the job may get many applications or it may get a few. Why not apply for the job and in your cover letter state that you are currently undertaking the qualification and expect to be fully qualified by month x, year y? This will show that you're capable of taking the initiative, that you're continuously up-skilling yourself, and that you've a good grasp of current marketplace conditions. Why not take a chance? If you are sincerely considering enrolling to get the qualification, you are not 'cheating' in any way. (But make sure you do enrol.)

Instead of just saying, 'I can't ask for a pay rise,' ask yourself, 'Why should I get a pay rise?' What could you do today to become more valuable tomorrow? Dollarize it and ask the world to recognize that you're worth it.

In business terms, increasing the size of the deal has a technical name: it's called cross-selling. When customers have shown they're ready to buy from you, ask them whether they would like an additional item – one that is related to what they have already bought and will increase their enjoyment of it. This is the thinking that gave birth to one of the most profitable questions in business. McDonald's has made billions out of one simple question: 'Would you like fries with that?' If you were to look at your own offering, what 'fries' could you add?

I once spoke at an entrepreneurship event and made this very point. Afterwards, a caterer came up to me and told me that she had recently employed this technique, with wonderful results. It was April at the time and she was busy catering for a number of communions. As people made the booking, she went through everything with them and then asked, 'Would you like a cake with that?' More often than not, they said, 'Actually, that would be lovely.'

I met an accountant who had many clients who came to him with company accounts. He told me that he wanted to make the company more than one of the thousands that compute taxes and compile final-year accounts. He thought about it and then offered to do directors' personal income taxes also. Anybody who has an accountant will tell you that they invest time, money and trust in them. As a result, an accountant's client base is a captive audience, so it is easy for the accountant to offer an additional, very valuable service that saves time and eliminates stress.

I know of an off-licence owner who, in the depth of the recession, realized that he needed to do something else to stimulate the revenue performance of the company, as he couldn't just carry on as he had in the past. Sales were down and he had tried advertising, special offers, you name it, all to no avail. He thought about selling cheese with the wine. He brought in small portions of cheese, which were put into the chilled shelves with the white wine, so he didn't have to buy any additional coolers. After a while, he couldn't believe what started to happen. People were actually coming to him for the cheese alone. He expanded the food range to include chutneys, crackers, chocolates, etc. He then renovated the shop and created a dedicated area with all of these items in it. Following this, he began offering food-and-wine hampers to the retail and corporate market. He is certainly one businessman who says the recession in Ireland has served him and his business very well, as it forced him to do things better, differently and much more profitably.

Remember, it is your responsibility to come up with ways of helping your clients – not theirs.

Increase the number of referrals that I get.

- ⌒ *Employee: 'Put it out there' among your circle of friends and family.*
- ⌒ *Business person: Encourage referrals.*

If you're reading this and shaking your head saying, 'Where would I come up with any of these solutions?', ask for help. Drop it into the conversation with your family and friends that you have some free time, and that should they come across anybody who wants to learn how to play an instrument, wants filing done, is returning to work after maternity leave and wants to get their child minded – please tell that person you're available. You could also just say that you fancy doing something different and earning some money from it while making it fit in with your lifestyle, and ask if they know of anyone looking for someone like you.

At presentations, I often ask business people, 'How many of you have a sales team?' The number of hands that goes up often depends on the size of the companies that I'm speaking to. Naturally, the larger the company, the larger the pool of money available for a direct sales force. However, this is not the only sales team that a company has. If you're in business, you'll know that referrals are the cheapest form of advertising. I can sit in front of you and tell you how great my services are, but you are far more likely to believe this if a trusted friend or colleague tells you how they've benefitted from my great services. Consider this: every time one of your customers tells somebody about you, they are acting as a part of your dedicated sales team.

Do you thank them for that? Do you send them a card or a small gift to recognize their contribution to your bottom line? If not, do you think people would appreciate it if you did? Do you think people would be more motivated to refer you if you did? I know that I would be.

Also, do you ask people to refer you? It can be a hard thing to blatantly come out and say, 'Could you let other people know about me?' However, there are subtler ways of doing this. For example, if you're almost at the end of a contract, you could say, 'If you know of anybody else who might benefit from this service, I would be delighted if you could pass on my name.' I say 'almost at the end' because you need to ensure that their trust in you has been built up to the point where they are comfortable in recommending you.

However, and this is absolutely crucial if you are going to be 'referred', you must live up to what your 'sales team member' has said about you. I remember telling somebody excitedly that I had a potential customer for them who was waiting for their immediate call. I was delighted with my good deed for the day – only to hear a month later that the person to whom I gave the referral never made the call. If this happens, referrals will dissipate and you'll lose out both in business and in respect.

Once, at the end of a presentation, someone asked me a question. She said, 'I'm very lucky in that I get lots of referrals, but, to be honest, I'm not sure why they are referring me. How can I find out?' My answer was 'I'm not being smart here, but – just ask them.' If somebody is referring you frequently, take them out to lunch and say, 'I really appreciate that you're passing on this new business. It's fantastic. Might I just ask you what it is about my product or service that you really like?' Their answers may provide you with much better 'marketing speak' than you could have come up with on your own. You'll know exactly what's going on in your customers' heads. In fact, you may be in possession of a very special element that you're not even promoting, one that could bring you lots more customers.

19

Grabbing the low-hanging fruit and working towards your own money tree

In the previous chapter I explained the theory behind increasing your revenue. Now let's get down to a practical exercise, one that could be a warm-up for your revenue-generation efforts. Consider whether there is any money that is staring you in the face – some low-hanging fruit that you could harvest. These could be one-off opportunities or turn into small streams that come in handy 'now and again'.

Selling unwanted/unneeded goods in your home

Is there anything at home, recently purchased, that you haven't used and aren't going to use? If so, why not take it back to the shop and get a refund? Have you got things in the attic that are simply gathering dust that could be of use to somebody? If so, why not advertise them in the paper or online? Perhaps you might have text-books that you used while at college or some that the kids aren't going to use any more – could you put them on eBay for sale and turn them into money? This will not be a 'hard sell' – your buyers will be happy to pay you for these goods. If you decide not to take this step, it's like you not bothering to pick up a €50 note from the sitting-room floor.

Investing money in high-yield stocks or bonds

I couldn't count the number of people over the years who have told me that they have money sitting in an account doing nothing. Let's say that you have €1,000 in a current account that you are unlikely to need over the coming weeks or months: you could get a 4% return on that money. If you're not investing it, you're basically turning down €40. If I were to walk into your home right this minute and offer you €40, would you take it? If this amount increased to €10,000 and I offered you €400, would this be welcome? Think about how you could generate the highest possible income from your surplus cash in a way that fits in with your risk profile. If you don't know anything about investing in the stock market, now would be a good time to educate yourself. It's essential that, if you choose to invest money, you do it with your eyes wide open.

Getting paid for things you already do

Is there a particular cream that you've referred several times to your friends? Are you particularly happy with your phone, broadband or electricity company? Have you sent several people on a particular course, holiday or to a tourist attraction? If so, you could be getting money in exchange for what you're already doing. Many companies offer a 'tell a friend' incentive whereby you get a voucher or a cheque in return for essentially selling their services for them. Third-party referral fees are a great way to boost your business revenues too; you can engage in joint ventures with other companies that offer complementary products.

I knew someone who worked in a fast-paced job and had two children, so she didn't have any time at all to get another job. However, she loved to cook, and she had friends who liked to cook and share recipes. She loved to buy kitchen knick-knacks that made her cooking all the more pleasurable, colourful and fun. She found a company offering franchises: all she had to do was to set up a website, sell the company's products and collect a commission every time somebody bought the company's products through her. After all, she was telling her friends and family about this company anyway – why not get paid for it too?

Mystery shopping

If you want to get a product, service or trip funded, look into mystery shopping. This involves agreeing to test a product, observing the customer experience and writing about it. Take a look at some of the mystery-shopping companies in Ireland or abroad and ask them to send you information on how to get on to their books, the types of experiences that you would be reporting on, the flexibility of their hours, the remuneration as well as the skills and abilities they require. For example, you could get paid to go on a cruise worth thousands of euros in exchange for a well-expressed report on the various aspects of the holiday. On a much smaller scale, when I was at college, the campus newspaper offered to pay for a cinema ticket and related expenses in exchange for a well-thought-out movie review delivered by a certain deadline.

Using coupons/vouchers

Some people are of the opinion that coupons and incentivizing vouchers are for 'tight people'. I don't agree. Let's say that I walk into a shop and the cost of a handbag is €50. What would you think of me if I walked up to the counter and said, 'I would prefer to pay €60 please?' The shop assistant protests that there is no need, but I insist on paying the extra money. If you choose not to use coupons, that's exactly the scenario that you are playing out. Of course, coupons are a marketing strategy that shops use to make you buy more, or buy with them instead of with their competitor. So if you spend easily, coupons might make you buy things you may not have considered in the first place. Before you spend that kind of money, make sure you track down and use coupons only for things you already buy, or were planning to buy anyway.

Get paid for your opinions

I don't know anybody that doesn't have an opinion on something. If you Google 'money for opinions', you will find an array of market-research companies willing to offer you a small fee in exchange for taking the time to fill out a survey about what you buy, etc. As a student, I signed up to answer surveys online and I got paid in grocery vouchers. It took a couple of minutes in the evening, and it didn't take long for my credits to add up. Businesses wanted to get directly to the views of their target market, and the money was willingly handed over to me.

Sign up for clubcards, frequent-flyer points and loyalty programmes

If you're going to spend your money on goods and services, you may as well pick up any additional benefits you can. I travel a lot, and so by taking a couple of minutes to sign up for a frequent-flyer card I can now enjoy going straight to the top of the queue, lounges and (my favourite!) getting upgraded to business and first class on flights. My cousin got all her honeymoon flights and accommodation in a very exotic location paid for by building up these benefits. Once again, be aware that shops use these programmes to document your buying behaviour, so they are likely to send you offers based on what you bought in the past in order to make you spend more. Make sure the advantages you are offered are real advantages, and not just some paltry compensation for all the information you are going to be yielding in exchange.

Visit your local tax office to ensure that you are getting all the tax relief that you are entitled to

We pay tax on the goods we buy, the income we earn, the capital gains we make and many other financial transactions that we undertake. Perhaps you might like some money back from the government in the form of tax relief? Schedule some time to go into the Revenue Commissioners' office to speak with one of their officials about all of the benefits that you could be getting. If you have been overpaying tax and it is retrievable, you may find a cheque on its way to you.

Generating an income from your home

There are many ways that you could use the space in your home to generate money – after all, it's there anyway. Could you rent out a room or a portion of your house? If you *own* an area in which to park, is there a business close by or a commuter that would pay to use it? Could you take in some money for storing goods in your attic for a family who don't have much space in their current accommodation? (But avoid storing stuff for distant cousins whose sources of income are unclear but who seem to spend a lot of time in South America or South-East Asia!)

Government grants

There is a plethora of grants available from national and European agencies as well as various bodies. If you're thinking about doing anything from insulating your home, to taking care of an elderly relative, to researching a new product, to building a website, to running a community event, take a look to see if there is money available to help you.

*

Now I hope you've limbered up with this exercise and are beginning to see ways to make more money everywhere around you. Let's move on to the next level – how about setting up a business? Or recession-proofing the one you already have? I've already shown you how there are plenty of ways of turning aspects of your personality or hobbies or talents into saleable commodities (in Chapter 17). I'll recap a little here and then expand further.

What can I sell? Ask yourself this question and then think laterally. Do you like to read, travel, cook, write, design, paint, craft, manage people, learn about history, help people, speak languages, keep up with current affairs, plan, dance, spend money, go shopping? As a child, I dreamed of travelling the world. As a teenager, I lived abroad and loved it, but missed those at home a lot. I thought, wouldn't it be fantastic to be able to see various parts of the world, pop home often so that I wouldn't have the heartache, and also get paid for it? Funnily enough, this is exactly what life looks like as managing director of an international financial-training company. Don't for one second think that your dream career isn't possible. It absolutely is, but you won't find it unless you know what it looks like.

What are your skills? This is similar to, but not the same as, the last question. Make a list of what you are good at doing, and make sure to reach into your memory of compliments received. Can you speak a language, deliver an excellent presentation, stick to a plan, manage your time well, defuse tense situations, pick clothes for people that suit them, accessorize a plain dress into an amazing outfit, host a very entertaining dinner party, understand the needs and wants of a disabled person? Your skillset doesn't have to be a short list; keep writing until you're exhausted.

What are people always asking you to do? I have *lots* of cousins. Whenever there is a family gathering, there is 'a cousin for everything' – one who will always be asked for help in organizing, another who is an amazing cook, another who makes hand-made invitations, another who has a phone book like the *Golden Pages*, another who is the life and soul of the party, and I could keep going. Look in the mirror and ask yourself, 'Why do people call on me?' What is it that people feel that, in any circumstances, they can ask you to do? Something they can rely on you to do competently – from picking up the kids at school, because you're always punctual, to making a fantastic banoffee pie if they are having a dinner party, to organizing a party when they don't know where to start? This can give you a real start in finding your commercial talent.

On the other hand, you can also look outwards for these clues. Remember my story about my very first foray into business? I was coordinating investment clubs and people continually asked me questions about the technical areas of their own online trading, understanding the stock market and managing their affairs. After a while, I started a mentoring service to answer the need that I saw. Have you noticed that people are always asking you to do something – is there a spark of business in that?

Next, we need to move from looking at your skills, talents and abilities to the needs and desires of others. Take some time to write down a list of ways in which you could make the following happen.

Can you save people money? For example, if you act as an outsourced bookkeeper for a company, this can save them accountant's fees. Could you act as a mystery shopper for a company to check they are providing the best customer service possible and not losing out on the custom and referrals they would receive from happy clients?

Can you make people money? Could you go into people's homes and help them turn their clutter into money by showing them how to sell their 'no-longer-needed' goods online? Could you teach somebody French to business standard to improve their career prospects?

Can you ease pain for people? Could you take the stress out of planning a wedding or a party? Could you give some students grinds in a subject they are having difficulty with in order to minimize their frustration and ease their fears about doing badly in an exam?

Can you create pleasure for people? Could you give facials or manicures? Could you hold a dance class in the local community centre to give your attendees some fun and fitness?

Can you create something that is better than what's out there at the moment? Are you absolutely fed up with the lack of facilities available in some area of your life? Maybe there aren't enough kids' activities in your area. Maybe you want a service, but don't have the time to get there and back in the window of free time that you have. Perhaps there are more people than you in this situation and you could think about bringing this service to people's homes instead.

Can you save time for people? Can you do something for somebody that would save them a lot of time, and hence money? For example, you could be an outsourced personal assistant for a busy professional – processing emails, making calls, managing diaries, and all from the comfort of your own home during pre-specified hours. Could you do the design for a room in somebody's house, go out and buy all the new materials, follow through on your plan and make something special happen to that space?

In all of the above, I have asked you to look at how you might initiate your own additional revenue stream or business from scratch. However, there are other ways to hit the ground running.

Agent/Affiliate Marketing

You could become an agent for an existing company and sell their products. This can be a great way of making some extra money if you find yourself telling your friends about a product that you use often, and they are buying it. You could easily be making a commission on that.

Franchising

Instead of trying to start and build up your own brand, you could piggy-back on another by setting up a branch of an existing company. As a result, you could be part of a large purchasing group and benefit from the parent company's advertising. However, you may have to pay them an annual fee as well as a portion of your profits each year. Remember to use the P&L exercise to make sure this is worth your while.

Commercializing research

If you are an ambitious person with business acumen and are looking for a product or service to sell, you could contact your local college. Each year, there are millions of euros spent on research, but academics don't bring their innovations to market, as this is not where their skillsets lie. You could pick up where they are happy to leave off. In addition, there are often additional funding opportunities from governments in the form of 'Innovation Partnerships' to encourage this sort of joined-up thinking.

Businesses for sale

Businesses face extinction for many reasons – because of financial pressure, the model growing stale or the drivers of the business entering a more senior phase of their lives without having anybody to take over the enterprise. As a result, at any given stage, there are often several thousand businesses available for sale. If you would like to take over an existing, operating entity, perhaps this could be an option for you.

How can you sell? Is it a product? A service? Are you a consultant?

Now that we've thought in depth about what you could be selling, let's think about how you could sell it, and why people would buy from you. You need to think about all the ways there are to skin a cat. For each idea that you have, write a list of ways that you could derive a revenue stream from it. By way of example, here's what a would-be interior designer might come up with. She could:

- provide interior design as a service to people or companies who need to renovate a room or property;
- provide a specialized service to people who are trying to sell their house and want it to put 'the best face forward';

- develop her own version of a tool with which people can simulate on a computer screen the type of room they would like to see;
- deliver training courses in interior design as evening courses or at a post-Leaving Certificate college;
- act as a consultant for other interior designers in a niche area;
- buy an existing interior-design business;
- start a blog on interior design, build up the number of people that read it and sell advertising to companies that would be interested in this audience;
- sign up as an agent to get a commission on the products that she uses and would encourage others to use also;
- talk to her local college to see if they have any new, exciting research that an interior designer could get funding to commercialize;
- work with an interior-design magazine and grow its profile;
- write a book about interior design.

Apply this to every single idea that you came up with in the exercises above. After a while, you'll have built up quite an extensive list of revenue-generating ideas, ideas that have sprung solely from your own creativity and thinking. Then it's simply a matter of working through that list, finding out what works and what doesn't, and building momentum.

Why would people buy from you? What value do you bring? What problem do you solve?

The very first step in getting people to buy from you is that *you* have to believe in what you're doing. You have to be totally confident that you can deliver this product or service. After all, if you're not sure that you can do the job, you wouldn't expect anybody else to be.

Next, people need to realize that they have a need or a want. This isn't always obvious. In some cases, people will not see this, even if you can see it standing out a mile. It may be difficult to persuade them that they need you. For instance, a person may clearly need some training in digital marketing if sales via traditional means are falling. However, they may not be aware of this because:

- They may not even realize that customers are now looking for their products online.
- They might be blaming competition, economic circumstances and internal issues in the business. All of these might certainly be contributing to falling sales, but they could make a significant impact on their top line if they followed in the direction where their target market was leading them.
- They might just be too busy – answering calls, replying to emails, having meetings – to step off the treadmill and really evaluate the way their company is going.

The people that you want to speak to are those who not only acknowledge they have an issue, but who are actively doing something about it and looking for a solution. These people are far more likely to appreciate your help. Therefore, it's very important that your product or service actually fits their particular needs. If you feel that you can help them, all that's left to do is prove that what you can do for them is worth more than the money you're charging.

Why would people buy from you over all the others? What is your unique selling point?

In some cases, people will buy from you because you're in the right place at the right time. Let's say that you're walking down a city street and going for a coffee. You would like to get a newspaper to read – what do you do? You look around and find the nearest one.

That's all that comes into your head. Similarly, if you put yourself within viewing distance of your customers, business is far more likely to come your way. Hence, it's terribly important to know where your target market is likely to be looking, both physically and online. This could be via search engines on the internet, key industry events, magazines, networking events, exhibitions, etc. The first thing that you need to do is to make it easy to buy from you, and being visible is key.

The next thing is to differentiate yourself from others. You don't have to make a superhuman effort to find some undiscovered corner of your market. You simply need to think about how you are different. Do you have a certain specialist knowledge area? Do you have experience of a certain role or project? Do you practise what you preach? Do you offer extra value over your competitors? Do you offer supreme customer service? Is your method easier to follow? Have you worked with the leaders in your industry? Write a list of each and every way that your offering is defined and you'll find your unique selling point, or the way in which you distinguish yourself from others.

Why would people buy from you again? How good is your customer service? Do you have any upsell/cross-sell/subscription or retainer offers?

Business research reveals that it is four times easier to sell to an existing customer than to obtain a new client. If somebody is ready to hand money over to you in exchange for a product or service, you have built up a sufficient level of trust for the transaction to take place. If you make good on the agreement, that trust is cemented and leaves the door open for you to give further help to that customer. However, if this trust is broken on either side, the relationship is likely to suffer or disappear. As a result, the bedrock of any business that hopes to continue is to do what you say you will do and to do it well.

Do you ever give a moment's thought to 'How could I spend more money at the butcher's?' or 'How could I spend more money with the travel agent?' or 'How could I spend more money at the bookshop?' I doubt it. Instead, I think that these thoughts would pass through your mind: 'What will I give the kids for their dinner?' or 'Where will we go this summer on holiday?' or 'There is a "buy-one-get-one-half-price" – I might just buy the second one in that case.' Can you spot the difference? Customers don't spend their days thinking about how to spend more money with you; it's your job to show them how. How can you make it easy for your clients to spend more money with you?

Also, how can you encourage your clients to tell their friends and family that they too might benefit from your service? Again, it is of absolute importance that you live up to expectations. If a supplier disappoints a client, it's bad. However, if a supplier disappoints a friend or family member of a previous client, the impact is seriously compounded.

20

Nine steps to your first €100 of extra income

Now that you have an idea about what you have to offer, the next job facing you is to get it to market. Like everything else in this book, it's not that complicated if you break it down into simple steps. If you follow the nine steps below, before you know it your concept will have taken off and you'll be generating more income or you'll have laid the foundations for building your business.

Step 1: Articulate your offering

You need to put what you're offering into words. Have you heard of the 'elevator pitch'? This is what you would say to someone if you had to give them a clear, pithy and still comprehensive account of what you do in the time spent sharing a moving lift. A couple of 'dos and don'ts':

- Do keep it simple: five or so words should suffice to make your listener want to know more. If you're successful, the door will open and you'll have the chance to go into a little more detail.
- Do test it out on some (honest) family and friends. In sixty seconds or less, explain what you do and ask them to tell you what they heard. If this is completely at odds with what you thought you said, go back to the drawing board.
- Don't start off with: 'We do a lot of things really . . .', as this means that you are going to confuse your listener.

If you're not able to articulate your offering concisely, your listener is not going to be able to understand it immediately.

～ Don't spend ten minutes explaining your revolutionary technology, or the highly intricate processes of some form of mechanics or psychology, because all the other person will hear is 'Gobbledegook, blah, blah, blah.' Cue nodding, smiling, platitudes like 'Oh that's very interesting.' Then they walk away from you with no intention of ever getting in touch.

A useful formula is: 'I [solve this problem] for [that group of people] which has the impact of [state the benefits of the product or service] for them.' This forces you to concentrate on benefits, rather than on features, to show clearly why people want your service (what problem you solve), and who your target market is.

Step 2: Figure out the characteristics of your ideal customer so that you can recognize them

Identifying your target market is absolutely crucial and the more you know about them the better. A good way to start this exercise is to write down a list of groups of people who are not likely to be customers of yours. Once you've excluded people not likely to buy from you, focus on those who are left. Can you answer the following questions about them? If you do the exercise well, you should feel a bit like a stalker! Yes, that's how much you should know about your target market.

～ What age range is your target customer?
～ Are they male or female?
～ Do they work? If so, in what industry?
～ What are their hobbies?
～ What are their worries at this stage in their lives?

- Do they have children? If so, what ages are they? What are they doing at that stage in their lives?
- Do they have a lot of time? Money? Stress? Constraints?
- Where do they meet their friends?
- What media do they tune into? What time? Why?
- What is the best way to communicate with them?

Step 3: Where can you find your market?

If you can answer the questions prompted by Step 2, you'll have a head start on this answer. We are now zoning in on your market research and at the start of the process of working out your marketing strategy. Think about the following questions:

- Does your customer use the internet? For what? What are the 'keywords' that they are likely to search for? What problem do they have, and what words do they use to describe this problem?
- Where does your customer regularly go – a specific shop, crèche, street, holiday destination?
- What exhibitions is your customer likely to be interested in?
- What newspapers or magazines does your customer read?
- Whose opinions are trusted by your customer? Those of their friends, their favourite celebrities and media personalities, their peers, their superiors, as well as those of market-leading companies?
- What scarcity does your customer experience? Time? Money? Time on their own? Company? Opportunity? Self-esteem? A social life? Attention? Growth? Energy?
- What pleasures are sought by your target market? Success? Beauty? Good exam results? Calm? Social interaction with their peers? Time for their hobbies? Sleep? Financial security? Prestige?

Have you ever heard the phrase 'Seek first to understand and then to be understood'? Your customers are very important people in your life. After all, your customers pay your bills. Care for them. Invest time in understanding their lifestyles, worries, concerns and what makes them happy. You're going to start making their lives better in exchange for a slice of their income. Ensure that you do the best job that you can by taking an interest in their lives.

Step 4: Find a way of speaking to them

Building on the previous step, design your marketing strategy. Are you going to connect with your market:

- *online?* Are you going to use search-engine optimization (SEO) strategies to put your site in front of your customer? This means that when customers search using certain terms, yours is the business that comes high up in the results. For example, if you were searching for 'restaurants in Letterkenny' in Google, the ones that appear at the top of the list have been 'search-engine optimized', because you're far more likely to look through these options than those that are ten pages later. Are you going to create a blog, use social media, or offer to write articles for the forums and sites that your customer visits?
- *at networking groups?* Are you going to shortlist the networking groups that your target customer is going to be at, whittle it down to a list of people, companies or sectors, pitch to them when you meet them and follow up afterwards?
- *by advertising in offline media?* Are you going to advertise, generate interesting PR, write thought-provoking articles and use special offers to motivate people to contact you?
- *through people?* Are you going to ask your contacts to connect you with your target market? Are you going to call people or email them directly to engage with you and your

company? Are you going to ask your existing customers to refer you to their family, friends and colleagues?

~~~ *physically at the places they frequent?* Are you going to take a stand at a show or exhibition they are likely to visit? Are you going to go to events where your customer is going to be and strike up a conversation? Are you going to put posters and other informative content at their eye level in places where they pass through very often?

Of course, you could always use a combination of all of the above, but the important thing is to have a plan.

Step 5: Take ten sales actions every day

This could include sending an email to a potential customer, making a call to a lead, attending a networking meeting, publishing a blog post, distributing a press release, etc.

Note that I don't mention strategizing, writing a press release or researching good advertising media. At this stage, the only thing that counts is actually connecting with your potential customer. I would be very surprised if at least one of these actions does not bear some fruit. If they don't, investigate why they didn't work in whatever way you can and repeat with another ten tomorrow. Repeat until you get your first customer.

Step 6: Provide the service

As soon as the customer commits, work out the logistics of delivery with them. When is the product going to be delivered? When is the service going to take place? What needs to be organized from both of your sides, in advance? Do your utmost to deliver a superior customer experience because the greatest advertising of all is your own handiwork.

Step 7: Send the invoice and follow up on payment, if it's not forthcoming

As soon as the job has been done or the product has been delivered, send the invoice and set out your credit terms (if any) on the invoice. Let's say that you stipulate all payments must be made within thirty days and you don't receive payment within that time-frame. Call the customer and say, 'I'm just following up on invoice number . . .' There may have been a misunderstanding, a problem with their processes, a communication issue or somebody simply forgot. Unless you bring this to their attention, you have little chance of its being resolved. If they get slightly annoyed, don't let that stop you. You did the job and you deserve to get paid.

Step 8: Say thank you

After each time you do business with somebody and you get paid, say thank you. Without your customer, there is no business, no revenue and no continuity. They are highly important people and companies, and they'll appreciate your not taking them for granted. Depending on the size of the order, call them just to say thank you, send them a card, a hamper or something that could be useful to them.

Step 9: Suggest other ways of helping them

After the job has been done successfully, is there a way in which:

- you could provide the product or service again in the future?
- you could provide additional products or services?
- any of their friends, family or colleagues could benefit from your product or service?

And that's it. Lather, rinse, repeat, as they say. These steps are the bare bones of conducting business. Whenever you feel overwhelmed, refer back to them to get you going again. Deep down, business is nothing more and nothing less than doing the nine steps above, over and over again.

And now: a word of warning. Can you spot the difference between a business and a busy mess? It's very easy to become very busy and deceive yourself into thinking that you are being productive. You can spend the day driving to a networking meeting where you don't meet any potential business connections at all, returning to your office to colour code your folders, spending an hour updating your business page on Facebook, chatting to your friend and then reading reviews on TripAdvisor of a hotel that you're going to next month before going home. What have you achieved for your business with all those hours? Absolutely zip.

Let me give you another scenario. A woman has the ambition of bringing in €1,000 of revenue in her first month in business. She registers her business in July. She spends August setting up an email account, creating a Facebook page, drawing some pictures of what she would like her website to look like and doing a course on Twitter marketing. The kids are back to school in September, so all she finds time to do is research a list of logo designers, web designers and local networking groups. In October she contacts the web designer and discovers that he can't do a lot until she chooses the colours she wants in her logo; she also finds out that she has to write all the copy for her website herself. In November she puts up her first couple of posts on her Facebook page, gets her logo sorted, gets her business card designed and passes on these developments to her web designer. In early December she puts together the first draft of her website copy and then Christmas takes over. In early January she gets a great burst of enthusiasm and signs off on the website, gets her business cards printed, goes to some networking meetings and makes her first sales calls. In February she pays an accountant to file last year's accounts for her and she gets her first commitments from customers (from her calls in January). In March she turns over €1,000 and is delighted that she met her goal – to make €1,000 in her first month in business.

Can you see the problem here? She is nine months in business, according to Companies Registration Office. She spent a full half-year 'getting ready'. Ultimately, her first bit of turnover came from those sales calls she did in January. She chose to spend the previous six months faffing about with peripheral details rather than simply contacting her target market to tell them about how she could supply their demand.

Make no mistake – business is all about sales and cashflow, not about having a state-of-the-art website or impressive business cards. You can spend countless hours in your office doing a lot and getting nowhere. As soon as you know what you want to do and who you want to sell your product or service to, your mind should focus on sales-generating activities right from the outset. Everything else can wait. As you bring in your first couple of customers, get a logo and a business card designed. Continue to focus on sales and then organize your website.

On the other hand, I would absolutely not advise diving straight in by picking up the phone book and calling round to sell your service. It's crucially important that you first put words and numbers around your offering – as outlined at Step 1 above – and then figure out how to allocate your time, resources and energy. Take a while to develop your product, learn to articulate your business offering, find out who your target market is and go for it. If you don't know who your customers are, you could waste a lot of time trying to sell to the wrong people. Schedule some time for sales activities daily and also look at your cashflow each day. Only afterwards should you look after everything else. Without sales and cashflow, the rest is irrelevant.

Before I send you on your way, let me give you one last checklist – ten business pitfalls to avoid.

1. *Doing the work and not invoicing for it.* This might sound totally bizarre, but it happens. People and businesses can go through the

process of sourcing the work, securing the deal, honouring a contract and then forgetting to send an invoice for weeks or months. It
is important to keep on top of your documentation for the following reasons:

- If you don't comb through the invoices to be sent and those
  to be followed up on, there is a much higher risk that you'll
  forget to ask to get paid.
- If you happen to run into financial difficulty or are presented with an opportunity that requires investment, you
  can't just send out invoices today and expect to get paid
  tomorrow. However, if you always get your invoices to your
  customers immediately on completion, they can get payment to you from that point onwards, as opposed to being
  asked only weeks later.

Let's say that I turnover €10,000 a year and I always leave my invoices
until a month after I do the job. Further, let's assume that I could get
an interest rate of 6% on any cash balances that I invest or save. If I got
the money that is due to me in my account a month earlier, just by
sending my invoices earlier, it could spend more time in my account,
and I would earn interest on it. By my inaction, I am choosing not to
earn an extra €50 that year for absolutely zero work. This may sound
like a nominal amount, but it's still money that you're leaving on the
table and you're going to have to send out the paperwork anyway. Of
course, the more I earn and the longer I leave my invoices unissued,
the higher that figure becomes. Personally, I would rather the €50 go
towards a bill in our company than straight into the ether.

2. *Leaving money on the table.* You'll remember I pointed out
that most people choose the most difficult and least profitable route
of constantly trying to find new customers, rather than simply
searching for more business through existing channels. I have often
seen business people become frustrated because they can't find or
convert new leads; and yet there were untapped opportunities to be
found in their previous ten phonecalls.

3. A one-time-hit sort of business. As a teenager, I did a short stint of work experience in a shop that sold furniture. The owner began to specialize in 'baby furniture', branded herself accordingly and began to stock baby clothes, soothers, sheets, etc. I asked her why she decided to change her business model (although at that time I wouldn't have used that phrase). She said that people will invest in a table and chairs that will be used for five years, but babies grow out of clothes within five weeks. It's important for a small business to build sustainability into the model via fast-moving stock, a strong referral incentive or a recurring fee, as otherwise, every day, you're starting from scratch.

4. Not listening. I remember having a conversation with a man about finding external financial supports from state agencies and European bodies. At the time, his business was much bigger than mine and he had turned over many multiples of what I had. I often asked him for his opinion on business matters as my own business was growing. I valued his opinion very much, as he had given me valuable advice many times. However, I had been much more successful than he had been in obtaining this type of funding for my business. I thought it would be helpful if I highlighted some avenues that he could investigate. He didn't let me get to the second sentence before telling me the road was too hard, fraught with paperwork and probably fruitless anyway. I protested saying that this was completely contrary to my experience, but he was closed to the idea.

I suggest that you listen to everybody who is willing to share some of their experiences with you. You don't have to act on everybody's advice, but there can be a nugget in every story. At this point in the book, you probably won't be surprised to learn that I have been known to talk at great length, in great detail, on a great number of topics. But, despite what you may think, I listen far more than I speak: there is an abundance of wisdom within earshot.

5. Seasonality. Seasonality is both a threat and an opportunity. Ice-cream can sit for months in freezers around the world waiting for the sun to shine and consumers to perspire. Tourist operators and accommodation providers often shut down altogether during the quieter seasons, as there simply isn't the business to warrant running a full staff. However, this week I met with a budding businessman, who happens to be a relative (you guessed it – yet another cousin!), and he is turning the issue of seasonality totally on its head. He sells parts for, and repairs, farm machinery. He didn't want to be anxious about weakening revenue at certain times of the year, so he set about creating an offering that could cater to the different needs of his target market as the seasons changed. For example, spraying and fertilizer-spreading is done from March to May, and silage and hay are harvested from May to August, and so on. He sourced the facilities needed to service this target market throughout each phase of the farming calendar. He lets his customers know in March that he understands the products and repairs they are likely to need in April, and that he has the capacity to provide them. He has proven to his customers that he is one-step ahead of their problems and that he has the physical inventory and technical expertise with which to deliver on his promise. Essentially, he is morphing several different seasonal offerings into one enterprise and giving his customers a reason to go back to him on a monthly or biannual basis. If you're looking to work a couple of weeks or months in a year, a seasonal revenue stream might be perfect for you. However, if you want to generate revenue evenly throughout the year, be careful of a product or service that turns out to be seasonal

6. *A costly revenue stream.* It's very easy when you start in business to get so excited about bringing in new revenue that you totally forget about the costs. You run up high phone bills, excessive mileage on your car and unbilled time on customer service, because you want to drive your enterprise onwards and upwards, and what do a couple of client meetings matter along the way? Remember to keep a very close eye on your P&L for every customer and don't forget to cost your own time to ensure that you're allocating your resources

(including your own mental and physical energy) in the most effect-ive ways.

7. *Burning out.* If you are the business – the only person who gen-erates sales, provides the product or service and you do everything else as well – remember, then, that the business is you. If you burn out because you've poured out all your enthusiasm in one go, the whole enterprise that you built on adrenalin has to go to ground while you catch up with yourself. It's so important to take care of yourself, recognize when you need a break and to take it.

If you find, like many women do, that you're being pulled and dragged in all directions – as a business woman or employee, mother, wife or girlfriend, sister, daughter and friend – it can appear that somebody has forgotten to give you your fair share of 'me-time'. 'Me-time' is time you give to yourself. So if you're not getting it, you need to find a way of creating it. If you feel the universe isn't appreciating you, maybe you need to help it out a little. Find ways to nourish, reward and appreciate yourself. As I write this, it's Friday evening, I'm on the way to my board meeting, and I've had an immensely busy week. It saw lots of things done, new contracts secured and countless hours poured into the business yet again. If I don't take a break at some stage this weekend, I'm not going to be worth tuppence by the time the week kicks off on Monday morn-ing. And this is the case even though I love my work and I'm looking forward to another week: burnout doesn't care how great your enthusiasm is.

8. *Lack of delegation.* A lot of businesses could grow into new and exciting forms, but the very person who started the enterprise may be holding it back. Entrepreneurs are feisty people. They don't have a lot of patience, they don't hang around for others to make things happen, and, given the right opening and a sprinkling of luck, they can make a lot happen with few resources. This is all important in the start-up phase. However, as time goes on, they have to spread themselves rather thinly and problems can arise unless they can bring other people into the organization, train them and trust them. Otherwise, they'll stay stuck on a treadmill of running to stand

still – always dreaming of moving onwards and upwards but not willing to let themselves and those around them get there.

9. *Lack of self-discipline.* Business requires a lot of self-discipline. In the early stages, many business people start to fall in love with the flexibility of their new lifestyle and find themselves on the golf course absorbing the kudos of being a 'company director', at the gym or in the shops more often than in the office. There is absolutely nothing wrong with admitting that being in business isn't for you and that instead you would rather be less formal about generating extra revenue, but recognize this rather than blaming the economy, the sector, the address you have or the cereal you eat for breakfast. If you want to set up a company that will grow into a multinational, employ people or turnover substantial figures annually, there is a huge amount of self-discipline involved and don't expect anything less. Don't set lofty aspirations of bringing in millions by spending a couple of hours here and there. The amount that you can bring into your life is in direct proportion to how smart you are in doing so and the effort that you direct towards that ambition. If you want it, it's out there for you, but you have to walk, run, hop or skip to get it.

10. *Not changing with the times.* It is important not to resist what is staring you in the face, but to move with it. This can mean learning about social media or e-commerce. It also means that if you notice that you're getting bigger and busier, you have to talk to mentors who can help you to understand your new paradigm, examine your processes and procedures, and really capitalize upon the opportunities in front of you. If you see that your business model isn't working any more, you have to look to the biggest and boldest in your industry and see what you can learn from them. Life is exciting because it changes. With every ending, a beginning presents itself and it's crucial to surf the waves – otherwise you'll be caught unawares by the backwash. But not changing with the times shouldn't be a problem for you – now that you've read this book, you know how to deal with moving out of your comfort zone.

Conclusion

And this is it, the end of the book. The book may have ended, but your journey to financial freedom is just starting. My wish is that you will use this book as your very own financial satnav, returning to it every time you need to check where you're headed and how to get there. I would love for this book to turn into a kind of logbook, so that every time you achieve one of the goals outlined, every time you take a step, you take a coloured pen and write in the margin of the corresponding passage *I did it. I nailed that goal* – with the date, of course. Then the book will become a physical reminder of your achievements.

I have given you several examples of times when I found it difficult to take the first step – I was nervous, I was striking out into the unknown, it took me a long time just to put one foot in front of the other. However, it's not just me. I have mentored hundreds of people who were getting started in the stock market. I've sat in many houses listening to clients say to me, 'I would like to learn how to buy and sell shares, but I'm afraid that I won't be able to do it/I will press the wrong button and end up owing millions/I'm just uncomfortable with it.' I've shown them how to do a dummy trade on a simulator and then I've asked to swap seats. I've talked them through each step. I've then asked them to do it on their own, and if they got stuck I pointed them in the right direction. By the third time, I was drinking tea and eating biscuits because they'd mastered it. I have so often watched the look of surprise and pleasure at their achievement as they say, 'I think I could do that.' I meet these people months or years later and they tell me how they're happily managing their own accounts and have taught their children to do the same. I was sitting at the back of a presentation one day and a man made a beeline for me at the end just to say, 'The trading platform is actually very easy to use when you get used to it.'

Similarly, I meet people who have been in the audience when I spoke on the topic of entrepreneurship. They see me afterwards and tell me that they've started to ask their clients if they can provide even more benefit to them, and to their amazement their clients say, 'That would be great actually.' They tell me how they shut their eyes as they make what they think is a cheeky offer on the phone, in case they're forced to face rejection. Instead, they hear kind replies such as 'Not at the moment, but that's an interesting idea' or 'We may consider that', followed by questions to get more information. I remember one woman said to me, 'I never realized an extra 10% in revenue was just waiting for me to ask for it.'

Can you remember your first day at college? Your first day in a new job? Starting a new class? Going on a night out with a group of people with whom you have only a slight connection? Walking into a networking group? Going on a date? Think back to all the times that you put one foot in front of the other in the face of uncertainty. Think back to all those times that it paid off. I was living with my cousin when I started college and she nearly had to physically push me out the door, such was my apprehension about walking into this new world. On my second night, she rang me at 7 p.m. to ask me where I was. I said, 'I'm having coffee with the lads here – I'll be home there later on.' I had assimilated that fast. Think about a job where you felt a dread in the pit of your stomach about starting, and by the time you left you cried because you loved the people and the surroundings so much. Think about the time that you made a friend for life by taking a risk. Think about the great nights out that you might never have had if you hadn't pushed yourself out that door.

But sometimes the first step is the most difficult, so let me help you . . .

Let's say that I want to save money by stopping a direct debit for a service that I don't use any more. The gap between wanting to do that and actually achieving it is a single phonecall. I don't think that I need to explain how to lift a handset, dial a number, initiate a conversation and carry one out until the matter has been discussed. Everybody reading this book knows how to use the phone. Therefore, the gap between thinking, 'I must do that some day' and doing it is tiny.

Let's say that I want to get information about setting up a business. The gap between wanting to do that and actually achieving it is a couple of Google searches. I don't think that I need to explain how to switch on a computer, open a web browser, go to Google's search page and type in 'Setting up a business – what do I do?' You all know how to do that. Therefore, the gap between thinking, 'I must do that some day' and doing it is tiny.

Let's say that I want to take a client out to lunch and ask them how I can offer more benefit to them. The gap between wanting to do that and actually achieving it is a single call. Therefore, the gap between thinking, 'I must do that some day' and doing it is tiny.

Let's say that I want to find some restaurant vouchers or special offers. The gap between wanting to do that and a less expensive dinner and night out is a Google search. Yet again, the gap between thinking, 'I must do that some day' and doing it is tiny.

Let's say that I want to meet my boss about my existing pay arrangements. The gap between that and achieving it is an email with the following words, 'Could I pop into you some time this week?'

I hope that you see that the actions themselves aren't difficult – it's the will behind them that makes the difference. Of course, actually carrying out those actions is simple – it's fear and uncertainty that hold us back. Acknowledge that fear and try this: just do the action in a mechanical, automatic way, as if you were hypnotized. You might be surprised by the results.

Have you ever been in a situation where you thought 'I didn't know I had it in me'? Life has its own way of forcing things out of us. You have deep reservoirs of talent and ability within you that can make amazing things happen. All you have to do is pick up that phone, send that email, search for the information, ask the questions and act on the answers.

And still, despite our best efforts, sometimes uncertainty drives us to procrastinate. So what do you do then? How about . . .

~ Setting a timer for five minutes. You might say 'I will just work five minutes – only five short minutes.' By the time the timer rings, your initial resistance will have been broken and you'll be well into the task.

~ Doing something related to the task that is not the task itself. You could make a plan of action for the next half-hour: 'To tackle this, I will first do *x* for ten minutes, then *y* for ten minutes, then *z* for a final ten minutes', e.g., reread what you did on the task the last time so you can pick up where you left off; look for one piece of information related to the task, etc. It's a way of easing into it.

~ Talking yourself into it: you could open a text document and begin writing to yourself, saying, 'I really don't want to do this thing. I see no way I could possibly enjoy doing it. It's boring. I don't want to do it. I hate everything, every-thing about it. Everything . . . Let's see . . . What is each of those things? Of course, I might perhaps do *x* to make it more enjoyable . . . Wait, I'll just do that, see how it goes and report back.' And of course just by saying, 'I can't possibly enjoy it,' you start thinking of ways to make the task more enjoyable . . .

Let me share with you my personal arsenal for dealing with pro-crastination and fear.

I strategize. As you know, I love developing systems, making plans and setting out goals. If I'm reluctant to get into something, I simply write down a list of things to be contained within it. I question how I would like to approach it, style it, explain it, make it interesting, personalize it, make it interactive, make it snazzy and make it excit-ing for me to do it. After all that, I'm interested in putting my ideas into action and I'm motivated to do just that.

I deconstruct a task. This increases the feeling of gathering momen-tum. If I feel that I'm getting nowhere, I write a list of every single thing that I could possibly do to move forward. If I'm actually get-ting nowhere because I'm involuntarily busying myself with doing irrelevant time-fillers, I break down everything that I need to do to complete the project and then focus on one simple, enjoyable task. If I have to write a report, I break it down into its sections. If I have a list of calls to make, I write down each name. If I have to prepare a presentation, I break it down into the key concepts. In essence, I 'start at the start' and increase the number of ways that I can tick a box to say, 'That's done now.'

I call my boyfriend. There have been days when I do the above, but it just isn't happening. He is the most wonderful friend and I have been known to phone him at 11 a.m. on a Monday morning to tell him that I just can't get into it. He asks me exactly what's wrong and we figure out a way to get back on track. Typically, we find the one small step needed to get going again and then I'm off. He'll often ring an hour later to see how I'm doing but by then I'm flying.

I stop. Sometimes I just have to stop everything and acknowledge that now is just not the right time to work on a particular task. I had a writer's block one day when writing this book and I turned the laptop off. I looked through my cookery books and thought about what I would like to make. I made my shopping list, came home and whipped up a fantastic spread. After my creativity had expressed itself in these ways, it was ready to manifest itself in the written word again. Sometimes, you need to stop and start again. Has your computer ever crashed and then when you reboot it, it's fine? Maybe like your computer, you've simply overworked yourself and you need to give your brain, ingenuity, effort, ambition and inner self a breather.

The main thing is that I never have the intention of giving up, if I believe in the task at hand and/or the goal that I'm striving for.

Believing in the goal is crucial. If you're questioning the entire process or the journey, as opposed to the particular task, that's a whole other ball game. If you feel that you're slacking off on 'doing the things to get you there', question the goal that you're moving towards. Has its shine worn away? If so, why? What would be better and do you need to change what you're doing now in order to get there? If not, do you simply need to be reminded of your goal? How about rereading your favourite bits of this book for a pep talk?

I was mountaineering up the Mourne Mountains with a group from college years ago. I remember thinking how hard it was, how cold it was and how hungry I was as we got closer to the top. However, the only way to keep going was by looking at how far we had come and how much nearer the top of the mountain appeared. Similarly, throughout this journey, stop and congratulate yourself often on the steps that you have made. Remember, that's what the 'R' is for in SMARTER goals. Also, ensure that you regularly dream about where you want to be and why you want to get there. This isn't a sprint but a marathon that becomes progressively easier.

Now, before you close the book, do this: take your diary. Decide to take one, just one, of the actions below. It doesn't really matter which, just pick one to start with. Then decide how long it will take you and put down in your diary the day and the hour that you're going to carry out that action, with the time-frame next to it.

Your road to success is just a matter of doing exactly this: choose an action, choose a date, choose a time-frame and carry out the action, over and over and over again. So, what is the one small thing, the one totally easy and non-scary step you'll take to move forward?

You could . . .

- Go for coffee and dream about what sort of a life you would ideally like to have.
- Arrange your first board meeting.
- Write in your diary where you want to be in a month's time.
- Look at your receipts for the week and enter them into the Excel spreadsheet from Chapter 6.
- Arrange a meeting with the tax office to see what benefits you aren't claiming.
- Have a meeting with your bank manager.
- Write a list of insurance providers' phone numbers to call.
- Decide to cut one unnecessary expense (one that doesn't bring any benefits or any pleasure).
- Set up a direct debit into a savings account, for €50 a month.

- Search the internet for restaurant vouchers.
- Sign up with a company to answer surveys online.
- Come up with one innovative way to do your hobby differently that is less expensive.
- Write a list of ways to reward yourself that don't involve money.
- Look at what you would like to throw out of your home and where you might sell it.
- Ask for an appointment at your County Enterprise Board to have a preliminary meeting with a business adviser.
- Ask a friend or relative what the one thing is that you do so well they would be willing to pay you to do it.

Once you have taken one of these steps, what is the next small step you can take?

The journey that I'm inviting you to take is pretty much mapped out for you. If you tap your destination into your financial satnav, put effort into driving towards it and open your mind to the possibilities along the way, you will succeed. I have given you the steps and I'm happy to go the distance with you through my website – I would be delighted if you shoot me an email to tell me of your achievements.

We are all rooting for your success, so go for it!

Acknowledgements

In a most heartfelt way, I want to thank everybody who worked with me on this book, including Michael, Patricia, Donna, Cliona, Patricia, Brian, Keith, Holly Kate, Lisa and all of their teams. I have thoroughly enjoyed each and every word of this book, and I thank you all for your continuous help throughout the process.

I would like to thank Julie Duran-Gelleri, who acted as my sounding board from the beginning, read each building block of each chapter, has been a mine of education, advice and support, helped me to sew it all together, held me accountable and has always been at the other end of a Skype line to listen to me talk excitedly about each new stage.

I would like to thank the Culleton family for their support, encouragement and engaging discussion about the book over dinner on a Sunday night, my friends for giving me insights into their financial tales over the years as well as all my professional colleagues whose individual contributions of education formed a large part of my own.

I wish to express my profound appreciation to Mam, Dad and Conor as well as all of my aunts, uncles and cousins. There is no greater start in life than to be born into a family of thinkers, talkers and teachers of life's lessons, but who most of all offer the most wonderful friendship. Thank you all for your financial (and otherwise) vignettes!

Finally, I would like to dedicate this book to Ardle Culleton:

To the man who has been most inspirational in my life, is of such infinite wisdom and a perennial source of support, drive and motivation.

To the man who is such an amazing life partner with whom to share my dreams, my stories, my experiences.

I love you, Darling – my 'hero'.